The Aftermath of the Cassinga Massacre

Basel Namibia Studies Series

VILHO AMUKWAYA SHIGWEDHA
Foreword by Ellen Ndeshi Namhila

The Aftermath of the Cassinga Massacre
Survivors, Deniers and Injustices

Basel Namibia Studies Series 18

Basler Afrika Bibliographien 2017

Basler Afrika Bibliographien
Namibia Resource Centre & Southern Africa Library
Klosterberg 23
PO Box
CH-4051 Basel
Switzerland
www.baslerafrika.ch

CARL SCHLETTWEIN
STIFTUNG

The Basler Afrika Bibliographien is part of the Carl Schlettwein Foundation

Efforts were made to trace the copyright holders of illustrations and maps used in this publication. We apologise for any incomplete or incorrect acknowledgements.

Cover photograph: Road sign at the entrance to Cassinga, the town in Southern Angola which was home to a SWAPO base attacked by the SADF in the 70's. July 2008.
Photographer: Johann Van Tonder

ISBN 978-3-905758-80-1
ISSN 2234-9561

Contents

Appendices

Basel Namibia Studies Series

In 1997, *P. Schlettwein Publishing* (PSP) launched the *Basel Namibia Studies Series*. Its primary aim was to lend support to a new generation of research, scholars and readers emerging with the independence of Namibia in 1990.

Initially, the book series published crucially important doctoral theses on Namibian history. It soon expanded to include more recent political, anthropological, media and cultural history studies by Namibian scholars.

P. Schlettwein Publishing, as an independent publishing house, maintained the series in collaboration with the *Basler Afrika Bibliographien* (BAB), Namibia Resource Centre and Southern Africa Library in Switzerland. All share a commitment to encourage research on Africa in general and southern Africa in particular. Through the incorporation of PSP into the *Carl Schlettwein Stiftung,* the series, by then a consolidated platform for Namibian Studies and beyond, was integrated into the publishing activities of the BAB.

Academic publishing, whether from or about Namibia, remains limited. The *Basel Namibia Studies Series* continues to provide a forum for exciting scholarly work in the human and social sciences.

The editors welcome contributions. For further information, or submission of manuscripts, please contact the *Basler Afrika Bibliographien* at www.baslerafrika.ch.

Foreword

The Cassinga massacre, as the author duly put it, represents the darkest and most unresolved chapter of the colonial violence committed against Namibian civilians during the struggle for independence and democracy. The Fourth of May 1978 is commemorated annually as a national holiday, but what does this really signify? As one of those who were lucky enough to escape at least physically unharmed from the hell of Cassinga, I am privileged to write the foreword to this insightful piece of work that takes the reader through the mass killing of Namibian civilians by the South African military on 4th May 1978. The book raises the painful memories that the massacre continues to generate in the hearts and minds of the victims of that experience. It is within this context that Vilho Shigwedha attempts to explore the unacceptable afterlife of that episode beset with the aggressive perpetrators' denial of the killing of innocent civilians, the absence of restorative justice to encourage the victims to deal with the trauma of loss and their recurring nightmare of experiencing and surviving the killings of their comrades, friends and relatives in Cassinga.

In an exploratory manner, the book navigates the reader through the conundrum of survivors' ongoing painful testimonies of the Cassinga massacre in contrast with those perpetrators who remain obstinate and unremorseful, celebrating the killing of innocent women and children in Cassinga as a great military achievement. This inflames the victims' anger and bitterness. It also raises a concern that the ongoing suffering of the Cassinga victims is as a result of post-colonial Namibia's failure to encourage the victims and perpetrators to negotiate the past openly and hold those responsible for the violence accountable. In attempts to disentangle these challenges the author grapples with the persisting physical and emotional trauma of the survivors with the absence of closure for friends and families, but also with the unresolved scars the massacre left in the minds of the perpetrators. Because – and this is noteworthy – not all the South African soldiers involved in the attack share the unrepentant attitude of General Breytenbach and his ilk, and they have their own nightmares to deal with.

Shigwedha juxtaposes and contrasts different sources such as testimonies from survivors, oral and written narratives of perpetrators and photographs from different archives. With an incisive analysis of the content, use, and interpretation of selected "iconic" photographs, he demonstrates how the widely disseminated image of the mass grave obscures the tragedy behind it, and how the South African photos intended to hide the truth about the massacre does, on the contrary, evoke the vivid memory and wrath of a survivor.

By doing so he intends to and succeeds in opening a discursive space in which the dominant national versions of the Cassinga massacre that circulate in Namibia, and the too long afterlife of the SADF version of the massacre, may be challenged and interrupted so as to allow for more open-ended narratives. Such narratives, as the author convincingly demonstrates, elaborate and critique colonial-apartheid violence yet evade the co-option of justifying or redeeming a postcolonial national or nationalist framing. As the central argument accumulates from one chapter to the next, a vast and deeply contested social, sensory, embodied and discursive landscape of ruin and devastation painstakingly emerge. The 'accumulative' structure of the book is persuasive and allows the argument to gather force. By the time the perpetrators' narratives are engaged in Chapter 5, a meticulously close reading of primary sources, including the few from the South African military archives, which the author was finally permitted to access, exposes the disinformation campaign that was already designed in the planning stages of "Operation Reindeer," the military codename for the attack on Cassinga. The author explores in detail how the denials, contradictions, lies and disingenuous claims that circulate in public versions of the massacre associated with the perpetrators' public narratives operate.

The book is based on extensive oral testimony. It is disconcerting to read the survivors' attempts to disclose, via testimony, their individual experiences of continued pain and suffering and their cry for justice to help alleviate their suffering and their tangible and explicit everyday misery. As they attempt to make their pain and suffering known, they experience insurmountable difficulties with the testimony's incapacity to expose their predicaments fully. They communicate traumatic flashbacks that are more ambiguous than what the victims intend unpacking for the public understanding. The kaleidoscopic fragments of their experience in Cassinga and thereafter, combined with the obvious silences and outright misinformation on the apartheid South African Defence Force's side together with the gaping holes in the archival record that have been hidden or destroyed, cannot be pieced seamlessly together to create a clear narrative of "what really happened."

This is not to contradict the fact that the testimony of the survivors is valid, and their indignation about the continued rationalization of this war crime (Shigwedha avoids using such ostentatious labels) by the top brass of the apartheid military is justified. Whatever challenges the narration of the Cassinga massacre presents, it remains crucial that the voices of the survivors are not drowned and pasted over in a hollow understanding of "reconciliation" as forgetting and absence of justice. The photographic evidence of the neglected and crumbling remains of the mass grave symbolizes the need for closure and restorative justice beyond the token of declaring the Cassinga day, a national holiday.

Ellen Namhila, University of Namibia: Pro Vice Chancellor

Acknowledgements

This book emerged out of my PhD research project with the University of the Western Cape, Cape Town. Since its inception in 2007, it has received support from different people who assisted in different ways throughout its endeavors. Without assistance, I could not, alone, have overcome the numerous difficulties encountered in the course of gathering archival data for my Doctoral thesis and finally this book. I would single out the former SADF archive in Pretoria, which gave me a tough time and delayed my archival research for a period of two years before finally approving my application to consult documents of the Cassinga attack. I thank Sello Hatang, the former Director of the South African History Archive (SAHA), for coordinating links and lobbying for the release of some of the Cassinga declassified documents. Steve De Agrela and Gerald Prinsloo, the principal archivists at the former SADF archive in Pretoria, were invariably helpful during my frequent research trips to the SANDF archive. They had limited power, however, to influence matters. They had no authority to release unscrutinized, although declassified Cassinga files. The support I received in Johannesburg from John Liebenberg, Jo Ractliffe and Verne Harris is immeasurable. Patricia Hayes, thank you for introducing me to these wonderful people and many others.

I am grateful to Dag Henrichsen for allowing me access to the Namibia Resource Centre & Southern Africa Library in Basel, Switzerland. I am indebted to Giorgio Miescher and Lorena Rizzo for hosting me in their house throughout my stay in Basel. Martha Akawa, I am very grateful for your support in Basel.

In May 2011, I had the privilege of attending the South-South Exchange Programme for Research on the History of Development (SEPHIS) workshop on visual methodologies in Cairo. Part of my work benefitted from the intellectual expertise and critical analysis of Hanan Sabea, Mark Westmoreland and fellow participants in the two-week workshop in Egypt.

I spent the last five months (August – December 2011) of my study at the Interdisciplinary Center for the Study of Global Change (ICGC), University of Minnesota in Minneapolis, USA where I met academics with intellectual proficiency and extraordinary inter-personal rapport. I found myself in a very supportive academic and family-like environment with the following wonderful people: Eric Sheppard, Karen Brown, Helena Pohlandt-McCormick and Sara Braun. Allen Isaacman showed interest in my project. Unfortunately things do not always go according to plan. Helena Pohlandt-McCormick provided immeasurable mentoring support during my stay at the University of Minnesota. She read parts of my work with profound interest and suggested ways of improving critical areas.

Terence Mashingdiaze's coordination of the ICGC brown bag presentations was exceptionally helpful for the critical analysis of my work. Kate Griep Kulhanek acted professionally and passionately with the distribution of the bi-weekly finance and fixing errors. Thank you! Cecilia Aldarondo facilitated access to affordable yet good quality clothing for the harsh winter – thank you for showing Okechukwu and me the way to the Salvation Army stores around Minneapolis.

Okechukwu Nwafor, my colleague at UWC and flat-mate in Minneapolis, I am indebted to you in many ways. You not only shared my pain and suffering when I fell sick, you played a brotherly role in ways that cannot be expressed. But as the saying goes, a friend in need is a friend indeed!

This project would not have been completed without the Carl Schlettwein Foundation in Basel, Switzerland, which funded the first three years of my study. Jeremy Silvester, thank you for introducing me to the Schlettwein Foundation during my MA programme with the University of Namibia. I am grateful to the National Archives of Namibia for funding my initial field trip to northern Namibia to interview survivors of the Cassinga massacre. The Centre for Humanities Research (CHR) at the University of the Western Cape (UWC) provided immense financial support for this study. Thank you for granting me the two-year doctoral research fellowship.

I can not fail to list names of academics, colleagues and friends with whom I spent time at UWC and who enriched both my academic and personal growth. Patricia Hayes, Premesh Lalu, Ciraj Rassool, Leslie Witz, Nicky Rousseau, Heidi Grunebaum, Okechukwu Nwafor, Olusegun Morakinyo, Heike Becker, Anette Hoffman, Paolo Israel, Christian Williams, Zuleiga Adams, Suren Pillay, Annachiara Forte, Geraldine Frieslaar, Memory Biwa, Loide Shifula, Michael Akuupa, Kletus Likuwa, Napandulwe Shiweda, Charles Kabwete, Nduduzi 'Mdu' Xakasa, Stanley Baluku, Steve Akoth, Janine Brandt, Jane Smidt, Lameez Lalkhen, Margreth Wazakili, Rebecca Amollo, Kaikai – the list is long. In fact, writing an acknowledgement is about producing exclusions and absence of much of the assistance I received over the years.

This book is indebted to the professional expertise of Patricia Hayes, my supervisor. She responded to each chapter draft with analytical acumen and gratifying insights. Thank you for your insightful comments and useful guidelines. Thank you for organizing platforms such as colloquia to present my work and receive audience feedback. Such meetings, discussions and debates enabled me to revisit my work in a more critical and scholarly manner. I really consider myself fortunate to have worked with you over the years.

I must not fail to acknowledge the numerous contributions made by my interviewees. In particular, this book owes a great deal to the support and contributions made by survivors of the Cassinga massacre. Regrettably, interviews invoked your suffering and bitterness by switching on your difficult memories of that episode and its uninterrupted aftermath. I regret the emotional and psychological suffering you experienced in remembering Cassinga as you tried to reveal your experience to the inexperienced other. But that is the price you pay for the world to hear your uninterrupted suffering and forfeited justice.

To Joolokeni, Hafeni, Kadhila, Katopi, Namupolo, Iikondja, Lazarus, Shatika, Lugambo and Mweupandje, I am grateful. Lastly, I dedicate this book to memory of my parents, Jonas Kadhila Martin and Aina Napaasita Martin, who both passed away in 2014. Also to the memory of my younger brother, Shigwedha Martin Christmas Shigwedha who passed away in 2011.

Ondapandula.

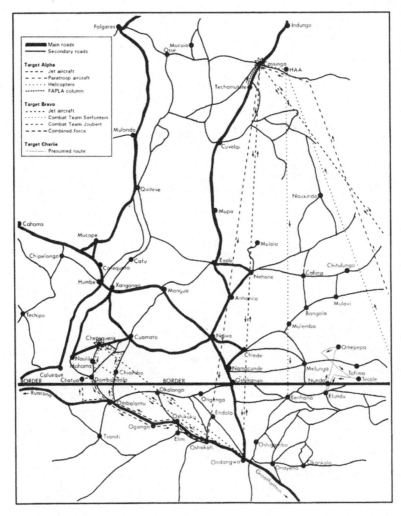

'Operation Reindeer,' 4–10 May 1978, showing SADF bases in northern Namibia and targets in southern Angola.

1 Introduction

Overview

The collection of data for this book began with my visit to the institutional archives in Pretoria, South Africa, which I frequented between 2007 and 2010. I expected to mine the archives for photographs, written documents, field diaries and other forms of documentary information that the South African Defence Force (SADF) recorded or captured during the attack of Cassinga on 4 May 1978. During the first trip, I visited the National Archives and Records Service (NARS) of South Africa and the South African Police Museum and Archives, both located in Pretoria. In Cape Town, I visited the Western Cape Provincial Archives and Records Service and the Mayibuye Centre at the University of the Western Cape. In Namibia, I visited the SWAPO Party Archive and Research Centre (SPARC) and the National Archives of Namibia in Windhoek. I collected a substantial number of interviews with the war victims, in particular survivors of the Cassinga massacre across Namibia's thirteen political regions. However, I concentrated mainly on the four northern regions (Omusati, Oshana, Ohangwena and Oshikoto). This is where most survivors of the Cassinga massacre were born and continue to live. I went to visit survivors with photographs and other documents I had collected from the institutional archives in Namibia and South Africa. It was intriguing to learn that the photographs and other documents I handed out to some survivors of the Cassinga massacre turned out to be irrelevant to their personal experience. Surprisingly, survivors interpreted such images as casting obscurity over complex realities of the Cassinga episode. Ironically, while survivors deplored what they called the sheer absence of the tangible experiences of the Cassinga brutal massacre in what photographs show, their personal testimonies of the Cassinga episode too failed to uncover tangible living memories of that episode.

The lack of visual, oral and historical accounts to support the complex and dynamic experience of the Cassinga massacre implies that the actual experience of the Cassinga violence does not resonate with the way Cassinga is narrated, remembered and commemorated through different techniques that attempt to represent that event. In fact, to paraphrase Cathy Caruth on trauma and its role in literary texts, the experience of the Cassinga massacre lies not in what can be disclosed or concealed through different techniques of narrating and attempting to show the experience of that event. Rather, the life and living memories of an event lies in the "inherent latency within the experience itself"[1] that can no longer be

---

[1] Cathy Caruth, Unclaimed experience: trauma, narrative and history (Baltimore: Johns Hopkins

1

displayed to others who did not experience it. In retrospect, things did not work out the way they were originally understood and outlined in the research proposal preceding my experience in the field. In this connection, dialogues and analysis presented in this book are particularly shaped by the ambivalence and the silence, which the visual, oral and written testimonies would certainly articulate when attempting to communicate memories of the Cassinga massacre.

Nevertheless, this traumatic event is the most commemorated day of the lives lost during Namibia's war for liberation. Regrettably though, its commemoration during which verbal, visual and other testimonies of that episode are recited and exhibited does not present the audience with anything tangible for them to fully experience, understand and reflect on the individual and collective memories of the pain and suffering as experienced by the victims. Against this background, one of the aims of this book is to untie the problematic relationship between the representation of the Cassinga massacre through images and political rhetoric and the reality of Cassinga as experienced by survivors. This approach is intended to create a new way of thinking and seeing the economy of violence beyond the confines of the conventional oral and visual representations of the Cassinga event. In exploring the impossibility of understanding the violence through oral, visual or written exchange, this study relies mainly on interviews conducted with a number of survivors, archival photographs and, to some extent, individual perpetrators' written accounts of the attack.

Individual survivors' testimonies of the Cassinga massacre as well as each survivor's reaction to the photographs I presented to them provided me with important indications and insights about the challenge faced by any sort of testimony (visual, oral or written materials) to fully corroborate survivors' personal memories of that event and its afterlife. Interestingly, the voices of the interviewees were translated from Oshiwambo into English, transcribed, and the text then edited. These changes raise some serious concerns about the final version of this book. For instance, the ways in which the original voice is transformed and reconfigured brings into question the text's ability to capture, contain and communicate violence to the reader as represented in the original voice of the victims. In fact, the text eliminates the voice, its rich content and crucial details of violence articulated by the victim's actual voice, in relation to the crucially informative residues of violence that the victims' body may also narrate in the presence of the interviewer.

University Press, 1996), p. 17.

Introduction

Namibia experienced a series of massacres of civilians, inside and outside the country at the hands of the South African Security Forces during the war for liberation from apartheid South Africa (1966–1990). Whilst the focus of this book is on the massacre of Namibian civilians at Cassinga in Angola, it is equally important to think about similar traumatic experiences that involved the massacre of civilians throughout the period of the war for Namibian liberation. Some of the mass killings of civilians notably include, Singalamwe 1968, Epinga (Omundaungilo) 1972, Oshatotwa 1976, Vietnam 1978, Oshikuku 1982 and Oshakati (Barclays Bank) 1988[2], to mention but a few. According to the Truth and Reconciliation Commission of South Africa Report (TRC)[3], the Koevoet (a special police counter-insurgency unit) was arguably responsible for numerous murders and human rights abuses before Namibian independence and operated with impunity.[4] In addition to the Koevoet, there was the South West Africa Territorial Force (SWATF), formed at the beginning of the 1980s. SWATF conscripted Namibians into the force intending to Namibianize the military conflict. Some of the recruits were children below the age of eighteen who had been trained as soldiers to fight against the South West Africa People Organization (SWAPO)[5] combatants, who had taken up arms to liberate the country from apartheid South Africa colonial rule. Unannounced visits (which often resulted in interrogations, torture and arrests of teachers and students on suspicion of aiding SWAPO soldiers) by the SA security forces to schools prompted many students to stay away from schools. In particular, it was mainly male students who stopped attending school to avoid forceful recruitment into the South African security forces. That situation compelled many students and teachers to flee Namibia into neighbouring, independent countries.

---

[2]   In addition, untold numbers of individual civilians lost their lives and property throughout the Namibian liberation struggle. Equally so, countless members of the People's Liberation Army of Namibia (PLAN) died fighting in numerous combats with the South African security forces. This included hundreds of combatants who were captured by the enemy and thrown, alive, into the Atlantic Ocean. According to Chandre Gould, who testified before the TRC, "the prisoners were given an overdose of the muscle relaxants, scoline and tubarine, before they were thrown out of an aircraft into the sea." See Chandre Gould, "More Questions Than Answers: The Ongoing Trial of Dr. Wouter Basson, November 2000, Disarmament Diplomacy 52," available at www.acronym. org.uk/52trial.htm. Accessed on 26 August 2015.

[3]   The Truth and Reconciliation Commission of South Africa Report, "The State outside South Africa between 1960 and 1990," Vol. 2 / Ch. 2 (1998).

[4]   *Truth and Reconciliation Commission of South Africa Report*, "The State outside South Africa between 1960 and 1990," Vol. 2 / Ch. 2 (1998).

[5]   Namibia's internationally recognized liberation movement. In other words, SWAPO's struggle to liberate Namibia was waged with the full support of the international community, including all the organs of the United Nations.

Certainly, the independence of Angola in November 1975 caused waves of mass exodus of civilians from Namibia into Angola to seek refuge, education opportunities and support of the international community against South Africa's illegal occupation of Namibia. In response to the unprecedented number of civilians arriving in Angola, SWAPO established and administered a cluster of civilian camps in southern Angola[6]. Cassinga, situated some 260km from Namibia's north central border with Angola, became a SWAPO civilian and reception centre in 1976. By 1978, Cassinga had developed into SWAPO's largest permanent civilian camp in exile.

Before the Cassinga massacre in May 1978, more than 4000 Namibian civilians, the majority of whom were women and children, lived in the camp.[7] Here, it is important to give a brief account of the rise and fall of Cassinga from a witness' account:

> In March 1976 while on the hunt for Commander Dimo Hamaambo[8] we, a platoon of SWAPO combatants, came to Cassinga. By then, the Cuban soldiers had occupied it, there were no Namibians living there at the time. The mission to find Dimo aborted while we were at Cassinga. From there we went back to Huambo without any clues about the army Commander. In just over a year, on June 15, 1977, a group of about five hundred of us, men and women, left for the former Soviet Union for advanced military training. We returned on December 4, 1977. A few of us stayed behind, on the real front, the rest of our group members went to the war fronts/ SWAPO military regions in southern Angola, closer to the border with Namibia.[9] I was sent to Cassinga for administrative purposes. By that time, the civilian population arriving from Namibia had increased tremendously. They were in thousands and newcomers were

---

6   According to Tor Sellstrom, "in the early 1976 the MPLA government allocated various sites – including the abandoned mining centre at Kassinga – to SWAPO in the southern Huila and Cunene provinces, where the organization could set up reception centres for refugees pouring out of Namibia, as well as military bases." Tor Sellström, *Sweden and national liberation in Southern Africa: solidarity and assistance 1970 – 1994, Vol. 11* (Uppsala: Nordiska Afrikainstitutet, 2002), pp. 350–352.

7   International Defence & Aid Fund, "Remember Kassinga and other papers on political prisoners and detainees in Namibia." *Fact Papers on Southern Africa, No. 9* (London: Canon Collins House, 1981), pp. 30–31.

8   According to oral sources, one of the objectives of Operation Savannah was to capture Dimo Hamaambo. By then Hamaambo stayed at Oshitumba where SWAPO and UNITA operated as allies prior to the 1975 split. When the SADF launched Operation Savannah into Angola (end of 1975) Hamaambo escaped from Oshitumba. He, according to Paavo Max, spent months in hiding in the jungles called the Efitu Lyiiti yaNandjamba, an evil forest, until the situation normalized, that is when the Operation Savannah retreated towards the Namibian border.

9   According to Paavo Max, by 1978 SWAPO had three Military Operational Areas (regions) located closer to Namibia border with Angola. These were: the North Western Region (under the command of Wilbard Tashiya "Nakada"); Northern Region – East of Ondjiva (under the command of "Zulu" Nadenga); and the Eastern Region – Okongo, Eenhana area (under the command of Matias Ndakolo Mbulunganga). Source: author's interviews with Paavo Max, Efindi, 2008.

arriving from Namibia almost on a weekly basis. Because of Cassinga's geographical position and location, far from the Namibian border with Angola, we thought it was out of reach of the regular SADF incursions into southern Angola by land. We thought it was a safer place to settle civilians arriving from home. The massacre happened about a year and a half from the time Cassinga became a SWAPO civilian settlement. Therefore, by the time of the massacre, the camp was in the process of establishing itself fully as a community of displaced Namibians in exile. The growing community of the exiled civilian population needed support in terms of education, administration, health facilities, shelter, clothing, food and most importantly security and protection from the enemy. Security wise, we dug long trenches, omatelendja, in the camp, because the enemy attacks from the air were expected. What we did not expect was an attack by foot soldiers ... though we did have some concerns about UNITA, but not to the extent of the ruthless power that the Boers used against civilians. Education provision for the young ones and soliciting schooling opportunities in independent countries for the students leaving Namibia was our first priority. As the centre was in the process of developing, classes took place in the open space, under the trees: we needed everything, qualified teachers, books, you mention it. We ran adobe bricks-making project, to build classes, accommodation and other facilities required in the camp. Historically, Cassinga was a sort of a farm area, formerly a Portuguese settlement. As such, there were not enough facilities in terms of building structures. The settlement only had eight buildings, as far as I remember, abandoned by the Portuguese. One of the buildings was converted into the camp clinic, another building was used for the administrative purposes and the largest one was used for storage purposes. However, we erected additional facilities, basic accommodation structures such as the traditional thatched roofs to accommodate the growing number of people. We divided the camp accordingly. For example, young children stayed at a separate site, away from the centre of the camp. In view of its strategic geographical location between the Tobias Hainyeko Training Centre (SWAPO fighters' training base) and the combat regions, Cassinga was a crucial networking site, particularly in terms of transportation. There was a garage and a petrol station. All SWAPO vehicles traveling from Lubango to other places or from the combat zones were expected to refuel in Cassinga before proceeding to other places. In fact, the interaction between SWAPO soldiers and the civilian population was necessarily for the maintenance of family, community, cultural and national attachments to each other. So, PLAN combatants could not avoid traveling through Cassinga, they had to pass there and sometimes, especially when transport was not available or broken, they could spend days and weeks in Cassinga. For example, at the time of the attack a number of combatants from Zambia were on transit in Cassinga. They had just arrived there a few days, unfortunately they had no weapons when the attack came.

The attack

My residence in Cassinga was located next to the garage. On the morning of May 4, 1978, I woke up as usual, at five o'clock. I went for the morning exercise before returning to my room to dress up and prepare for the daily morning parade. Around seven o' clock that morning, I was done and ready for the parade. I had dressed up in full military uniform, okakonkola, and as usual, I always carried my gun and four rounds of ammunition with me. I was on my way to the parade / okapale when a sudden thundering sound rocks the space above me. When I looked up, I saw four planes. I immediately reckoned that it was an attack and when I looked at my watch, it was seventeen minutes to eight (07: 43). The four planes formed a cross in the air, one in front, another one behind and the other two flew opposite each other. They emerged from the direction of Lubango, north to south direction. In seconds, they descended on the parade – okapale where people assembled for the morning devotion. Suddenly there were heavy explosions at the okapale followed by thick crowds of dust, smoke, people's screaming and confusion at the parade.

When the planes dropped the first bombs, people were commanded to take cover, lay down flat on the parade. As the first wave of the bombings passed, we ordered everyone to retreat to the trenches. I immediately retreated to the guns. We had two anti-aircraft guns. One was a double-barrel and the other one a single barrel, Zek U 2 and Zek U 1 respectively. We also had a lighter British anti-aircraft gun, but that one proved ineffective, it jammed after firing a few shots. The one-barrel anti-aircraft gun was also put out of action immediately. However, the double-barrel anti-aircraft gun was located in a dugout, almost disguised and obscured from the direct enemy view and fire. It stayed intact for much longer. We however wasted a lot of ammunition, including small arms fire by firing at the planes. We thought the enemy would only attack from the air. We did not expect the drop of paratroopers inside the camp.

When the enemy dropped from the air, the crew at the only remaining anti-aircraft gun concentrated the fire on the advancing ground forces. That gun really caused trouble for them as it delayed the enemy advance into the camp for much longer. The temporary holdup of the enemy was significant in many ways. For instance, it enabled us to rescue some of our people to safety before the enemy moved inside the camp. Unfortunately, the anti-aircraft gun ran out of ammunition and the gunners were shot dead. Following the silence of the anti-aircraft fire, the enemy broke inside the camp and committed gruesome killings of so many innocent people. The enemy marched freely along the trenches shooting civilians inside the trenches at point-blank range and bayoneting them, ta ya tsu aantu nomagonga gokoond-jembo. They vandalized every existing structure; they burned everything they came across; the clinic, administrative office, food depots, accommodation facilities, cookery and utterly everything that survived the aerial bombardments was deliberately set on fire.

The rescuing task

A very few number of combatants volunteered to save women and children. It was a risky undertaking. Rescuers exposed themselves to many dangers, but it was important to save the lives of women and children. This tiny blemish you see on my face is a bullet mark! It was fired from a very close distance as I cut my way through the bushes. It was painful but I did not succumb to it. I did not feel the pain immediately.

The violence was so unbearable that one became insensitive to injuries on the body. Pain, hunger and thirst were just not there until the violence subsided. People were running with critical injuries and I contemplate about it a lot until today: I find no explanation as to how it was possible for the victims to sustain such deep injuries, lose much blood, yet they sustained a life ... Many of the people we rescued or failed to rescue were in total panic and confusion. The situation in the camp was horrible; dust and smoke oozed everywhere, people could hardly see each other and many people crumbled under chemical emission/gas that made many of them insentient and insensible instantly. Nevertheless, we tried the best we could. I personally rescued four successive groups to the riverside before the Boers stormed inside the camp. Mbolondondo was another rescuer who played a significant role. He evacuated most of the children from the other side of the camp, where most of the young children were located. He took most of them (the pre-school kids), across the river where we also whisked Dimo Hamaambo.

Hamaambo could have died or captured in Cassinga. He stubbornly refused initial attempts to escort him to a safer place outside the camp. We acted in accordance with the ethos of our army that senior commanders must be covered and provided with maximum protection in case of precarious situations that risked their lives or allowed them to fall into the hands of the enemy. We were fighting a war with the mightiest army in the region, maybe in the continent. It has always been our principle that the safety of our leaders was the first priority. In engaging such a powerful enemy, it was imperative that we keep our leaders safe in case of the enemy threat. Their safety was crucial – so that they can guide and lead us through the revolution as they successfully did. We took Hamaambo across the river, to a hidden location, where he stayed with his bodyguard "Nakadila" and others. We ordered the noncombatant civilian population to retreat to the western direction of the camp. That was the only possible route to escape from the camp, provided the escapees avoided the open terrain. There was an open space and a path extending from the centre of the camp towards the riverside. We instructed people to follow the densely vegetated area to the riverside and avoid the open space. Unfortunately, people were scared of escaping through the thick bushes. Instead, many of them ran across the open terrain, oya matuka mongalangala, to the riverside. As a result, many of them were shot dead as they tried to run across that open terrain. That terrain without bushes became a rich hunting ground for the predator and the prey an easy catch.

The most difficult part of the rescue mission was dealing with many people who refused to leave the trenches. Many of them, despite shouting and urging them to move out of the trenches to safer places, to leave the camp under our escort, did not respond to the command. People were terrified and shocked. They would have reasoned that it was much safer inside the trenches than running across the burning and exploding camp. It was a very tense situation, heavy smoke, deafening bomb blasts and gunshots all over the camp. Some children went into very dangerous hideouts, such as seeking shelter under their beds, inside the pit toilets and other dangerous enclosures. Most of the thatched roofs that served as dormitories were bombed and set ablaze with people inside them. There was another challenge. People were falling asleep while on the run for safety. I think, something was inhaled that made people weak and unconscious. Many people were falling asleep instantly while on the run, but if you slapped that person, he would wake up but in a confused state. When the Boers flooded the camp, it became impossible to continue with the rescue work. I retreated to the western side of the camp. I stayed in the riverbed until the Cubans arrived.

The Cubans' intervention

The Cubans' base at Oshamutete (often spelled Techamutete) was the nearest military camp, about 20km from Cassinga. At the inception of the 'paratroopers' drop at the outskirt of the camp, Uhuru,[10] the camp secretary, was dispatched to Techamutete to notify the Cubans about the attack and to request for military assistance. Unfortunately, Uhuru did not return to Cassinga, he was killed when the SADF Air force attacked the Cuban military convoy on its way to Cassinga. However, the second attempt by the Cubans succeeded. They arrived very late though, around two in the afternoon. The Boers were still in the camp just before the Cubans entered Cassinga. They retreated the moment the Cubans moved inside the camp. After assessing the deplorable situation, the Cubans took some of the wounded people to their clinic at Oshamutete. We did not receive any assistance from Lubango [Angolan help] that day. That late afternoon while we were going around the camp, with the Cubans, collecting the critically wounded, I found the body of Commander Jonas Haiduwa, the deputy Commander of PLAN, pierced with bullets and mutilated. I did not know how he re-entered the camp, because we also whisked him to a place of safety when the enemy started dropping soldiers in Cassinga. Surprisingly, I think, he should have experienced a moral dilemma, surviving at the cost of women and children. I also found the body of my sister, Anna Max, among other bodies in the trenches. We also rescued four girls at the spot where I found my sister's body. They were like dead: their entire bodies smeared in the blood of their dead comrades: they were very confused and shivered feverishly. A few other people were still alive among the dead bodies inside the trenches as well as at other places around the camp. Survivors were so shocked that they did not respond regardless of our efforts, shouting and appealing to anyone alive to report to us. When darkness came, we could hear multiple sounds of people groaning and some were calling for help. Many of them were wounded and terribly cold: it was very cold at night since it was the beginning of the winter season. We were fortunate, however, to find enough blankets not destroyed by the fire. The ground enemy set all standing structures ablaze, deliberately. Before the nightfall, the Cubans went back to their base to assess their own losses. They left us in a very desperate situation. Some of our comrades (combatants) with whom we were supposed to share responsibilities fled the scene. Some of them went as far as Jamba about 42km from Cassinga. That night almost everybody, except for the seriously wounded and corpses, deserted the camp. People were scared of spending the night in the camp. The number of us left in the camp was about four. There was a

---

10   Golden Uhuru, Paavo could not remember Uhuru's middle name. It also appears that "Uhuru" is not Golden's surname.

concern that UNITA, the most important ally of South Africa in Angola, might sneak into the camp at night and execute survivors. Six of us spent the night inside the camp, the four who made up this number were not soldiers, we just recruited them to help stay on guard of the camp overnight. One of these boys works at the State House – where I also worked before my retirement. We call each other comrades in arms, in the memories and remembrance of that horrible and difficult night of May 4 through to the morning of May 5. It was a long night of much pain, horror and of the horrible stench of death.

The following day

SWAPO soldiers from Lubango called Omakamufelendja arrived in Cassinga on the morning of May 5. We were very much relieved when they came. We shared responsibilities in collecting the corpses all over the camp and in organizing the mass burials of the dead. By then, the dead bodies had begun to decompose. I received instructions to count the bodies as we buried them. First, we buried One Hundred and Forty Four, 144, bodies inside a trench located near the clinic. This is where we usually dumped the clinic disposals to maintain hygiene in the camp. The site for this mass grave is located between what used to be the clinic and the tailoring workshop managed by Meme Veronica. The other trench was much larger; we planned a storage dugout at that site. Five hundred and eighty three, 583, bodies are buried in that trench. That one is located in the western direction of the camp, at the outskirts of the crop field, between the field and Hamaambo's residence. The total number of the bodies buried in the two mass graves, as I counted them, stood at Seven Hundred and Twenty Seven, 727. People have been giving misleading and conflicting reports about the exact number of the bodies buried in the two mass graves. I counted the bodies and recorded the exact figures of the dead in the mass graves. After the burials, I gave Tate Uushona alias Komanda Yeekomanda (who commanded the SWAPO soldiers from Lubango to Cassinga) the printed report, hand-written, of the number of the dead bodies buried in each of the two mass graves. It is saddening that innocent civilians were killed, but it is also correct that a small number of soldiers were also killed. These included the camp administrators and some soldiers deployed in Cassinga for the security of civilians. However, it is also obvious that a significant number of the victims of the Cassinga massacre are not buried in the two mass graves. Many people escaped from the camp with terminal injuries and are suspected to have died in the bush. Many people also drowned in the big Cubango River – I saw people washed away by the strong water. People jumped into the water in attempts to swim across the big Cubango River. Most of these victims were women and children who could not swim but tried to save their lives.

Not surprisingly, the Boers call the Cassinga massacre a battle and a victory against SWAPO terrorists: because they could make no distinction between the SWAPO combatants and noncombatants and between children, women and terrorists. Of course, in war-torn Angola, they would not have expected SWAPO to abandon its civilian population without providing security for them. We had a responsibility to keep the civilian population away from the flashpoints of violence. Providing civilians with security was also not a crime, but a humanitarian obligation. We also did not use civilians as human shields as the enemy alleges, but we tried to protect and shield them from the enemy attacks and indiscriminate killing. SWAPO fighters were trained to use the guerrilla combat tactics. Therefore, it is almost unthinkable that SWAPO kept such a large number of combatants at one place, let alone at the war fronts. It is indeed quite unnerving when the enemy deconstructs Cassinga into a military camp and the victims as combatants. It is hurtful, particularly for us who have seen the unfolding horror of the Boers' indiscriminate and pitiless mass killing of women and children. Eembulu, the Boers did not drop into Cassinga to fight any battle, they knowingly went there to slaughter civilians. Indeed, for us who witnessed it, what they did to those people, most of them very young and the majority of them women constitute a war crime. It was indeed political and racial killings. The majority of our people died from close range shots, some bayoneted to death. However, the SADF chronicling of the Cassinga event is deconstructive, intended to obliterate their shameful and inhuman actions against the innocent civilians. The official stand taken by the SADF since the Cassinga massacre is however not surprising, they had never admitted to killing civilians throughout their occupation and militarization of Namibia.[11]

Historically, long before the Angolan war for independence, Cassinga existed as a centre for mining iron ore, which was a practice of artisans in certain communities in north central Namibia. Blacksmiths from the Oukwanyama communities frequented Cassinga for iron ore extraction. This happened before the Portuguese appropriated and developed Cassinga into a modern mining site. Oral history gives no clue about the exact period when local artisans frequented Cassinga for iron-ore extraction. Nonetheless, it appears that following the collapse of Portugal colonial rule in Angola, the mine at Cassinga, buildings and other facilities were abandoned at the start of the Angolan Civil War in 1975. The abandoned buildings at Cassinga were temporarily occupied by the Cuban soldiers before they relocated to a permanent base at Oshamutete (this local name is often spelled Techamutete). This was before it became a SWAPO refugee centre. According to SWAPO's documents, Cassinga was often referred to as Moscow. This is while the SADF documents for the planning of the Cassinga attack referred to Cassinga as "Alpha." Interestingly, the renaming of Cassinga into Moscow, the capital city of the former Soviet Union can be understood as putting emphasis on the importance of the Soviet Union in providing political and military support to SWAPO during the liberation struggle.

---

[11] The author's interview with Paavo Max, Efindi, 2008.

Why Cassinga?

As early as 1976, SWAPO took a strategic decision to transfer its military bases from Zambia to Angola. That move was strategically important for the People's Liberation Army of Namibia (PLAN)[12] as it allowed them to infiltrate northern Namibia more effectively than before. Because PLAN military bases[13] were located a few kilometers from southern Angola's common border with northern Namibia, it improved communication between SWAPO guerrilla fighters and the civilian population in northern Namibia. This situation created a conducive environment for the SWAPO soldiers to effectively mobilize local communities to support SWAPO's project of liberating Namibia. It was as a result of the SWAPO guerrillas' interaction with local communities in northern Namibia that many people recognized the importance of joining the liberation struggle. As a matter of fact, there were two equally important motivational factors that encouraged the youth to join SWAPO in Angola: the desire for better education opportunities abroad and military training to confront the enemy militarily. In many instances, civilians crossing the Namibian northern border into Angola did all their preparations with the assistance of SWAPO guerrillas who did the mapping for possible escape routes and securing enough logistical material for the long and arduous trek to Angola. In most cases, civilians were first taken to FAPLA camps,[14] closest to the Namibian border, for rest, food, medication, logistics and would wait there for transportation to SWAPO camps. The PLAN fighters who escorted them then returned to their operational areas in northern Namibia.

The journey into Angola was nevertheless risky and very often resulted in loss of lives. A distance of 10km, on both sides of the border, was uninhabited due to forced removal of people who had lived there before the war. The South African Defence Force (SADF) had removed all vegetation and proclaimed the desolated space a no-go area. The distance along the border was fenced with steel wires. Nonetheless, SWAPO fighters demolished the fence regularly, at particular points, to allow access and exit into both countries. So, although the SADF had a strong presence of combat troops along Namibia's north western and north central border with Angola, which resulted in unaccounted-for loss of civilian lives, the long

---

[12] PLAN used guerilla warfare to fight the powerful South African army and security forces in Namibia. Prior to 1966, PLAN was named South West Africa Liberation Army (SWALA). This army was again renamed the Namibian People's Liberation Army (NAPLA) and, subsequently, the People's Liberation Army of Namibia (PLAN). At independence, members of PLAN joined the new Namibian Defence Force comprising of former erstwhile fighters.

[13] SWAPO had three military Fronts or Regions along southern Angolan border with northern Namibia. These were: the North Western Front, Northern Front and the Eastern Front.

[14] FAPLA stands for Forças Armadas Populares de Libertação de Angola / People's Armed Forces for the Liberation of Angola (English translation).

border between the two countries was nevertheless porous. It was not always possible to maintain a security presence at every point of the border, especially at night. This is how many people fled from Namibia into southern Angola, into SWAPO camps, as refugees.

In response to the unstoppable exodus of civilians crossing the border to seek refuge in Angola, the SADF army and air force frequented Namibian exiles' camps with deadly attacks from the air and land. This is how on 4 May 1978, Cassinga suffered the heaviest single day loss of innocent civilian lives during the entire period of the Namibian armed liberation struggle. As presented in Max's account above, the Cassinga massacre started with the SADF Air force bombardment of the camp. This was followed by a drop into the camp of SADF paratroopers. According to available records, "370 combat troops" jumped into the settlement.[15] This number (370 paratroopers) contradicts other sources. Edward Alexander reports that on the evening before the Cassinga massacre, 498 paratroopers were transported by eight large transport aircraft: four C-130 Hercules and four C-160 Transalls from Bloemspruit in South Africa to the SADF's large operational rear-area logistics base at Grootfontein in northern Namibia.[16] According to SWAPO, "a combat force of 1500 South African troops was involved" in the attack.[17] It is however not reported how SWAPO obtained its figures. Nonetheless, the precise number of paratroopers involved in the Cassinga attack does not concern this study as much as the level of unacceptable killing of unarmed civilians that the paratroopers are accused of inflicting on innocent civilians.

Survivors told me that the explosives from the aerial bombardment wounded more people than they killed: the greater number of people were killed by the "merciless" paratroopers who landed in Cassinga and shot or bayonetted civilians to death. However, the exact number of people reportedly killed and missing in Cassinga fluctuates. In *To be Born a Nation: the liberation struggle for Namibia*, it is reported that "out of 3000 (which contradicts the figure given above) people living there, 867 were killed and 464 wounded and over 200 taken prisoner and hauled off to prison camps in Namibia."[18] However, according to survivors, the SADF took no captives from Cassinga: except in 'Vietnam' or Osheetekela (commonly spelled as Chetequera)[19] where over 200 Namibians were rounded up by the SADF

---

15 Jan Breytenbach, *Eagle Strike: the story of the controversial airborne assault on Cassinga 1978* (Sandton: Manie Grove Publishing, 2008), pp. 152 & 242.
16 Edward Alexander, "The Cassinga raid" (UNISA: unpublished MA Thesis, July 2003), p. 117.
17 International Defence & Aid Fund, "Remember Kassinga and other papers on political prisoners and detainees in Namibia." *Fact papers on Southern Africa, No. 9* (London: Canon Collins House, 1982), p. 31.
18 Department of Information and Publicity (SWAPO of Namibia), *To be Born a Nation* (London: Zed Press, 1981), p. 242.
19 Chetequera is perhaps the Portuguese way of writing the name, which the South Africans appropriated in their planning documents for the Cassinga attack. Osheetekela or "Vietnam" was situ-

and transported overland to prisons in Namibia.[20] The report by Peter Katjavivi breaks down the figures as follows:

> 612 Namibian refugees killed (147 men, 167 women and 298 children); 12 Angolan soldiers and 3 Angolan citizens killed. 611 Namibian refugees wounded; 63 Angolan soldiers and 15 Angolan civilians wounded.[21]

Mvula ya Nangolo and Tor Sellstrom replicate the figures provided by Katjavivi. They reported "612 dead." Of this number, "298 were children, 167 women and 147 men. Another 611 ... were physically wounded, while many more were affected by gas and most of the Cassinga survivors ... were mentally traumatized by the gruesome events they had witnessed."[22] Survivors (those I have interviewed) feel that the number killed in Cassinga is much higher than the published figures. Some written reports corroborate the survivors' position. According to Nangolo and Sellstrom, "the precise number of those killed at Cassinga might never be known as some of the wounded who died in foreign hospitals were not recorded as Cassinga victims and others disappeared during the attack."[23] Much like the exact death toll of civilians, which remains unknown, the exact number of the missing is also unknown. The general perception in northern Namibia, Owamboland, where most of the Cassinga victims came from, is that each family has lost a family member(s), relative(s) or neighbour(s) in Cassinga.

---

ated in the area of Oshikango shaPopawa, about 2km from Namibia's northwestern border with Angola. This is where the headquarters of PLAN's northwestern front which at the time of the attack was commanded by Wilbard "Nakada" Tashiya was located. The attack on 'Vietnam,' was launched by land and air on the noon of 4 May1978. The commander of the raid was Frank Bestbier. Nonetheless, in spite of being a military camp, "Vietnam" also served as a transit camp for civilians escaping from Namibia before they were transported to Cassinga. As such, the majority of the people captured in "Vietnam" were civilians, en-route to the Cassinga refugee camp. For a summary of the Vietnam attack see Appendix E: the author's interview with Rev. Samwel Mateus Shiininge, a survivor of the Vietnam attack (interviewed at Etunda, 2008); also available in the interview with Rev. Andreas Shomawe, survivor of the Vietnam attack (interviewed at Okahao, 2009).

[20] Department of Information and Publicity, *To be Born a Nation*, p. 242.

[21] Peter Katjavivi, *A history of resistance in Namibia* (London and Paris: James Currey, UNESCO Press, 1988), pp. 110. Cited in the People's Republic of Angola "White papers (presented at the UN General Assembly session in 1983) on acts of aggression by the racist South African regime against the People's Republic of Angola, 1975–1982 (Luanda, 1983), p. 15.

[22] Mvula ya Nangolo & Tor Sellstrom, *Kassinga a story untold* (Windhoek: Namibia Book Development Council, 1995), p. 36; Tor Sellström, *Sweden and national liberation in Southern Africa*, pp. 352–357.

[23] Annemarie Heywood, *The Cassinga event* (Windhoek: National Archives of Namibia, 1994), pp. 36–37; Mvula ya Nangolo & Tor Sellstrom, *Kassinga a story untold*, p. 36.

The systematic planning to kill civilians

The planning for the Cassinga massacre involved five men. It was conceived at a secret meeting held on Thursday, 29 December 1977 when five key people in the government of Pretoria met with B. J. Vorster, South African Prime Minister. They were the Minister of Defence (P. W. Botha), the Minister of Foreign Affairs (R. F. 'Pik' Botha), the Chief of the South African Defence Force (General Magnus Malan), the Secretary of Foreign Affairs (Brand Fourie), and the Chief of the South African Army (Constand Viljoen)."[24] The subject of their secret meeting was the negotiations around South West Africa (Namibia) and specifically how to ensure that the South African supported Democratic Turnhalle Alliance (DTA) could win the UN supervised elections planned for Namibia in 1978. During this meeting, Alexander argues that P. W. Botha reasoned as follows:

> To win the political battle in Owamboland (the most populous part of Namibia and SWAPO's stronghold since the liberation struggle) the Ovambo people would need to be convinced of which side was the strongest. Political success in Owamboland therefore depended on military success. Botha felt that SWAPO needed to be dealt a blow and that the SADF should be given the right to go into Angola effectively and to sort out SWAPO bases once and for all (... *om effektief in te gaan en klaar te speel met basisse*).[25]

According to one military report, "On 27 February 1978, Magnus Malan submitted a request to the Minister of Defence (P.W. Botha) to launch an attack on five SWAPO bases in southern Angola ... Four of these bases were between 8 and 39km from the Angolan/Namibian border."[26] The fifth, Cassinga, was further north as indicated above. The other four bases within the 40km radius were Eheke, Mulemba, Dombondola and Chetequera complexes.[27] However, Malan's request only received approval to attack four SWAPO bases, "Cassinga was turned down."[28] This exclusion was based on the reason that there was "less enthusiasm from the ranks of ... political bosses" to attack a civilian camp.[29] Hence, the political front found it quite challenging and a dangerous undertaking to attack and annihilate the SWAPO civilian camp at Cassinga. Edward Alexander writes the following:

---

[24] Edward Alexander, "The Cassinga raid," pp. 80–91.
[25] *Ibid.*, p. 80.
[26] Chief of the South African Defence Force. "SWAPO ontplooiing in suid-Angola ten noorde van Owambo" (Top Secret). Ref. No. AANH A by H / LeeR/ OPS/ 301/2 DD, Feb 78. Source: SANDF Archive, Pretoria.
[27] Chief of the South African Defence Force. "Military politieke situasie in Suidwes-Afrika" (Top Secret). Ref. No. HS OPS/301/2, February 1978. Source: SANDF Archive, Pretoria.
[28] Edward Alexander, "The Cassinga raid," p. 82.
[29] *Ibid.*, p. 80.

It had been very difficult to get Balthazar Johannes (John) Vorster (the South African Prime Minister at the time of the Cassinga massacre) and his Cabinet to agree to the raid ... and even the Minister of Defence, P. W. Botha was unhappy with the plan."[30]

It is reported that B. J. Vorster, himself, "had painful memories of how the political failure of Operation Savannah had destroyed years of covert effort ... (for South Africa) to reach a form of détente with neighboring states."[31]

Interestingly, post-1976, following the independence of Angola, South Africa had embarked on an all-out effort to sway world opinion in its favour. Thus, as reported by Dries van Heerden, a former SADF member:

> A number of counter intelligence gurus such as Major Piet Muller wrote fake Swapo newsletters and publications and designed posters for anti-SWAPO rallies in Windhoek and elsewhere. The strategy was rather crude – they would intercept SWAPO publications and reprinted them in Windhoek with some unsubtle disinformation slipped in between the paragraphs. They even faked the official SWAPO calendar and other posters... Muller had a fairly sophisticated litho printing press at his disposal and I was asked once or twice to proof read the copy and correct his English.[32]

In particular, the John Vorster government was central to what became known as the "Information Scandal." It relates to the use of the apartheid government funds for pro-apartheid South African propaganda. "This became particularly evident in investigations ... of the late 1970s, when it was disclosed that the government was funding groups such as the Right wing Christian groups. These groups, among others, espoused extreme conservative politics and justified them with Christian symbols ... The most obvious example of a faith community propagating state theology was the Dutch Reformed Church."[33] Vorster was therefore anxious that attacking Cassinga "would provoke an international outcry and place great diplomatic and political pressure on South Africa."[34]

Vorster's initial advice to the SADF not to "carry on" an attack on Cassinga vindicates the argument that the SADF went to Cassinga with the knowledge and authority to kill civilians.

---

[30] *Ibid.*, p. 92.
[31] Edward Alexander, "The Cassinga raid," p. 80. 'Operation Savannah' was a name given to the South African Defence Force's 1975–1976 covert intervention in the Angolan civil war. The intention of this operation was to overthrow the MPLA (supported by the former Soviet Union and her allies) government in favour of installing a UNITA (supported by the west since the start of the Angolan civil war, 1975–2000) led government in Luanda.
[32] Dries van Heerden, "Cassinga Photos," 14 August 2012.
[33] *The Truth and Reconciliation Commission of South Africa Report presented to President Nelson Mandela on 29 October 1998. Volume Four, Chapter Three*: "Institutional hearing: the Faith Community." p. 59–93.
[34] *Ibid.*, p. 82.

In a tussle between the SADF and its political front, Constand Viljoen, the Chief of the South African Army, was reported to have threatened to abort the whole operation into Angola if Cassinga were to be excluded from the SADF planned attacks on the SWAPO military positions.[35] Some SADF sources stated that Viljoen "aggressively lobbied" against the decision regarding the exclusion of Cassinga from the list of the SWAPO bases listed for the SADF attacks. He, and perhaps other generals, are reported to "have persuaded" the South African Minister of Defence, P.W. Botha, who in turn "persuaded the Prime Minister, B. J. Vorster for the inclusion of Cassinga in the list of the SWAPO bases to be destroyed."[36]

On Wednesday 8 March 1978, Constand Viljoen sent a memorandum to his immediate senior, Magnus Malan (the Chief of the SADF). The memorandum heading reads: "Die rol van Cassinga in the Militeêre aanslag teen Suidwes-Afrika" ("The role of Cassinga in the military onslaught against South West Africa").[37] This document contained 22 items implicating Cassinga as a military camp. Viljoen argued rigorously for the inclusion of Cassinga, in fact as the principal target, for the SADF planned destruction of SWAPO bases in southern Angola. Amongst other reasons Viljoen insisted that Cassinga should be destroyed included his argument that "the Commander of PLAN, Dimo Hamaambo, had his headquarters at Cassinga, from where he planned and coordinated the execution of all operations against South West Africa (Namibia)."[38] Viljoen alleged that Cassinga provided a space for activities such as the planning, control and coordination of all SWAPO military operations against SWA. He further argued that Cassinga's role included the intelligence aspect; the logistical planning and physical provisioning of SWAPO bases in the eastern Cunene province of Angola; the planning and provision of supplies, weapons and ammunition to insurgents operating inside central and eastern Owamboland; and that infantry and mine-laying refresher courses were presented at Cassinga.[39]

---

[35] By late March 1978, the SADF planned to attack six SWAPO forward operational bases forming the complex at Chetequera / Vietnam. This was code named 'Operation Bruilof' (an Afrikaans word for a wedding). It was to be the first SADF military offensive into Angola since Operation Savannah, but targeting SWAPO military bases in southern Angola only. Operation Bruilof, however, did not materialize. One reason for its cancellation was that any attack on SWAPO bases, without targeting Cassinga [which the SADF considered the 'backbone' of SWAPO] as the primary target would not give a devastating blow to SWAPO.

[36] Edward Alexander, "The Cassinga raid," pp. 82–84.

[37] "The role of Cassinga in the military onslaught against South West Africa," In the "Memorandum from Chief of the South African Army to the Chief of the SADF" (Top Secret), Ref. No. H Leer/309/1, 8 March 1978. Source: SANDF Archive, Pretoria.

[38] "Memorandum from Chief of the South African Army to the Chief of the SADF" (Top Secret). Reference, H Leer/309/1, 8 March 1978. Source: SANDF Archives, Pretoria.

[39] "Memorandum from Chief of the South African Army to the Chief of the SADF" (Top Secret).Ref. No. H Leer/309/1, 8 March 1978. Source: SANDF Archive, Pretoria.

The items listed in Viljoen's memorandum to Magnus Malan dominated "the top secret military appreciation on the destruction of Cassinga."[40] The top-secret military document on the destruction of Cassinga was finally "drawn up by the Chief of Staff Operations and submitted to the Chief of the SADF on 1 April 1978."[41] Items highlighted in that document included the following: "the role of Cassinga regarding SWAPO; location and weakness of Cassinga; occupants of Cassinga; Cuban and MPLA interference and enemy capabilities."[42]

Although the Cassinga attack was initiated and planned in Pretoria, the SADF wished to act as if the plan for the attack was unknown to them. Interestingly, according to the SADF planning of the attack, "the AG (Administrator General of SWA who represented the South African colonial government in Namibia) and the GOC (General Officer Commanding South African troops in SWA) would issue a joint or separate statement[43] to the media explaining why SWA attacked the Cassinga camp [see Appendices A, B and C].[44] Such statements would be followed by a statement by an RSA Government spokesman, with a preference for the Minister of Defence to avoid the appearance of over–reaction."[45]

The SADF mission for Cassinga was code named 'Operation Reindeer' replacing the aborted "Operation *Bruilof* [wedding]." The Citizen Force soldiers reported to camp in mid-April 1978 for training in preparation for the Cassinga attack. The training ground was outside Bloemfontein, the capital city of what was then called the Orange Free State (Free State Province in post-Apartheid South Africa). Colonel Jan Breytenbach and Brigadier Mike du Plessis were responsible for the training of the paratroopers. Breytenbach arrived in the camp on 17 April 1978 and commenced with the training immediately.[46] The timeline for the training was very short, as the D-day for the attack ... was initially scheduled to take place on 1 May 1978.[47] On the morning of 3 May 1978, according to McGill Alexander, General

---

[40] Edward Alexander, "The Cassinga raid," pp. 52–54.

[41] Chief of the South African Defence Force. "Vernietiging van SWAPO basisse." Ref. No. HS OPS/310/4/KOSTUUM (Top Secret). Source: SANDF Archive, Pretoria.

[42] Chief of the South African Defence Force. "Vernietiging van SWAPO basisse" (Top Secret). Ref. No. HS OPS/310/4/KOSTUUM. Source: SANDF Archive, Pretoria.

[43] The 'AG' and 'GOC' were the highest ranking political appointees of the South African apartheid government in South West Africa (SWA, now Namibia). They were the authority of apartheid-colonial administration and Military operations in Namibia. At the time of Cassinga massacre, Jan Geldenhuys was the General Officer Commanding South West Africa Military. The administrator-general of South West Africa was Marthinus Theunis Steyn (1977– 79).

[44] Chief of the SADF, "Guidelines for statement by GOC SWA: Appendix A & B to PSYAC planning directive No. 3 / 78: suggested approach for statement by the Minister of Defence" (Top Secret). Source: SANDF archives, Pretoria.

[45] Chief of the SADF. "PSYAC Planning Directive No. 3 \ 78: Operation Reindeer. Phase Three (D Day to D plus approx 4)" (Top Secret). Also see, Appendices A, B and C of this book (AG and GOC statements following the Cassinga attack). Source: SANDF Archive, Pretoria.

[46] Jan Breytenbach, *Eagle Strike,* p. 168.

[47] "Memorandum from Chief of Staff Operations to the Chief of the SADF" (Top Secret). Ref. No. HS

Constand Viljoen issued the order to "execute Operation Reindeer. D- Day 4 May 1978." On the night of 3 May, the paratroopers boarded aircrafts at Bloemspruit near Bloemfontein. Under the cover of dark, they flew to Grootfontein in northern Namibia. In the early hours of the morning of 4 May 1978, the SADF paratroopers took off from Grootfontein to Cassinga.

OPS/310/4/Reindeer, 21 April 1978.

2 Mass Burials: The "Iconic Photograph" and Other Witness Accounts

Around noon, May 4, 1978 comrade John Kawaalala[1] left Lubango with two companies of PLAN combatants or Omakoma who, at the time of the Cassinga attack were in the process of completing their military training, to evacuate survivors to safer places and bury the dead in Cassinga. Most of the combatants were new intakes at the Tobias Hainyeko Training Centre[2] near Lubango, a distance of 278km North West of Cassinga. Their attempt to reach Cassinga on the day of the massacre was unsuccessful. Their convoy was bombed by the South African Air Force (SAAF) and forced to retreat back to Lubango. On the night of May 4, they regrouped and successfully arrived in Cassinga on the morning of May 5 under the command of Uushona alias Komanda yeeKomanda. As soon as they arrived, they started collecting the dead bodies for mass burials. We started with the smaller mass grave where we buried one hundred and forty four bodies. The badly mutilated and spoiled bodies were collected first and taken to the nearest burial site. This site was at the centre of the camp, near the clinic ... It was more easily accessible than the bigger trench that was at the far end of the camp ... where many civilians were killed. The smaller trench was very deep, but very narrow. This is why we buried the badly damaged bodies and other bisected human pieces inside that narrower trench. This could also be the reason why the photograph of the smaller mass grave in Cassinga appears not to exist. The second trench was much larger as it was meant for storage purposes[3] ... we were planning to build a storage depot at that site.[4] That one, the main mass grave, lies in the west of the camp closer to the maize field – a few meters away – on the left side of the pathway from the centre of the camp to the river side ... in the western direction of the camp. I counted five hundred and eighty three bodies buried in the main mass grave. The total number of the bodies buried in the two mass graves is seven hundred and twenty seven. This is the number I counted and submitted to the late Tate Uushona.[5]

---

[1]   John Kawaalala is a lieutenant in the Namibian Defence Force
[2]   The SWAPO Guerrillas Training Centre near Lubango in operation between 1976–1989.
[3]   According to my interviews with Max and Shikongo, the two trenches that became the mass graves were already dug before the massacre (see details later in this chapter).
[4]   According to some other survivors, there were also other trenches in Cassinga at the sites of the adobe bricklaying projects.
[5]   Around noon, 4 May 1978 John Kawaalala (John Kawaalala is a lieutenant in the Namibian Defence Force) left Lubango with two companies of PLAN combatants or Omakoma Most of the combatants were new intakes at the Tobias Hainyeko Training Centre (The SWAPO Guerrillas Training Centre near Lubango in operation between 1976–1989) near Lubango, a distance of 278km North West of Cassinga. Their attempt to reach Cassinga on the day of the massacre was unsuccessful. Their convoy was bombed by the South African Air Force (SAAF) and forced to retreat back to Lubango. On the night of 4 May, they regrouped and successfully arrived in Cassinga on the morning of 5 May under the command of Uushona alias Komanda yeeKomanda. As soon as they arrived, they started collecting the dead bodies for mass burial. Paavo Max who provided

Remembering Cassinga and the challenge of representation

In postcolonial Namibia, Cassinga is remembered as the worst massacre during the anti-colonial struggle against South African rule of Namibia. Generally, testimonies of individual survivors of that event, as well as the photograph of the Cassinga open mass grave in this chapter, are the most important means through which the experience of that event is narrated and communicated to the public. Interestingly, the relationship between the actual experience of Cassinga (as well as its living aftermath) and how that event is exhibited through the medium of various testimonies has not been interrogated. No existing written work on Cassinga has attempted to explore and examine how such testimonies relate to the reality of the Cassinga experience. Most existing literature on Cassinga had been written with the intention of unveiling "the truth about the Cassinga event" through "careful" or good research work. In explaining the aim of her book, *the Cassinga Event*, Annemarie Heywood writes that:

> When a group of us originally embarked on a book about the massacre at Cassinga, our aim was to search out, among the fragments of personal memories and the too-coherent existing narratives, the truth about the event. We assumed that a catastrophic event ... must possess an objective reality which careful research could uncover and record. We envisaged that the trauma of Cassinga, which we as a nation publicly commemorate each year, could be ... documented.[6]

In spite of asserting that the Cassinga "plain truth has been more difficult to uncover than we foresaw,"[7] Heywood has attributed this challenge to the absence of "survivors' voice" in her work. She claims that the SADF refusal to release images that they filmed and photographed during the 'entire operation' as another reason for the failure of her work to "uncover ... truth ... trauma ... and sufferings ..."[8] experienced in Cassinga. Heywood's claim that for oral and visual representations to stand a chance of reproducing violence for the other to equally experience it is problematic, but it does open a space for new kinds of thinking and exploration That is, to challenge the visual and the oral representations of the Cassinga

---

me with this account said that Dimo Hamaambo delegated the task of counting the dead bodies to him as they were interred in the mass graves. The late Jerobeam Dimo Hamaambo (1932–2002) who was in Cassinga at the time of the attack was the Commander of the People's Liberation Army of Namibia (PLAN) until its integration into the new Namibia Defence Force, comprising members from former erstwhile forces, in 1989. After independence, Hamaambo served as Namibia's first chief of the Namibian Defence Force (NDF) until his retirement in 2000. He died in September 2002. The author's interview with Paavo Max, a survivor of the Cassinga massacre, Efindi, 2007.

6   Annemarie Heywood, *The Cassinga Event*, p. 5.
7   *Ibid.*, p. 6.
8   *Ibid.*, p. 9.

massacre in view of their limitations in trying to represent the Cassinga brutal massacre and the suffering of the victims that has exacerbated over the years. This chapter explores such techniques and methods (visual and oral) as ultimately unyielding when it comes to Cassinga victims' and historians' efforts to reclaim the Cassinga violence. It challenges the claims that careful social research (to paraphrase Heywood) could uncover and record an "objective history" or "truth" of the Cassinga massacre.[9] The reasoning here is that the sufferings and experience, in particular, of the victims of the Cassinga massacre are so diverse, different from one victim to the other, and tangibly not obtainable or accessible by the other.

Christian Williams' doctoral thesis on "Exile history: An ethnography of the SWAPO camps and the Namibian Nation"[10] in particular, a chapter about the Cassinga camp and the attack that annihilated it, as well as his subsequent article on "Remember Cassinga?"[11] raises a number of problematic issues. One of such problems emerges from the photograph of the Cassinga open mass grave which as Williams notes:

Became the most enduring symbol of Cassinga. Taken from the grave's edge, the mass grave photos are close enough to the corpses for individual bodies, and in some cases the clothing, wounds and flies covering them, to be discernible. The photos demand a visceral reaction. In the weeks following the attack and for years to follow, SWAPO and solidarity organisations published texts alongside the photos that directed this reaction by imputing meaning to the bodies in the grave. Texts drew attention to the 'civilian' qualities of the bodies, the suffering of Namibians under colonialism, and the violence committed against oppressed people in other settings. In so doing, they associated the mass grave at Cassinga with the history of the refugee camp.[12]

As Williams recognizes, the photograph of the Cassinga open mass grave is an enduring symbol of Cassinga's violence. But this assumption is only meaningful when one takes into account the context of this photograph as the most widely published and disseminated of all the Cassinga attack photographs. Likewise, it is problematic to suggest, as Williams did, that the publication of "texts alongside the photo" of the Cassinga open mass grave is a way of "imputing meaning to the bodies in the grave." This book contests this argument. Centrally, the photograph of the Cassinga open mass grave does not, in any way possible, draw "attention to the 'civilian' qualities of the bodies in the mass grave (the same as the use of text along the photograph of the open mass grave), the suffering of Namibians under

9 Annemarie Heywood, *The Cassinga Event*, p. 5.
10 Christian A. Williams, "Exile History: an ethnography of the SWAPO camps and the Namibian nation" (Unpublished Ph.D. Thesis, University of Michigan, 2009).
11 Christian A. Williams, "National history in Southern Africa: reflections on the 'remember Cassinga?' exhibition." *Kronos: Southern African histories*, Vol. 36 (November 2010), pp. 207–250.
12 Christian A. Williams, "Exile history," p. 74.

colonialism, and the violence committed against oppressed people in other settings" as Williams argues. Instead, the use of visual and other techniques of documenting the Cassinga massacre should be understood as ways through which violence and its dynamics are deconstructed. Photographs collapse and taint acts of violence with a near absence of factual evidence. The 'near absence of factual evidence,' which the photograph of the Cassinga open mass grave exhibits, obscures the traumatic experience and suffering of those who survived the massacre as they narrate it.

The emphasis put on photographs as a means of exploring painful memories of the Cassinga massacre deserves a closer examination. In attempts to authenticate the Cassinga experience when told to an audience during official commemoration of this day, emphasis is put on "bloodshed," indiscriminate killing of innocent civilians, etc. Interestingly, as war rhetoric supposedly depicting death and loss of innocent lives, they are instead ambivalent. In fact, testimonies whether in the form of photographs, rhetoric, etc. disclose nothing: they reveal no 'bloodshed' nor the grief that they lament. Instead, they create dialogues around which the authentication of Cassinga massacre through images and language is debated and contested. This is what James Howe, on a different subject, referred to as "verbal dispute"[13], which suggests that memory of violence is beyond language, description or any act of attempting to picture it beyond the confines and frontiers of the self or the restricted personal memories of the witnesses.

I am not suggesting that testimony merits no recognition. Notwithstanding the fact that violence transcends the reach of testimony (which attempts to bring violence back to life), that makes it problematic. For example, when survivors' voices are transcribed into a text, considerable damage is done to the original content of the voice: the text obscures all emotional sentiments, which would have been evident when the victims narrated their stories in the interviews. I do not claim that my work is an exception here, but it challenges and interrogates the relationship between the actual Cassinga experiences and the different storylines of its telling. In so doing, I expect my work to unlock the barriers that disconnect and separate the conceptual representation of Cassinga from the tangible experience of violence suffered by the victims.

The "iconic photograph" and the search for the familiar

Cassinga was a small camp where everybody generally knew everybody except for the newly arrived who had not yet been introduced to the rest of the camp residents. In fact, Cas-

---

[13] James Howe, "Argument is argument: an essay on conceptual metaphor and verbal dispute," *Metaphor and symbol*, Vol. 23/1 (2007), p. 1.

singa was a community of Namibian exiles consisting of family members, relatives, people who knew each other from home and so forth. Yet, picturing the Cassinga open mass grave, no survivor recognizes anybody among the dead. This is while the media, that sympathized with the victims of the Cassinga massacre called the photograph of the Cassinga open mass grave "iconic" and making it the most widely published, circulated and exhibited in newspapers and other publications with the intention of sparking an international outcry over the human cost of lives in Cassinga. The iconicity of this photograph is however problematic as it creates tension between the actual seeing and remembering of individual victims killed in Cassinga, who are believed to have been buried in this mass grave, and the impossibility of recognizing anybody in the picture. Put differently, the photographic framing of the Cassinga open mass grave invokes a number of problematic trajectories because this image manifests itself across a range of conflicts and contestations with the Cassinga witnesses' memoryscape. This scenario invites many questions, such as do images literally depict violence? Is there a relationship between the visual and oral accounts of same events that both the camera and survivor have pictured?

In this relation, some key theorists of photography such as Roland Barthes, Walter Benjamin, Susan Sontag, Siegfried Kracauer and John Tagg have explored the relationship between photography and reality by analyzing photographs as "certificates of presence" or "truth," to doubting the truthfulness of photographs as sources of historical evidence.[14] In this connection, this book argues that the 'discipline' of attempting to capture scenes of violence and, belatedly, present them to an intended audience through the medium or art of photography does significant damage to the authenticity of the violence that survivors wish to present in its original form and space. Photographs jam, flatten, blur, obscure and are visibly oblivious to the multiple realities that individual survivors experienced. By contrast, some studies theorize photographs as embedded in the discourse of "authenticating" events or, to follow Caroline Brothers, disclosing the "exact physiognomy"[15] or actual pictures of the events shown in photographs. How exactly photographic images validate and relate violence to the actual life of the things they aspire to represent, however, appears problematic.

---

[14] Roland Barthes, *Camera Lucida: Reflections on photography* (New York: Hill and Wang, 1981); John Tagg, *The burden of representation: essays on photographies and histories* (Minneapolis: University of Minnesota Press, 1993); Roland Barthes, "Shock-photos." In *The Eiffel Tower and other mythologies* (Berkely, Los Angeles and London: University of California Press, 1977); Susan Sontag, "In Plato's Cave." In *On photography* (New York: 1977); Walter Benjamin, "The work of art in the age of mechanical reproduction." In Philip Simpson, Andrew Utterson, and K. J. Sheperdson (eds.). *Film theory: critical concepts in media and cultural studies,* (London and New York: Routledge, 2004).

[15] Caroline Brothers, *War and photography: a cultural history* (London and New York: Routledge, 1997), p. 5.

Fig. 1: The "iconic photograph" of one of the Cassinga open mass graves, 1978. According to Tor Sell-strom, who was in the UN team (UNHCR and WHO) that came to Cassinga a week after the massacre, this photograph was captured between May 5 and 6 by Gaetano Pagano, an Italian cameraman. At the time of the Cassinga massacre, Pagano was shooting a documentary film on Angola for a Swedish Television (SVT).

In attempts to explore and challenge the metaphoric assumption that images do convey the actual life of events and people, this chapter utilizes the image of the Cassinga open mass grave (figure 1) to explore this theory. This approach is informed by survivors' responses to the various images of the Cassinga massacre that were presented to them during the interviews.

The position presented in this chapter that violence is in the knowing of the individual victims of the Cassinga massacre, not in a photograph or other forms of testimony (it appears this sentence has no meaning). To rephrase Thomas Hawley, who writes on a different subject, a photograph is not a transparent tool to represent reality but is instead opaque (dense). Hence, the art of using photographs to narrate events is viewed as productions of meaning rather than reflections of reality.[16] Here, I argue that if a photograph discloses nothing tangible other than ascribing a shadow to reality, then it is obvious that the meaning of a photograph translates into absence of reality, thus making reality not only ambivalent but also ambiguous. In the interviews, survivors invoked this scenario by lamenting the way that the use of the visual as a method of attempting to elicit violence for the experience of others pushed them into insurmountable difficulties of not being able to see their individual experiences in Cassinga in the "iconic" photo. In fact, this photograph's attempt to describe the complexities of survivors' experience of brutal violence and suffering during the Cassinga attack and afterwards produces dissonance and ruptures. This is because the complexity of the violence and suffering since the Cassinga massacre exceeds that which the photograph is able to articulate and authenticate. Certainly, the moment the process of documenting (through the visual, oral or printed forms) commences, the tangible violence which such techniques intend making public begin to fall apart and disintegrate. "Analogies fall woefully short; definitions seem impossible [and] explanations are simply inconceivable."[17]

Dominick LaCapra adds the following: when documenting violence, "loss goes with writing ... absence and loss become palpable through discoursing ... 'It is here that events ... are omitted from the language of the writing but are made present in the absence of writing.'"[18] LaCapra's description, when applied to the photograph in this context, infers that an image not only roasts evidence, but it completely burns into ashes the original subject of the storyline. Therefore, the way Cassinga is remembered and narrated through the medium of visual representation fails to disclose the victims' uninterrupted emotional

---

[16] Thomas M. Hawley, *The remains of war: bodies, politics, and the search for American soldiers unaccounted for in Southeast Asia* (Durham & London: Duke University Press, 2005), p. 7.

[17] Peter N. Goggin and Maureen Daly Goggin, "Presence in absence: discourses and teaching (in, on, about) Trauma." Cited in Shane Borrowman (ed.), *Trauma and the teaching of writing* (Albany: State University of New York, 2006), p. 36.

[18] *Ibid.*, pp. 34–35.

and physical sufferings, which have been ignored and exacerbated over the years. However, in spite of the considerable limitations of visual testimonies in attempting to represent the experience of the Cassinga massacre, such techniques are still perceived as having greater significance.

The purpose of picturing the open mass grave and contested representation of violence

Acting on the request of SWAPO, photojournalists from a number of Scandinavian and former Eastern Bloc countries travelled to Cassinga to photograph the dead bodies before they were buried in mass graves. Images of horror from Cassinga were destined to invite a strong international opposition to South Africa's illegal occupation of Namibia. In the following weeks and months, following the Cassinga massacre, a single photograph of the Cassinga open mass grave made headlines, as 'a document of horror', in international newspapers such as *Basler Zeitung*. However, what it showed restricted the viewer's understanding of the Cassinga violence within the perimeter of the photographic gaze. This chapter explores the way this photograph's representation of the testimony of the Cassinga massacre discloses a conflicting relationship between the story of the photograph on one hand, and testimonies of survivors on the other hand. It uses testimonies from interviews with survivors, especially from those with first hand accounts of the burial process thus adding their individual voice to the attempts to disclose the complexity of the Cassinga massacre beyond the limits of visual testimonies.

At this stage, it could be argued that this photograph's significance is not what it reveals, but the complexity of the violence it is oblivious to. In other words, there is more than meets the eye when this image is compared to the actual experience of the open mass grave. This image does not represent living memories of the open mass grave as witnessed by survivors, representing instead a staged reality of the scene of horror. In spite of the fact that this image does not show us the life of this horrific scene as witnessed, it nevertheless remains the "most important means through which the experience" of the Cassinga massacre is narrated and communicated to the public. As explained in the following excerpt, personal experiences of survivors of the Cassinga massacre challenge the reality that this image exhibits as represented in the following excerpt:

> I cannot comment anything about the content of this photograph ... suffice it saying that besides the reality that this photograph attempts to represent, there are multiple unknown graves of the victims of the Cassinga massacre. There are two mass graves at Cassinga. Where is the second one? Also, survivors who escaped from the camp tell stories of comrades who were badly injured, lost blood profusely and left to die

alone in the bush. The bodies of such victims were never recovered, but there are also reports that some of our people's remains were discovered by Angolans who buried them in the bush. But, I want to stress that what you see in this photograph is nothing, apa kape na sha apa!! This image has no resonance with the practical dynamics of the brutal violence on the ground: the memory pictures of the critically wounded comrades who succumbed to pain and loss of blood as others watched on, the screaming and anguished voices of despair of the wounded victims trapped in thatched dwellings under fire, the horror in the trenches where the bayoneting and shooting at close range of civilians unfolded predominantly. People suffered deplorable damage: physically, emotionally and psychologically. I have a friend of mine, Angelina Angula, a survivor of the Cassinga massacre and currently a teacher at the Mweshipandeka Senior Secondary School in Ongwediva. I would advise that you visit and interview her. She survived the massacre inside the trenches, covered by dead bodies – these terrible things remain vivid and troublesome. I personally remain in the shock of the horrific picture of mutilated bodies of women and children bayoneted to death inside the trenches ... as well as roasted bodies of women and children burned inside pit toilet holes and other shelters where they went in attempt seek protection. My memory of such unbearable picture, of those innocent Namibians slaughtered cold-bloodedly, is infinitely and permanently wounding me with no end in sight to it![19]

By claiming that the iconic photograph is "nothing," Mwatilifange is not dismissive of the experiences and narrative of this image. Rather, her discontent raises one important theory, and possibly several others. It suggests that the reality of the Cassinga massacre as experienced and lived by individual survivors since then is immensely deplorable and tangible and exceeds the visual and oral techniques of its documentation. However, the use of nothingness about this photograph does not suggest that this image shuts the window that ventilates general feelings of pain and sympathy for the victims of the Cassinga massacre. Instead, the photograph challenges individual survivors' "mental picture." It suggests that the devastation and destruction of human lives, which this image is oblivious to, preceded the capturing of the scene that this photograph represents.

Therefore, in essence, this image produces dissonance and rupture between the divergent, disturbing practical realities in testimonies of individual survivors and the considerable exclusion of brutal violence demonstrated by the photograph. In this context, the living traumatic experience that survivors decry resonates with what Siegfried Kracauer calls the "monogram." Rosalind Morris explains "monogram" as a "memory image," the last recalled image of a person whose lived history and relation to others generate a sense of his or her "truth." Anything which does not signify something in terms of that truth – what is often

---

[19]   The author's interview with Martha Mwatilifange, Oshakati, 2007.

called the essence of a person or personality – is generally omitted from these images.[20] The "nothingness" or the obvious contradiction between individual survivors and the Cassinga iconic photograph points to this image's alienation or disconnectedness from survivors' "monograms," the dynamics of those aspects which survivors count as tangibly traumatic, unacceptable and permanently present in the everyday traumatic memories of the victims of the Cassinga massacre.

Nonetheless, it is important to recognize that although many survivors failed to relate their personal experiences to this image, they were nevertheless encouraged to conquer the photograph's obtrusive silences. That is, each individual survivor eagerly explored and interrogated deplorable elements that the photograph missed, obscured or failed to disclose and explain to the inexperienced viewer. Survivors for instance, interrogated the way this image covers up the identities of the bodies in the mass grave. This translates into survivors' claims, to give one example, that most of the dead bodies were violently mutilated by the attackers. Moreover, the dead bodies were spoiled as they were left unattended for over a day before the mass burials.

In fact, the people affected by the Cassinga massacre see the iconic photograph as producing a shadow of darkness in the lives of the bereaved families. This shadow relates to the way this image represents the dead bodies of the victims of the Cassinga massacre. Yet, affected families find no explanation; nothing in this photograph can console and help them find solace in the loss of their loved ones. In essence, this image suggests that the 'truer' or tangible disastrous human carnage and personal identities of the Cassinga victims is something that nobody will ever recover and explain through the visual representation of that event.

If this image is a silhouette or shadow of the actual traumatic experience of those innocent Namibians buried in the mass grave, then it should not be perceived as representing the organic world of the Cassinga massacre in totality. Any testimony (unlike memory) about traumatic past is constructed under distinct limitations. To paraphrase Allen Johnson, in a different context, whether the aim of testimonial accounts (such as the case of the iconic photograph) is to tell how it really was or how it really came to be, such records can never reach mathematical certainty or a high degree of probability or explain the dynamics of the violence as experienced in actual life.[21] Instead, it should be understood as mnemonic,

---

[20] Rosalind C. Morris, *Photographies East: the camera and its histories in East and Southeast Asia* (Duke: Duke University Press, 2009), pp. 3–4; Siegfried Kracauer, "Photography." In *The mass ornament: Weimar essays* (Cambridge: Harvard University Press, 1995), p. 51.

[21] Allen Johnson, *The historian and historical evidence* (New York: Charles Scribner's sons, 1926), p. 141.

something that triggers survivors memories to interrogate this photograph's silences and exclusions of personal memories of that event. Consider the following account:

> The bodies in this mass grave (in the photograph above) are buried in layers. But, I must admit that most of them were not handled with the respect they deserved. Many of them were in very bad shape, especially those buried in the smaller mass grave as well as underneath the bigger mass grave: they were badly mutilated. The top layer that appears in this photograph contains the less mutilated bodies ... what is at the bottom of this photograph is horrible ... you cannot see it but – believe what I tell you! ... Pieces and parts of human flesh ... our soldiers from Lubango, who collected the bodies for burial, were instructed to bury the bodies accordingly, in respect of our customs and rituals. For example, the heads of the dead facing the West ... we detached shoes from their feet and removed the belts, as it is a custom that one cannot bury a dead body, oshimhu, wearing a belt or shoes. Regrettably, the task of collecting the bodies was enormous and quite challenging. The stench was unbearable and we had no special equipment and tools other than using bare hands and wooden sticks to carry the bodies ... The enemy abandoned some stretchers in the camp, but they were not enough. We cut wooden sticks to carry the bodies across the length and breadth of the camp ... and you know there were close to eight hundred dead bodies, not counting parts and pieces of human flesh. We tried the best we could, but it became too difficult to properly manage and control the distressful situation. It became almost impossible to bury the dead, procedurally and accordingly. It was a miserable moment ... We were confronted with uneasiness to do things accordingly. The unprecedented number of mutilated bodies ... the unpleasant stench of human blood and flesh made us drowsy, nauseous and very much uncomfortable. However, we managed to speed up that difficult and challenging task. We hurried to cover the mass graves to reduce the stench of the decomposing bodies. There was an urge to finish, at once, and move away from the horrible smell, away from the qualms of the unpleasant pictures of human misery and total destruction of the camp and property. Unfortunately, after we have closed the mass graves, we received instructions to display the bodies for journalists to view and document the massacre. People stepped on the bodies, removed sand and prepared the bodies for the journalists viewing and photographing. The mass graves were left open ... we covered the top of the open tombs with branches of Eucalyptus trees until the arrival of journalists from Luanda. It was a horrible experience, very difficult and emotional moment to remember: people dead with their grieving eyes and mouths widely open and fixed on you, which is customarily incorrect![22]

While the photograph of the Cassinga open mass grave may bring to our sight some prearranged images of blurred dead bodies, whose identities are difficult to recognize even with the assistance of survivors' interviews, this photograph cannot describe the agony of the dead persons buried in it. In the same way, this image fails to recognize personal identities of the corpses, which remain shrouded in the mystery of unknown persons. As Susan

---

[22] The author's interview with Darius 'Mbolondondo' Shikongo, Ondangwa, 2007.

Sontag would contend, "many of the canonical images of early war photography turn out to have been staged, or to have their subjects tampered with."[23] This trend in photography resonates with the way the photograph of the Cassinga open mass grave sparks conflicting statements when it is read by Cassinga survivors. The following account may help elucidate this conflict or ambivalence:

> My sister, Anna Max, was killed in the attack ... I was fortunate to discover her dead body and assessed how she was killed. She had two bullet wounds in the back of her head through her forehead. My analysis is that she was shot point-blank from behind while hiding from the enemy in the trenches. I, myself, laid her dead body on the top layer of the mass grave, but it is difficult to recognize and identify it in the photograph. But, for sure her body is there.[24]

The fact that this photograph converts the dead bodies into unknown and mysterious figures generates a particular trajectory of conflicting truths. Hence, the genre of truth documented in this photograph drifts away from the personal survivors' realities. This pertains to the witnesses' personal encounter with the physical recognition and emotional presence of the dead people during the burial process, not only mutilated but decomposing and issuing a terrible smell, with maggots and flies, all of which are not tangibly evident when one reads this image. Certainly, by producing silences about the dead bodies (and their personal memories) that it hosts, this image not only hides memories of the Cassinga massacre and denies inexperienced viewers an understanding of anything about the history that this photograph presumes to disclose, it says nothing about its authorship, dissemination and what impact it had among its audience. However, this image begins to get a life and context when others try to understand the unknown history of this image. Gary Baines explains:

> The "iconic photograph" of the Cassinga open mass grave, in black and white was widely syndicated and published by newspapers such as *Basler Zeitung* under the caption 'Ein Dokument des Grauens,' which translates into English as, 'a document of horror.' In June [1978] SWAPO issued its eponymous bulletin with the same image appearing on the cover with the byline ('Massacre at Kassinga: climax of Pretoria's all-out campaign against the Namibian resistance').The picture was included in the Kassinga File, a collection of images compiled by Pagano and Swedish filmmaker Sven Asberg.[25] The file circulated through a network of agencies and organizations affiliated to the international anti-apartheid movements. These organizations distributed and displayed the images of the mass grave at pub-

---

[23] *Ibid.*, pp. 46–48.
[24] The author's interview with Darius 'Mbolondondo' Shikongo, Ondangwa, 2007.
[25] Sven Asberg appears to have visited Cassinga in the company of Gaetano Pagano. He is often quoted as Pagano's co-author of some of the photographs of the Cassinga massacre photographed by the journalists who visited Cassinga after the attack.

lic exhibitions and in publications. The shot became emblematic of the Cassinga massacre. It was also reproduced on a number of posters commemorating Kassinga [or Cassinga] Day produced by solidarity organizations such as the International University Exchange Fund (IUEF) and SWAPO's own Department of Information and Publicity poster entitled 'Massacre at Kassinga' which must have been produced fairly soon after the event.[26]

Because this visual image conceals much, it pastes a blurred and ambiguous reality onto different accounts that attempt to remember, authenticate and historicize its origin. Consider the following account in response to my attempts to find facts about this photo:

> The photo [of the Cassinga open mass grave] was captured between May 5 and 6 by Gaetano Pagano, an Italian. He was at the time shooting a documentary film on Angola for a Swedish Television (SVT). We / the UN team (UNHCR and WHO) and two journalists from the GDR only arrived in Cassinga a week or so after the attack. By then all the mass graves were already covered.[27]

The history of this photograph continues to be twisted and casts a blurred version when Per Sanden who arrived in Cassinga before any other photographer told me that he is not the author of this image as previously claimed by some authors:

> I cannot, of course, answer for all the other photographers who visited Cassinga after the massacre. In my own case, I did not develop my photographs (most of which were shot in Cassinga a few days before the attack) until I arrived in Stockholm (Sweden), about a month later. When it comes to the film rolls they were all processed in London, a couple of days later, since I sent them there for processing and dissemination, owing to the fact that South Africa claimed they had attacked a military installation and not a refugee settlement. BBC in London processed the 16 mm films and used them together with my other material taken in Cassinga before the attack. This was fast considering the availability of laboratories, flights to Europe, etcetera, when there were no portable professional video equipment that time and no linking of 16 mm film material directly to various stations around the world, which is the case today.[28]

---

[26]   Source: BAB, A.A3, SWAPO Collection, 78aSPR2, 16 May 1978. Also in Gary Baines, "The Battle for Cassinga: Conflicting Narratives and Contested Meanings," 2007. Visit: http://eprints.ru.ac.za/946/1/baines_Cassinga.pdf

[27]   The author's email interview with Tor Sellstrom, 2009. Tor Sellstrom, a Swedish citizen, "coordinated official Swedish support to the Patriotic Fronts (ZANU/ ZAPU) of Zimbabwe, SWAPO and to the ANC of South Africa." SIDA provided crucial humanitarian support (such as education and health facilities) to SWAPO civilian centres of exiled Namibians during the liberation struggle.

[28]   The author's interview with Per Sanden, Windhoek, 2009. Per Sanden was possibly the first photographer to arrive in Cassinga after the massacre. Prior to the Cassinga attack, he had spent time in Cassinga documenting the everyday life of refugees in the camp. He was there until 3 May 1978. Cassinga was attacked a few hours after he had left. He was prompted to go back to Cassinga to document the massacre. Unfortunately, due to logistics and security concerns, he only

The authorship of this image is not an issue here. Of course, the importance of this image lies in the undisputed fact that this photograph is testimony to the mass burials of innocent Namibians killed in Cassinga. However, the evidence of this image becomes problematic because it is self-contained and self-actualized. And, although this image represents a scene that was seen and captured live, nothing of such practical kind reaches the audience in the same way that the violence was experienced by different agents of witnessing and the accounts this generated. In fact, generally, all visual images dilute violence. As Liisa Malkki writes, in a different context, "photographs and other visual representations ... speed up the evaporation of history and narrativity."[29] This implies that "to photograph is to frame and to frame is to exclude,"[30] conceal and damage evidence. This is exactly what the photograph of the Cassinga open mass grave does. This is further explored in the following interview:

> I arrived back in Cassinga on 6 May 1978 together with units of PLAN from Jamba, a mine town southeast of Cassinga, where we arrived in the evening of the 3rd of May, 1978 from Cassinga. Traveling back to Cassinga in a heavily armed convoy of Volvo jeeps, Land Rovers and trucks with plenty of PLAN soldiers we all speculated about what was going to meet us there. ... We drove up and offloaded at the big parade ground in Cassinga where I had delivered a short speech, during my first visit to Cassinga, in front of hundreds of women and children who gathered at the parade.[31] I had seen dead people before, during the years from 1973, when I first crossed into Namibia with PLAN combatants, and onwards. Nevertheless, this was more devastating than anything else I had experienced before. The smell was evident; it lay across the place as a fog. I knew I came back with a purpose. I went into action without hesitating. The Aaton camera was prepared like I always used to do, cleaned the lens, checked the battery level and extra cassettes, placed it in its special belt around the waist, extra batteries in the jacket pocket, off I went [to the mass graves]. PLAN soldiers had removed the huge branches that had covered the pitches, which were all full with bodies. There it stopped for me. I got the camera up to the right eye, I watched through the ocular the horrific sight of war fought with terror. People I had met just three days earlier! I could not do the normal shots, close ups, wider pictures with perhaps a panoration [sic], as any other camera operator could have done, I suppose. I did not even zoom in to set focus and then zoom out. I felt like I intruded a space with its own rules. Here hundreds of people were laying, they could receive

---

arrived in Cassinga on 6 May with SWAPO combatants.

29 Liisa Malkki H., "Speechless emissaries: refugees humanitarianism, and dehistoricization." In Hinton Alexander Laban (ed.), *Genocide: an anthropological reader* (Malden, MA: Blackwell, 2002) p. 353.

30 Susan Sontag, *Regarding the pain of others*, p. 41.

31 Parade or Okapale, in the Oshiwambo language, is where daily roll calls were made prior to resuming daily activities in and around the Cassinga camp. The Okapale was the main target of the first wave of the surprise air bombardments that hit directly on crowds of people assembled at the morning parade.

recognition, perhaps of their mothers and their fathers and their children, who could feel offended by my zooming down into their misery. I took a few wide shots of the two pitches [sic], well describing the magnitude of this crime. [Well], it turned out that my wide shots were not so common among all the other camera operators flown there from Luanda. We moved away from the pitches [sic] that became the graves of Cassinga.[32]

The reality of the Cassinga open mass grave, as Per Sanden suggests, resides in the personal memory of those who experienced it. This involves the physical and emotional engagement with dead bodies, the inconceivable reality of human suffering, agony and anguish of traumatic death. These experiences are almost impossible to transmit to others through visual techniques. Practically therefore, what happened in Cassinga, in terms of human loss and suffering, is beyond the reach of any photographic narration. That is, no photograph can explain or show anything regarding the human suffering and misery, which the dead bodies in the Cassinga open mass grave endured. In this context, one may reason that Per Sanden's apprehensiveness not to shoot accurately or 'zoom in to set focus' and shoot at the bodies (similar to the gun shots at close range) derives from the notion that to do so would be akin to disclosing nothing. Put it differently, picturing the bodies in the mass grave is a way of obscuring the horror that actually transpired at Cassinga.

This places emphasis that the mutilation and the decomposition of the bodies were so gruesome that even a close-up shot would not have helped anyone to successfully capture and identify every dead body. "They [the mutilated bodies] could receive no recognition" by photographing them, as Per Sanden put it in the interview above, which would cause further emotional damage to the affected individual families and, possibly, shut the door to any closure or serenity of the families whose loved ones went missing following the Cassinga massacre. Individuals could establish no link between the actual events and the image the photograph has pictured and framed. Affected people would look at such a disturbing image of violence in an attempt to identify people they know, to find nothing and remain haunted by the ambivalence and the complete absence of answers they had expected to find in photographs, answers that would help explain unresolved questions about the Cassinga massacre. Alternatively, if photographs were able to name and identify the missing victims of the Cassinga massacre, affected families could accept the loss of their loved ones and possibly find some sort of tangible closure.

It therefore appears obvious that to photograph a scene of violence is not a way of showing evidence of what actually took place. Instead, it is an agency through which uncertainty and ambiguity become explicit as events and their subjects are removed and disconnected

---

[32] The author's interview with Per Sanden, Windhoek, 2009.

from their natural niche or life. Thus, to photograph the Cassinga open mass grave is an act of belatedly staging residues of violence. Hence this practice is fraught with considerable omissions, inexactitude and negation from the impact of violence.

With reference to the photograph of the Cassinga open mass grave, it can be said that this image does not convey the unadulterated experiences of violence to the intended recipient. In fact, it should be noted that the scale of damage and exclusion due to the camera's close or distant shots, as Per Sanden mentioned earlier, is high and carries negative implications. The closer the camera lens moves to focus on a specific area, the greater are the number of excluded elements. Contrarily, the further the camera lens moves away from the target of shooting, the more the photographed scene generates ambivalence and ambiguity to the viewer.

Closely connected to this line of thought is Per Sanden's perception of the association between the camera and its operator as producing a sense of betrayal, mistrust and the transgression of sympathy for the dead and the affected. Most importantly, since the dead bodies (most of which lay underneath and beyond the reach of the camera's eye or lens) in the mass grave were reduced to rubble and disfigured, photographic images from that scene could be manipulated by the other side or opposition. The ambivalent state of such images could inadvertently help create a fertile ground for the perpetrators to advance defensive claims, in desperate attempts to repair their damaged reputation for killing innocent civilians.

Such is the case regarding the existing claims by certain perpetrators involved in the Cassinga massacre. They are adamant the photograph of the Cassinga open mass grave provides no evidence to authenticate SWAPO's version of the event, namely that those killed in Cassinga or buried in the mass graves are beyond any doubt civilians, in particular, women and children. Consider the following scenario:

> In my opinion, however, this photograph proves conclusively that there was no massacre of the innocents as alleged by Alexander in his thesis ... that accusation was a propaganda ploy on the part of SWAPO and its sympathizers and that Alexander, if he was an unbiased investigator, should have arrived at the same conclusion. The relatively few female casualties found in the photograph(s) most certainly included the unfortunate ones ... used as human shields during the fighting in the trenches. Where is the mass grave filled with the bodies of well over a thousand refugees, mostly women and children? Alexander carefully avoided this thorny question but still made the accusation in his thesis that the majority of the people massacred in Cassinga were civilian refugees. Photographs to prove this shameful accusation are strangely not available.[33]

---

[33] Jan Breytenbach, *Eagle strike*, p. 563. Also read Edward Alexander, "The Cassinga raid" (UNISA: unpublished MA Thesis, July 2003).

Closely linked to this statement, Breytenbach purported that:

> SWAPO mutilated the bodies of its own people deliberately ... to underline the horror of the moment ... a deliberate ploy to claim that Cassinga was a refugee camp and not a most important military target. They wanted to hide the fact that they had suffered a huge military defeat by trying to turn it into a massacre.[34]

When different viewers engage with visual images, each viewer sees what he or she believes in, or wants the public to believe in, regardless of its inclusions and exclusions. As such, this image has become a much contested bone of contention between different agencies debating the Cassinga massacre. The following contradictory statements illustrate this problem of a dialogue that would take the viewer or reader nowhere:

> The images of corpses, some of whom are women, some young, and some wearing civilian clothing are evident to a cursory examination of the photograph.[35]

Countering this argument again is Breytenbach who maintains that:

> The so-called mass grave [photograph] shows a great majority of men, all [of] them combatants, with only three women barely recognizable among the lot and, significantly, without any evidence whatsoever of dead or mutilated children.[36]

It would have been interesting if Breytenbach were to disclose his own photographs of the Cassinga attack to substantiate, if possible, his claims. But it appears quite challenging for him to make public photographs that would undisputedly corroborate that Cassinga was not a civilian camp. Why? Analytically, Breytenbach's opinion does not deny the fact that his paratroopers killed and mutilated bodies of innocent women and children at Cassinga. But his statement resonates with the impossibility of the photograph of the Cassinga open mass grave to reveal the physical and emotional torture or suffering that the attackers brutally inflicted on civilians. Therefore, in considering this discourse, the conflict between the different agencies of seeing and commenting on the Cassinga iconic photograph is explained as credibly embedded in the darkness that this image elicits. Put differently, the enduring blackout that this image unleashes evaporates evidence and nourishes inconclusive dialogues between different witnesses, writers and commentators of the Cassinga event. The perpetrators claim that this image does not show the bodies of civilians confirms that

---

[34] *Ibid.*, pp. 543 & 564.

[35] Gary Baines, "The Battle of Cassinga: conflicting narratives and contested meanings." Accessed from *http://eprints.ru.ac.za/946/1/baines.Cassinga.pdf.*

[36] Jan Breytenbach, "Cassinga battle account reveals biased claptrap," *The Sunday Independent*, 3 February 2008, edition 1, p. 6 (See Appendix G of this book).

this photograph is not only ambivalent but also ambiguous. It allows viewers to attribute different meanings and interpretations onto it. As mentioned earlier, the failure of this image to provide indisputable evidence regarding the massacre of innocent civilians in Cassinga empowers the perpetrators to overwrite their wrong-doing in Cassinga with the aura of correctness and blamelessness.

Christopher Pinney, to paraphrase him, in his study of cultural production through images in India, problematized the space that photography occupies as ... "a place where faces can easily become masks and where reality can easily become invisible ...."[37] It is the invisibility of the actual dynamic space of violence in the photograph of the Cassinga open mass grave that the following excerpt alludes to:

> Many people fled to the trenches and most of them were killed inside them. The enemy went up to the trenches and moved along them bayoneting people to death. The trenches were constructed with the purpose of providing a saver passage to escape from the camp, in case of an attack. But most people just went into the trenches and bed down idle. Some people were wounded before they got into the trenches, therefore they could not move further. So the Boers bayoneted and shot them at point blank range, inside the trenches. We found many people with such wounds. Apart from that, the wounded and desperate victims were spread across the camp. I always remember an elderly man who was seriously wounded on the face. The entire foreskin peeled off from the face and it was covering his sight. What shocked me is that he was lying not far from us as we sat under a shade resting, because, we were very tired. He lay down flat and motionless like a dead person. But, suddenly, on hearing a command to collect his body for burial, he stood up ... which surprised and shocked most of us. He was taken to the hospital, Techamutete, and I did not know whether he survived. I swear we spent time in front of him thinking that he was dead and he was laying still like dead.[38]

Again, this description contends with the notion that the photograph of the Cassinga open mass grave eludes the tangible horror and complexities of the Cassinga massacre. I find this contradiction problematic; in view of survivors' comments on this photograph, tangible violence makes heavy concessions to photography. Of course, this image unleashes uncomfortable emotions to those affected by the Cassinga massacre, because it does not help affected families to find some closure. Perhaps, multiple images of the Cassinga massacre, including those taken by the attackers, would have presented the public with the supremely unacceptable scenes of the violence as reported by survivors.

---

[37]   Christopher Pinney, *Camera Indica: The social life of Indian photographs* (London: Reaktion books, 1997), pp. 8–15.

[38]   Author's interview with Darius "Mbolondondo" Shikongo, Ondangwa, 2007.

It is helpful at this stage to put into perspective why the Cassinga event is represented by the presence of a solitary photograph when the event is actually suffused with multiple experiences of brutal atrocities. Why was there no release of other photographs from different angles of seeing violence in Cassinga, as evident in survivors' testimonies? Why were no photographs taken before the arrival of foreign journalists who visited Cassinga days after the massacre? Why did SWAPO not work in partnership with the host government (Angola) to photograph and record the immediate aftermath of the Cassinga massacre? The following accounts would try to explore possible answers to these anomalies.

Interviewees had no clue as to whether the Cubans who forced the SADF to retreat from Cassinga and who were the first to arrive in the camp did take photographs of the violence. However, according to two informants,[39] a crew of Angolan photographers and journalists who arrived in Cassinga a few hours following the SADF withdrawal was denied access into the camp. They claimed that Dimo Hamaambo, who at the time was the commander of the People's Liberation Army of Namibia, had personally refused the Angolan television crew access to the camp. His decision landed him in trouble with the FAPLA. He and Greenwell Matongo, the chief political commissar of PLAN, were "summarily arrested" by the "irate FAPLA and detained at the headquarters of the 5th Military Region in Lubango on the order of Ivadi (according to Richard Kabajani), the irate FAPLA commander."[40] The arrest of Hamaambo and Matongo almost immediately following the Cassinga massacre is not surprising considering the following political squabbles between PLAN and FAPLA soldiers.

In the late seventies, political wrangles bedevilled the relationship between FAPLA and SWAPO over PLAN's forward operational bases in southern Angola. This trouble was anchored in FAPLA's suspiciousness around SWAPO's long-standing collaboration and comradeship with UNITA[41] prior to the independence of Angola. In many instances, according

---

[39]   The author's interviews with Paavo Max, Ogwendiva, 2007; Darius "Mbolondondo" Shikongo, Ondangwa, 2007.

[40]   Annemarie Heywood, *The Cassinga event*, pp. 54–55.

[41]   SWAPO was closely connected to UNITA whose support base was firmly rooted in the rural masses. This type of support base was akin to SWAPO's traditional base or political stronghold which had been, since the days of the liberation struggle, among the Aawambo, the largest population group of Namibia and who predominantly live in the rural areas of north central Namibia. In a similar way, UNITA's solid support came from the rural population of Angola, predominantly among the Mbundu, the largest ethnic group in the country. UNITA's political programme was also analogous to SWAPO's political programme of uplifting the lives of the rural poor and the exploited working class. This historical closeness between SWAPO and UNITA is explicable given that the mestiço-dominated, urban-based MPLA had its core of support in the intelligentsia of the capital city, Luanda, and Ovimbundu-speaking areas in north – west Angola. UNITA presented itself as the messiah for the oppressed peasants. Its constitution proclaimed that the movement would strive for a government proportionally representative of all ethnic groups, clans, and classes, and it "concentrated on raising the political consciousness of the peasants, most of whom were

to the General Reports of the Cassinga camp committee,[42] FAPLA had made serious accusations that the SWAPO civilian camp at Cassinga was harboring UNITA civilians and supplying them with provisions, mainly food and medicine. SWAPO soldiers at the forward military bases close to the Namibian border, from where they launched operations into Namibia, experienced regular harassments from the Angolan forces. In one such instance, FAPLA was reported to have arrested and disarmed PLAN "representatives" [members] at Cuangari, and then taken them to Pereirade Eça. This arrest followed the alleged clash between FAPLA and PLAN fighters at Oshitumbe on 9 June 1976 on allegations that UNITA members were seen being ferried in a PLAN lorry. According to the Cubans in Angola, FAPLA detained 58 other PLAN fighters en route to the front for the same reason.[43]

The General Reports of the Cassinga camp committee blamed the "enemy" for such incidents. It was noted that "enemies were trying hard to bring about friction and subsequently open conflict between the two progressive armed forces."[44] In the Cassinga camp General Reports of 5 May 1976, Commissar Ndafogwe Nopoundjuu reported the following: "when I met Shimbalanga, the head of the Information Department in Lubango,[45] at Cenjanca [sic] ... he almost burst out in rage; accusing us [SWAPO] of being obstinate in regard to orders given by the government ... he accused us of collaborating with UNITA. [He said] a senior UNITA commander was found at Cassinga and in the past [SWAPO] refused to hand over Nangonja."[46] In a similar report of the minutes of the Cassinga camp committee meeting held on 26 November 1976, it was reported that "the FAPLA comrades will not trust us [SWAPO] easily. They are now somehow convinced that SWAPO is not sincere about cooperating with them. Of late, the FAPLA at Canjanla [sic] recognized a former UNITA member called Hamala. He was in a group of sick people who were to receive treatment at Cassinga.

illiterate and widely dispersed." See Robin Hallett, "The CIA in Angola," *African affairs*, Vol. 78 /313 (October 1978), pp. 559–562; Christian A. Williams, "Exile history: an ethnography of the SWAPO camps and the Namibian nation" (Doctoral Dissertation, University of Michigan, 2009).

[42] These handwritten reports are contained in the "Cassinga General Reports," Available at the Basler Afrika Bibliographien (BAB) in Basel, Switzerland. Authors of the notes include Golden Uhuru and Mocks Shivute (the camp secretary and deputy secretary respectively). According to the archivist, these are some of the SWAPO documents that the SADF captured in Cassinga.

[43] BAB AA3 (SWAPO Collection), additional documents: "General reports" by SWAPO 1976–1978. Source: BAB SWAPO Archive, Basel, Switzerland.

[44] BAB AA3 (SWAPO Collection), additional documents: "General reports" by SWAPO 1976–1978. Source: BAB SWAPO Archive, Basel, Switzerland.

[45] BAB AA3 (SWAPO Collection), additional documents: "General reports" by SWAPO 1976–1978. Source: BAB SWAPO Archive, Basel, Switzerland.

[46] Statement by Cde. Shimbalanga [sic], head of the information department in Lubango, at Cenjanca before Commissar Ndafongwe Nopoundjuu on 3. 12. 1976, in the BAB AA3 (SWAPO Collection), additional documents: "General Reports" by SWAPO 1976–1978. Source: BAB SWAPO Archives, Basel, Switzerland. Godfrey Nangonya was liaison officer between SWAPO and UNITA, See Nangonya interviews with Patricia Hayes (personal communication, Patricia Hayes, 2009).

According to FAPLA, the man worked with a former UNITA commander, Hamupunda. They (FAPLA) therefore do not understand why these criminals are in our ranks. The man has been taken away."[47]

The minutes of the Cassinga camp committee meeting of 26 November 1976 brought to the attention of the committee that Major Zulu was forced by FAPLA to hand over "four girls [allegedly] former UNITA members, two from Namibia and two from within Angola.[48] During that meeting, Major Zulu admitted and expressed fear that FAPLA was preparing to make inroads into SWAPO bases for identification of former UNITA members."[49]

These developments might help to explain why Hamaambo refused to issue permission to the alleged crew of Angolan journalists. Such unpleasant incidents may also explain why FAPLA dealt with Hamaambo and other SWAPO commanders in a disrespectful manner, arresting him and his juniors for ambiguous reasons. Nonetheless, several other theories arise in the attempt to explain and understand why Hamaambo refused to allow the Angolans access to photograph and document the fresh scene of the Cassinga massacre. It is telling that Mbolondondo thinks that Hamaambo "was paranoid to have taken that decision."

Hamaambo's apprehensiveness to allow journalists free access to the camp is, however, better understood when the following circumstances are considered: the atrocities committed by the SADF in Cassinga were so gruesome and raised concerns about the impact such

---

[47]   BAB AA3 (SWAPO Collection), additional documents: "General Reports" by SWAPO 1976–1978. Source: BAB SWAPO Archive, Basel, Switzerland.

[48]   It is important to note that SWAPO, MPLA and UNITA all consisted of members from the Oshikwanyama ethnic group. Moreover, there had been incidents where former FAPLA soldiers and UNITA members (especially the Oshikwanyama speaking individuals) switched sides to join SWAPO based on the shared cultural bond and historical oneness before the colonial border divided the two countries. According to Hangula, "an agreement fixing the boundary between Namibia and Angola was reached, and a boundary convention was signed on 22 June 1922 in Cape Town between the Union of South Africa and the government of the Republic of Portugal." Lazarus Hangula. *International boundary of Namibia (1993)*, p. 41. See also Randolph Vigne, "The moveable frontier: the Namibia–Angola boundary demarcation." In Patricia Hayes, et al. (eds.), *Namibia under South African Rule: mobility & containment 1915–1946* (Oxford: James Currey, 1998), pp. 289–304. The agreement that fixed the boundary between Namibia and Angola bisected the Oshikwanyama-speaking people into two halves, allocating a portion of it on either side of the border but with the largest group of the Oshikwanyama-speaking people located on the Angolan side of the border. Many Oshiwambo-speaking people (which includes the Oshikwanyama-speaking groups) also fell into the hands of UNITA while trying to reach SWAPO bases in Angola. This means that many of them were waiting to defect to SWAPO when opportunity existed. Likewise, FAPLA experienced cases where their soldiers, especially those who spoke Oshikwanyama, defected to SWAPO. One instance is the case of the "heroic" PLAN commander, Matias Ndakolo Mbulunganga, who defected from FAPLA in the 1960s and became a prominent PLAN commander. Online at http://allafrica.com/stories/201008250672.html. "Namibia: Heroic battles of Matias Mbulunganga." Also in the *New Era*, 25 August, 2010.

[49]   BAB AA3 (SWAPO Collection), additional documents: "General reports" by SWAPO 1976–1978. Source: BAB SWAPO Archive, Basel, Switzerland.

images would create especially among SWAPO supporters at home. In the seventies, before combat clashes intensified between the SADF and SWAPO guerrillas, SWAPO fighters were, locally, associated with combat myths and supernatural power in fighting the colonialist army. This suggests that prior to joining SWAPO in exile, many civilians reasoned that once in SWAPO camps, it was no longer possible for the enemy to hunt them down and kill them. In this context, Hamaambo would have thought that the picture of the gruesome Cassinga massacre would result in the decline of the number of people joining SWAPO in exile and at home. The second reason could be that Hamaambo would have denied Angolan photographers' access to Cassinga on the grounds of being suspicious and mistrustful of the media and what their intentions were, or how they planned to use their captured images. The issue of security was another important factor. SWAPO was an armed revolutionary movement very suspicious and sensitive to possible enemy espionage. In this context, it could have been particularly difficult for Hamaambo and Matongo to verify the identity of the Angolan media crew as representing the MPLA government. It was believed that UNITA or its allies could disguise themselves as government agents. FAPLA was not to be trusted in view of the problematic relationships with SWAPO as presented above.

The other reason was the ineffective communication network. The SADF disabled Cassinga's link with places such as Luanda and Lubango. This suggests that Hamaambo and Matongo acted on their individual initiatives. However, Hamaambo's decision not to permit Angolans access into the camp suggests that he was possibly disappointed with the Angolans for not responding militarily to help Namibians against the attackers. Had FAPLA responded militarily, many lives would have been saved. Moreover, Hamaambo's decision underpins an ethos of strictly following combat norms. PLAN had strict combat ethics regarding the protection of identities of fallen fighters, especially senior commanders, for example those senior SWAPO commanders who were among the bodies of civilians, such as Jonas Haiduwa,[50] the Deputy Commander of PLAN, and Nalikonkole, the chief administrator of the Cassinga camp.

Finally, Hamaambo's alleged refusal to allow the Angolan journalist crew entrance into Cassinga should not only be viewed through the lens of the factors illustrated above. Issues pertaining to the social and cultural rites of the Namibian exiled community should be considered. Notably, photographing the dead bodies for public exhibiting and viewing may have been politically acceptable but was in fact culturally unacceptable.

---

[50] Haiduwa was appointed Deputy Commander of PLAN at the 8th meeting of the SWAPO Military Council, held on 04/ 01/ 1977, contained in the "Minutes of the SWAPO Military Council meeting, held on 4 January 1977, Mongolia (Angola)" in the SADF Chief of Staff Operations, Operation Reindeer *(Top Secret): H Reer / 309/1 DD MRT 78*, in file HS OPS/ 301/ 2. Source: SANDF Archive, Pretoria.

3 The Attackers' Photographs and the Eyewitness Testimony

In reading and analyzing different viewers' comments about photographs of the Okiek people of Kenya, Corinne Kratz contends that photographs were the "mnemonic that prompted people to talk about events ... beyond what is shown..."[1] The context of Kratz's analysis is not based on visual images of war and violence, unlike mine, but her view that photographs are "mnemonic" to memory is relevant here. Her analysis of how people relate to photographs, or how photographs relate to people in social practice is reflective of my experience of how photographs of violence relate to the Cassinga victims' experiences, as well as how the victims relate or locate their experiences of the violence beyond the perimeters of the photographs I presented to them.

My analysis of the Cassinga survivors' response to the photographs, mostly images taken by the South Africans in Cassinga, which I presented to them during the interviews, demonstrated how visual images triggered survivors' memories and presented them with the momentum to explore the hidden realities beyond the surface of some of the visual images that the enemy shot during the Cassinga massacre. In his book, *The Eagle Strike: The Story of the controversial airborne assault on Cassinga 1978*, Jan Breytenbach used a number of photographs, which the SADF shot in Cassinga. These photographs reveal no dead bodies of women and children shot dead by the SADF during that operation. The exclusion of civilians' dead bodies in Breytenbach's book appears deliberate, perhaps an attempt to corroborate the SADF rhetoric that the Cassinga attack was not a massacre of civilians. Hence, Breytenbach, who as the commander of the Cassinga attack, bears witness to the massacre of civilians, has a high regard for his publication as a "disclosure of truth" about the Cassinga event. Yet, how the truth of that event can "appear ... outside ellipsis and hyperbole,"[2] or how truth is made visible and tangible through photographs and texts, is deliberately left unproblematised in Breytenbach's book. For this reason, the SADF visual testimonies of the Cassinga massacre are particularly in conflict with survivors' testimonies that claim that the SADF killed civilians with intent, many of whom were shot at point black range or bayonetted to death, as they lay wounded and in need of immediate medical provision. In this relation, this chapter will focus on a photograph depicting Col. Jan Breytenbach and Brig. Mike Du Plessis, the two Cassinga commanding officers, to explore and raise interest-

---

[1]   Corinne A. Kratz, *The ones that are wanted: communication and the politics of representation in a photographic exhibition* (California: University of California Press, 2002), p. 148–149.

[2]   Pamela Marie Hoffer, *Reflets reciproques: a prismatic reading of Stephane Mallarne and Helene Cixous* (New York: Peter Lang Publishing,2006), p. 173.

ing debates about how the SADF attempts to use 'violentless' photographs as testimony to support their version of the Cassinga event. Before embarking on this central discursive theme, it is important to provide some background about how I accessed this photograph and a number of others.

I obtained this photograph, below, from the Department of Defence Archives in Pretoria. This institution was established as the SA Defence Force (SADF) archive in 1968, following approval by the Minister of Education for a separate military archive. It specializes in military history and houses the official records of the Department of Defence, as well as a collection of unique publications, unit history files, photographs, maps and charts pertaining to the Department of Defence and its predecessors dating from 1912. Accessibility to the archival documents is in accordance with the National Archives of South Africa Act (Act No. 43 of 1996) and in the case of classified documentation, accessibility is subject to approval of the Chief of Defence Intelligence of the Department of Defence.[3] This indicates that the now South African National Defence Force (SANDF) archive is highly bureaucratized as all documents (including photographs) must go through a process of declassification before they are made available to researchers. Documents already declassified are required to be re-scrutinized before researchers access them.

In my case, most of the archival materials, already declassified, that I have requested from the archives had not been released to me by the end of my field work in 2009. I have no intention to dwell on the politics of the colonial-apartheid archive in this book. But, as in Premesh Lalu's analysis of the colonial archive, it is pertinent to understand it in the context of an institution that the "discipline of history generally approaches ... with a measure of suspicion because of its supposedly inherent 'biases.'..." Indeed, the colonial archive translates into an institution that is embedded in "covering up the traces of complicity in violence ..."[4]

The SADF photographs of the Cassinga massacre, at least those I accessed, are shrouded in dubiously clean hands. This pertains to both the SADF and its archive. It is this sheer look of unblameworthiness, or the immaculateness of such images, that I explore later in this chapter. My numerous visits to the former SADF archive in Pretoria, between 2007 and 2010 revealed that, even after the collapse of institutionalized apartheid and violence, the colonial archive still validates and preserves the apartheid culture of constructing frontiers of obscurity around the histories which disclose apartheid – colonial acts of violence against its vulnerable subjects. In the same way as the colonial archive moderates the specific his-

---

3   Visit: *http://www.national.archives.gov.za/dir_entries_pg3.htm.*
4   Premesh Lalu, *The deaths of Hintsa: postapartheid South Africa and the shape of recurring pasts*(Cape Town: Human Sciences Research Council, 2009), p. 41.

tories surrounding the killing of Hintsa, to paraphrase Lalu, my efforts to dig up specific detailed histories in the former SADF archive about the killings of Namibian refugees at Cassinga in ways which depart from the SADF construction and justification of the colonial massacre were significantly constrained by the intransigence and pervasiveness of the discourse of the colonial archive.

The visual images unveiled to me for research, possibly in selective ways, consisted mainly of aerial photographs. Predominantly, these were images recorded by the South African Air Force (SAAF) Joint Air Reconnaissance Intelligence Centre (JARIC) before the Cassinga massacre. According to Edward Alexander, Canberra photo-reconnaissance aircrafts[5] carried out several reconnaissance missions over Cassinga prior to the attack. Ideally, these images corroborate survivors' oral accounts that a few weeks leading up to the Cassinga massacre, suspicious planes were noticed orbiting the aerial space around Cassinga. Such movements were noticed mainly in the early hours of the morning or at noon, as confirmed by many of the survivors that I interviewed.

Thus, there were very few traces of the photographs and no video footage of the SADF coverage of the Cassinga operation. This is despite the fact that the SADF mission for the Cassinga massacre was equipped with cameras and video equipment. According to Edward McGill Alexander, who has conducted a substantial number of interviews with the Cassinga paratroopers, "one paratrooper who was a photographer was given a 16mm cine camera and a still camera to take with him when he jumped into Cassinga. He received orders to record images of what took place. The man appointed to carry out this task, Mike McWilliams, claimed during an interview conducted with him, to have used the opportunity to take along an additional still camera of his own ... McWilliams claims that he handed the official cameras and films back to the military authorities at the end of the operation."[6] There are claims that individual paratroopers used personal cameras during the Cassinga massacre. Brigadier Mike Du Plessis is quoted as telling Sgt. Major Fougstedt in an interview that "Morne Coetzer of the SABC recorded some video footage, while many of us took photos with ordinary cameras. Many photos came out, but we weren't as successful as we had hoped to be."[7] Moreover, according to other sources, paratroopers recalled having been shown "a 16mm film footage [of the Cassinga attack] at a paratroopers' reunion some months after the raid and the film was, according to official minutes, shown at a debriefing conference ... However, the 16mm film footage could not be traced, nor could all the

---

5   Edward Alexander, "The Cassinga raid," p. 115.
6   Edward Alexander, "The Cassinga raid," p. 21.
7   Jan Breytenbach, *Eagle strike*, p. 494.

photographs."[8] In this regard, there is also a concern about the whereabouts of the documents that the paratroopers captured from Cassinga. The SADF official reports concerning the things captured in Cassinga state that the paratroopers "brought from Cassinga four trunks full of documents."[9]

According to the head of the photographic section at the former SADF archive in Pretoria, Gerald Prinsloo, the archive never entered any record of SADF-produced video footage of the Cassinga massacre. He told me that many of the Cassinga photographs available in the archive were deposited by individuals and not by the SADF as an institution. This is particularly so of the colour photographs that Mr. Prinsloo told me were donated to the archives in 2009 by one of the former Cassinga paratroopers who now lives in Europe (see Appendix D for some of these Cassinga attack photographs). Nevertheless, I considered it fortunate to have found a few essential photographs, relevant to the theme of my study. These photographs show the SADF paratroopers in Cassinga during its fall. Surprisingly, these images do not show the paratroopers' involvement in the indiscriminate shooting of civilians in the camp. These exclusions are crucial in attempting to explore the SADF deconstruction and packaging of the Cassinga massacre through visual images. The other concern is that most of the photographs do not contain crucial information such as the authors/photographers of the images. In the case of the photograph that I will discuss in this chapter, the only archival information it contained is a caption that reads: "Col J. Breytenbach (with radio) and Brig. Du Plessis at Cassinga." When I started drafting this chapter – focusing on this photograph – I sent an email to Prinsloo, inquiring about the author of this image and how the archive accessed it. He explained:

> It can be assumed that the photo was one of a group of official photos regarding Cassinga donated by the Defence Force to the archive. The film would have been developed and printed in the archive's own darkroom (now defunct). Unfortunately, we have no further specific information on the photo or photographer. Except for the following information: Indexed into the archive: 1980.[10]

Certainly, the failure to release documents of horror for public viewing in this case dilutes the SADF version of events that Cassinga was a sophisticated military base and the Headquarters for the SWAPO guerrillas in Angola. Moreover, the possibility that the SADF never deposited sensitive materials of the Cassinga attack in the SADF archives or removed them during the process of South Africa's transition to democracy suggests that the perpetrators' version of the Cassinga story is politically and defensively orchestrated. It is important to

---

8   Edward Alexander, "The Cassinga raid," pp. 21–22.
9   *Ibid.*, pp. 61–62.
10   Author's email interview with G. W. Prinsloo, September 30, 2009.

explore why the SADF visual images of the Cassinga attack, unlike the SWAPO photograph of the open mass grave that attempts to disclose the SADF merciless massacre of defenseless civilians, are constructed or staged in such a way that the assailants appear irreproachable in terms of killing innocent women and children. This is demonstrated by the photograph of the two top field commanders of the Cassinga massacre, who are now waging a fight about which of them was the actual commanding officer of the Cassinga massacre,[11] but who are equally adamant that their paratroopers did not kill civilians in Cassinga.

"Credible coverage" of the attack

During the preparations for the attacks on Cassinga (also known as Moscow by SWAPO and code named Alpha by the SADF) and Vietnam (code named Bravo),[12] the SADF was given clear instructions to make sure that photographic "coverage" of the operations, "especially Alpha camp," took place. An SADF planning document for the Cassinga massacre reports that "credible coverage and immediate release is essential to counter claims of SADF mass killings of civilians, especially women and children."[13] In general terms, it is without a shred of doubt that the SADF was well prepared and equipped to photograph and video tape the Cassinga operation in a manner that portrays it as a military camp. In essence, according to this document, the SADF photographers were expected to use manipulated images as tools to deconstruct, reconfigure and obscure things on the ground for political gains. Hence, the SADF cameramen should be understood as tools of apartheid machinery and thinking. Their agenda to photograph the Cassinga massacre was based on the SADF guidelines for the Cassinga attack which (in spite of the fact that the population in Cassinga was civilian and unarmed) were clearly spelled out as follows: photo coverage must show military features for example weapons, ammunition, communications, headquarter buildings; any dead must have weapons alongside them; any photograph of civilians must reflect humane

---

[11] Jan Breytenbach, *Eagle Strike*, pp. 546–7; Edward Alexander, "The Cassinga raid," p. 113.

[12] Vietnam\ Osheetekela was a SWAPO military camp, less than 30km from the Namibian northwestern border with Angola. The Vietnam base was attacked on the same date as Cassinga, alias Moscow. Unlike the Cassinga attack, Vietnam was mainly a land invasion. Although Vietnam was actually a SWAPO military base, many civilians escaping from Namibia to Angola could spend days in Vietnam waiting for transport to Cassinga and other arrangements. When the camp was attacked hundreds of civilians were found in the camp. It is estimated that over three hundred civilians died in the attack. Two hundred and sixty were captured and taken back to Namibia. The prisoners were detained at Mariental, 260 kilometers South of Windhoek and remained incommunicado for about eight years before most of them were released at the end of 1986. See Appendix E of this book: Rev. Samwel Mateus Shiininge's account of the Vietnam attack.

[13] Chief of the SADF, "PSYAC Planning Directive No. 3 \ 78, Operation Reindeer (top secret): Phase Three (Media coverage)." Source: SANDF Archives, Pretoria.

treatment, for instance being provided with food; and documents captured must feature prominently to add credibility to subsequent disclosures.[14]

Regarding the above, it is reasonable to argue that the photograph showing the two senior commanders of the Cassinga massacre, Brigadier Du Plessis and Col. Jan Breytenbach,[15]

---

[14] Chief of the SADF, "PSYAC Planning Directive No. 3 \ 78, Operation Reindeer (top secret): Phase Three (Media coverage)." Source: SANDF Archives, Pretoria.

[15] A scuffle is simmering among the Cassinga paratroopers about who actually commanded the Cassinga attack. At the centre of this disputation are Colonel Jan Breytenbach and Brigadier Mike du Plessis. At the time of the Cassinga massacre, Mike du Plessis had just been named first commander of the brand new 44 Parachute Brigade, comprising 1, 2 and 3 Parachute Battalions (see Breytenbach, Eagle Strike, p. 545). The account provided by Willem Steenkamp informs us that Brigadier Mike du Plessis was one of the two senior officers (the second one was Brigadier Hannes Botha, Director of Operations of the South African Army) who went to Cassinga without official permission. Du Plessis and Hannes Botha allegedly forced their way into the aircraft that flew Breytenbach to Cassinga. Because of their presence in Cassinga, it is not clear, today, who really was in overall command of the Cassinga massacre. Steenkamp reports that according to du Plessis, "Breytenbach was in command only of the two assault companies (Alpha and Bravo), while he, du Plessis, exercised overall tactical on the ground .... However ... there can be no doubt that Breytenbach was the commander of the whole battalion and that he appointed his second-in-command to control the assault companies ... Du Plessis himself admitted that the chief of the Army had expected him to exercise his command from an airborne command post. It is not clear why he did not do so." (In Willem Steenkamp, Borderstrike, p. 137). Mike McWilliams who was authorized to photograph and video record the Cassinga operation tells us that Jan Breytenbach, "the most respected, decorated and loved military leader in the South African (apartheid) airborne environment," was officially authorized to lead and command the Cassinga operation. A brief insight into Breytenbach's historical background of his career as a professional soldier, the loyalty and the respect he earned within the SADF inner circle during many years of unreserved service and commitment to the course of the SADF becomes crucial in understanding his role as the SADF kingpin in executing violence. (See Appendix J for Colonel Jan Breytenbach's role in regional violence and beyond). Nevertheless, the presence of Brigadier du Plessis, Colonel Jan Breytenbach's immediate senior (in rank) in Cassinga, created much annoyance for Breytenbach who accused du Plessis of doing things in Cassinga disrespectfully and unprofessionally. In his words, "the water spider," as du Plessis was nicknamed: following his accidental landing into the Cubango River during the Cassinga parachute drop where he almost got drowned, "was just a passenger" with no role assigned to him to play in Cassinga. He was unauthorized to go to Cassinga – "both Du Plessis and Hannes Botha jumped into Cassinga against Genl. Gleeson's will" – Gleeson was the Chief of the Army Staff Operations. (In Breytenbach, Eagle Strike, p. 547). According to Brigadier General McGill Alexander, Major General Ian Gleeson, the overall commander of the operation, was "emphatic that Du Plessis and Hannes Botha should never have been there [in Cassinga]." This was because, according to Gleeson, the two "wanted to go on a partridge shoot." In this respect, Breytenbach argued that du Plessis' presence in Cassinga made "the operation a ... bloody nuisance." (In Edward Alexander, "The Cassinga Raid," pp. 100–102). Breytenbach did not explain how Brigadier du Plessis made the "Cassinga operation a bloody nuisance" except to emphasize that du Plessis' conduct in Cassinga was highly "unprofessional." This statement could suggest that du Plessis' individual conduct in Cassinga was extremely brutal as alleged by Lazarus Cornelius later in this Chapter. Edward Alexander contends with Mike McWilliams and other sources that "the officer appointed to command it (Cassinga) was the most experienced and successful combat soldier in the SADF, Colonel Jan Breytenbach. Nevertheless, there was a long-standing sentiment of animosity between him and his immediate superior, Brigadier M. J.

was deliberately framed, its background and foreground considerably purged and eliminated to exclude the appalling scenes of violence against weaponless people. Therefore, this photograph suggests that the perpetrators had nothing to show as supportive evidence for its version of attacking Cassinga.

As I have presented above, it is not possible to find Cassinga represented as a comprehensive military camp in any of the SADF photographs that were made available to me during my frequent visits to the former SADF archive in Pretoria. This is while testimonies by sources close to the former SADF Darkroom appears to suggest the opposite:

In late April 1978 I was in Windhoek and ... I was asked to return to Oshakati to be on standby for the next few weeks because a major operation was imminent. Because of my low rank and existence outside of the structures I was never given details of what was planned – but it was apparent that "something big" was in the offing. A few days later I was called to the operational centre and handed a number of black and white film cartridges and told that they should be processed, developed and printed immediately. I spent about 12 to 15 hours in the darkroom – and I remember they posted a guard outside the door. When finished with the processing I had to hand over all the film negatives and the printed pictures to military intelligence. I was not allowed to keep any of the prints or the negatives but did manage to "hide" a few duplicates which I "smuggled" out in subsequent days. After this long explanation – these are the prints that are still in my possession. I assume they were taken at Cassinga by troops tasked to document activities and the aftermath. Your article in the *Mail and Guardian* prompted me to start searching for them and I eventually found some. I cannot vouch for the sequence but there are:• Two pictures of ground troops preparing to move;• Four very graphic pictures of killed Swapo soldiers apparently taken in some mealie field;• Nine pictures of captured and wounded Swapo soldiers – I cannot guarantee that they were taken at Cassinga – it might have been at another venue.• Four rather bizarre pictures of "soldiers" on a parade ground. It might be Cubans; it might be at Cassinga. I remember being told that some of the rolls of film I had to develop were "discovered" during the battle. They are rather amateurish – obviously taken from a distance. The prints are all 5" X 7" in size and fairly well preserved after more than 30 years. But you should note they were the "spoilt" prints which I did not hand over to the operational people. All in all I must have developed 10 to 12 rolls of film and made some 300 prints.

---

du Plessis, the brigade commander. This led to differences of opinions and a clash of wills." (In Edward Alexander, "The Cassinga Raid," p. 113). Breytenbach, himself, tells us that, in Cassinga, du Plessis demonstrated a "total lack of discipline ... (who) interfere(d) in my command ..." (In Jan Breytenbach, Eagle Strike, pp. 546–7). Breytenbach continued to testify that "I was given the command over several hundred paratroopers for the Cassinga battle by General Viljoen [Lieutenant General Constand Viljoen, chief of the SA Army]. Monty Brett, Lew Gerber, Johan Blaauw and Piet Nel with their troops came under my command. I prepared them for battle and I led them in the Cassinga Operation, which made me, and me only, responsible for the acts of every single one of the officers and men under my command at that time. After the battle I stepped back and they reverted to their previous commanders." (In Jan Breytenbach, Eagle Strike, p. 553).

The 19 prints are all that I kept and eventually brought back. After Cassinga, I stayed on and off in Oshakati and Windhoek for another nine months before returning to Pretoria to see out the last of my national service at *Paratus*. There is no reason why I want to keep the prints. I cannot fully vouch for when and where they were taken – but I can confirm that I did the processing in the day or two after Cassinga. You are more than welcome to take the prints – for what they might be worth. I assume they might be of some value for your own research. Please feel free to drop me a note if you are further interested. We can then arrange for me to mail the pics to you or hand it over to an associate of you in Gauteng.

In attempts to add credibility to the subsequent public disclosure of the Cassinga attack, as mentioned earlier, the SADF cameramen were instructed to take photographs that exclusively show military features in Cassinga. Pictures of the dead, according to one of such instructions, "must have weapons alongside them."[16] It is common knowledge that those who perpetuate violence against unarmed civilians are notorious for hiding from the public view any visual images that portray senseless torture and brutal killing of innocent people. Perhaps I should refer to a general case, for example, the wars in Iraq and Afghanistan. In these two countries, photographic images and video footage showing unacceptable violence against civilians by the American-led forces were not made accessible to the public, except through independent sources such as the leaked photographs depicting the US soldiers' torturing of Iraqis, civilian or "insurgents," at the Abu Ghraib prison which stunned and shocked the world in 2004. This argument follows Eliot Weinberger's observation when he wrote that:

> The Cheney-Bush 11 era has not produced a single poem, song, novel, or art that has caught the popular imagination as a condemnation or an epitome of the times. The only enduring image is a product of journalism: the hooded figure in Abu Ghraib photographs.[17]

As I have pointed out earlier, the Peter W. Botha government (1978–1989) which succeeded the John Vorster government (1966–1978) was determined to obscure and deny the public access to viewing photographs which could incriminate the SADF in acts of systematic brutal violence against civilians in Namibia, Angola, Zambia, Mozambique, South Africa and other neighbouring countries. In fact, and this is ironic, the SADF hated being branded

---

16 Chief of the SADF, "PSYAC Planning Directive No. 3 \ 78, Operation Reindeer (top secret): Phase Three (Media coverage)." Source: SANDF Archives, Pretoria.

17 Eliot Weinberger, "Comment," in Mahmood Mamdani, *Saviours and Survivors: Darfur, politics, and the war on terror* (Cape Town: Human Sciences Research Council Press, 2009), p. 61. Also see: Kari Andén-Papadopoulos, "The Abu Ghraib torture photographs: news frames, visual culture, and the power of images" (University of Stockholm, 2008). Online at *http://jou.sagepub.com/content/9/1/5.*

a "deadly force against" civilians. Consider the following statement following the Cassinga massacre: Irremediable damage had already been done ... to the paratroopers ... how do we rectify ... the perception that we acted like a bunch of blood thirsty murderers and rapists?[18] In this relation therefore, the absence of the photographs showing acts of appalling violence against civilians, as overwhelmingly conveyed in every interview with survivors, explains the SADF deliberate attempts to silence and distance themselves from the crimes against peace and humanity.[19] In this instance, the photograph that is the central focus of this chapter, creates numerous workable spaces for individual survivors to interrogate and challenge the SADF telling of the Cassinga event. That is, when the Cassinga photographic images are deliberately staged to obscure and silence the portrayal of the violence, survivors find it unacceptable. The nonviolent staging of the paratroopers' photographs incites disbelief and provokes individual survivors to give voice to the unacceptable violent practices that the SADF visual images hide from the public view.

This photograph was, most probably, shot shortly before the paratroopers' departure from Cassinga. As I have pointed out earlier, the SADF "media representatives (who)... accompanied the forces"[20] to Cassinga were instructed to avoid, by all means, taking pictures that in the post-Cassinga operation might implicate the paratroopers in the indiscriminate mass killing and maiming of civilians in Cassinga, especially women and children.[21] Arguably, this image is one of the SADF's foremost attempts to counter the popular narratives that implicate the paratroopers in the indiscriminate mass killing of civilians. In a more general approach to photographs, John Tagg compares the contradictory relationship between photography and historical events to the qualities of a "chameleon." The "chameleon-like" relationship is applicable to my analysis of why the unfolding of the Cassinga massacre is perceived in one way by survivors and other observers (including individual perpetrators of the massacre) of the Cassinga massacre, and differently in the way Cassinga is represented

---

[18]   Jan Breytenbach, *The eagle strike,* p. 544.

[19]   The International Covenant on the Suppression and Punishment of the Crime of Apartheid declares that apartheid was / is a crime against humanity and that inhuman acts resulting from the policies and practices of apartheid and similar policies and practices of racial segregation and discrimination, as defined in Article II of the Convention, are crimes violating the principles of international law, in particular the purposes and principles of the Charter of the United Nations, and constituting a serious threat to international peace and security. In Article 1 of the "International Covenant on the Suppression and Punishment of the Crime of Apartheid" (18 July 1976).

[20]   Chief of the SADF. "PSYAC Planning Directive No. 3 \ 78, Operation Reindeer (Top Secret). Phase Three (Media coverage), 25 April 1978." Source: The SANDF Archive, Pretoria.

[21]   Chief of the SADF. "PSYAC Planning Directive No. 3 \ 78 Operation Reindeer (Top Secret). Phase Three (Media coverage), 25 April 1078." Source: The SANDF Department of Defence Documentation Centre, Archive, Pretoria.

Fig. 2: Seen in this photograph is Col. Jan Breytenbach with bandaged wrist, and Brig. Mike Du Plessis with a shoulder bag. These two paratroopers were the top field commanders of the Cassinga attack. This photograph was most probably taken as the paratroopers prepared to leave Cassinga. For clues about the injury on his hand, see Jan Breytenbach, The Eagle Strike, p. 384–387.

in the various photographic images that the perpetrators captured and released for the public viewing.

In this context, the exclusion of the foreground and background in the photograph above becomes crucial. The unclaimed space of the catastrophic civilian casualties that this photograph deliberately obscures is intended to achieve some political leverage. Its purpose is to exert a confusion, create myths and wrest the perpetrators from accountability for the Cassinga massacre. Indeed, it is an attempt to eliminate anything that may show the paratroopers in the picture as guilty of "criminal and delinquent behaviours" against innocent civilians. That is, this image intends shunting or pushing away the shocking space, the multiple unpleasant features or landscapes of bloodshed and human carnage.

The fact that there are no records of the visual documentation of the Cassinga massacre in the former SADF archives in Pretoria does not mean that such historical documents never existed. Speculation is rife that the video footage and a substantial number of photographs showing the SADF violence against innocent civilians in Cassinga are in private collections of individual paratroopers. Another speculation is that the SADF might have deliberately damaged and destroyed the sensitive visual images of the Cassinga massacre. This could have happened following the closure and fragmentation of the apartheid institutions in Namibia and South Africa. Should these speculations hold any water, it would be credible to suspect that the SADF at this point was aware that the killing of hundreds of women and children in Cassinga was a morally disgraceful and unacceptable criminal act. The top echelons of the former SADF in particular were, and perhaps still are, afraid of the legal consequences of taking so many innocent human lives.

Of course, if the former SADF were to release the disturbing images of the Cassinga massacre for an unrestricted public viewing, this would unlock a different discourse and new debates about the Cassinga massacre. Implicit in this is the probability that, if made public, those potentially shocking images would disclose a level of extreme violence against civilians that the perpetrators of the Cassinga massacre adamantly refute as lies. Even in the absence of images that show violence, some survivors can still remember and relate some figures in the available photographs to acts of extreme violence against civilians in Cassinga.

Lazarus Cornelius is a survivor of the Cassinga massacre. In the excerpt below, his encounter with the photograph of the two top field commanders of the Cassinga massacre suggests how survivors' testimonies are involved in a conflict relationship with the perpetrators' visual representation of the Cassinga massacre:

> I saw this Boer on a shooting spree ... he was executing, *tasigula*, defenceless civilians who were critically wounded during the attack from the air that preceded the paratroopers drop in Cassinga. He was the only Boer I saw carrying this brown

shoulder bag. I believe that this bag does not belong to him ... It should be a SWAPO bag. When I saw him carrying this bag, I immediately thought about Commissar Greenwell Matongo who often carried a similar bag with him ... I suspected that this Boer took this bag from him or he found it somewhere in the camp ... I thought that way ... this is how I became interested in him and memorized his physical appearance and the unspeakable level of violence he committed on vulnerable women and children ... There was a moment when he came too close to me ... he should have thought that I was dead, because my body and clothes were smeared in blood. He was a matured man, walking alone ... alone ... unaccompanied by anybody and he was only armed with a pistol which he used to shoot the wounded to death: Tock! Tock! Tock! Tock! ... That sound remains intact in my ears ... Whenever I revisit that traumatic scene of the Cassinga massacre, my whole body collapses ... Yes, it is reconciliation, but the perpetrators still believes that it was right to kill, displace and maim innocent civilians in Cassinga ... why do they openly say these painful things? Is it because justice is on their side. Should we reconcile that way?

This account by Cornelius could be read and interpreted in diverse ways by a range of readers. But I wish to emphasize the way Cornelius encourages us to rethink photographs as severing ties between survivors and visual realities of the Cassinga episode. For Cornelius and other survivors, photographs are not the same as memory, they are in fact disconnected from the victims' memory struggle. Photographs can in fact produce oblivion and silence concerning the undisclosed human suffering of Cassinga. Such visual materials should rather be conceived as "sites of social inquiry." They generate questions about the missing historical facts, rather than disclose the complex realities of human suffering that they ostensibly seek to address. This unfolds lucidly in the narrative above.

The fact that Cornelius sees mass atrocities that the photograph of Du Plessis and Breytenbach conceals and which is completely hidden from the inexperienced public sight, awareness and understanding, conveys another important lesson. From this, one may construe that the act of staging photographs with the intent to disseminate a certain manipulative discourse is not effective. In fact, Cornelius' dialogue with the photograph above suggests that the experience of the Cassinga massacre does not reside in the packaged content that the Cassinga visual materials convey. Rather, the meaning and the understanding of the Cassinga massacre is inherent in the critique of the framing and exclusion of violence that photographs, as historical narratives, fail to disclose. Photographs should be understood as conveying a narrow and stereotyped reality in relation to the actual landscape of mass atrocities, personal human suffering and collective trauma of the victims.

If visual realities do obscure and undermine the complexity of the Cassinga experience and human suffering, then the efforts by the former SADF to impound and hide the visual materials that it fears are sensitive are wasted. My thinking is that whether such images are accessible or inaccessible for public viewing, they unravel no complex human suffering and experience of the Cassinga violence. In the same way that the victims are not impressed by the politicking around the Cassinga massacre, survivors are not interested in the simplistic appearance of the visual realities of the Cassinga attack. What concerns the victims most are issues of humanitarian importance. Survivors and affected families are by contrast making specific demands. They ask repeatedly for social recognition within Namibia, and for a formal apology from the perpetrator. This includes full accountability for their enduring suffering, the loss of their loved ones, and forfeited human dignity.

The fact that this photograph obscures the excruciating landscape of human catastrophe places this photograph in opposition to other photographs, which intend to disclose appalling scenes of the unnecessary loss of lives and other sufferings incurred by the victims of the Cassinga massacre. For example, the way the immaculate photograph is staged clearly distinguishes itself from the "iconic photograph" of the Cassinga open mass grave . The "iconic photograph," in contrast, carries a message of a humanitarian crisis and appealing for the public to render a sympathetic response to the suffering of Namibian refugees.

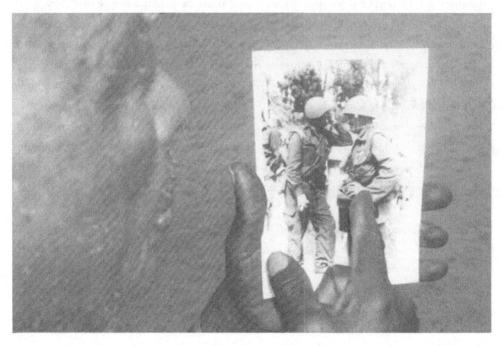

Fig. 3: Lazarus Cornelius, a survivor of the Cassinga massacre. He claims that the information bag carried by Du Plessis belongs either to Jonas Haiduwa or Greenwell Matongo or another SWAPO officer who was in Cassinga. It would be interesting should Brigadier Du Plessis himself or Colonel Jan Breytenbach comment on this scenario.

Therefore, it is obvious that whilst the photograph of the Cassinga open mass grave evokes pathos about the innocent killing of civilians, the central focus of the SADF photographer(s) is to tilt or shift away from the difficult and hard realities evident in the neighbourhood of the camera operators.

Ideally, the aura of innocence that this image suggests denotes the actual "white propaganda," a "public relations technique" employed by the SADF to keep the public in the dark about the humanitarian atrocities carried out by the agents of the apartheid state and colonial rule in Namibia. Nevertheless, the SADF use of photographs in the context of advancing "white propaganda" intended for public consumption appears ineffective. This accords with Caroline Brothers' view that "propaganda can only work successfully by resonating with those beliefs already held by the individuals it is meant to persuade."[22] As I have outlined earlier, if Du Plessis and Breytenbach's photograph was indeed constructed as a tool of state "white propaganda," then the spotless appearance of this photograph presents a "tangential relation" to violence. That is, it contradicts survivors' reports of the paratroopers' rampage and indiscriminate killing of civilians in Cassinga. Therefore, if this photograph is staged in a manner that the perpetrators appear exonerated from the brutal violence that they were observed committing in Cassinga, then its reality becomes unacceptable to individual survivors of the Cassinga massacre.

To enter into these dialogues, my interest in writing a chapter about this photograph was aroused by my interview with Lazarus Cornelius. Cornelius came across this photograph (the immaculate picture above) in the album of the Cassinga photographs that I presented to him at the end of interviewing him at his homestead, Etunda, in 2008. Cornelius claimed to have recognized one of the men in the photograph, Brig. Mike Du Plessis (according to the SADF archives caption). He claimed that he was alerted when he observed Du Plesssis indiscriminately shooting to death, at point-blank range, the critically wounded victims with a pistol.

In a more general approach, Corinne Kratz observed that "photographs do not 'speak for themselves' or provide a transparent 'universal language.'"[23] They embrace open-ended narratives. This means that the look, content and purpose of a photograph provokes and determines the meaning that individual viewers attach to it. In particular, inasmuch as photographs attempt to decontextualize the Cassinga violence from its actual experience and historicity, photographs also, concurrently, invoke survivors' opposition to the SADF

---

[22]   Caroline Brothers, *War and photography*, p. 35.
[23]   Corinne A. Kratz, *The ones that are wanted: communication and the politics of representation in a photographic exhibition* (California: University of California Press, 2002), p. 118.

photographs' attempts to reconfigure the paratroopers' ruthless practice of violence against unarmed civilians in Cassinga. The argument here is that, inasmuch as many of us, the inexperienced, cannot see beyond photographs, especially images which we are not familiar with, some survivors of the Cassinga massacre do see beyond the confines of photographs. Survivors can see and tell stories about hidden realities which do not protrude from the surface of photographs when inexperienced viewers engage them. As this chapter will explore, individual survivors recorded and filed individual paratroopers' (as individuals or as a collective) deliberate killings of defenceless civilians in the camp. Like the disclosers of WikiLeaks, survivors reveal undisclosed secrets that the SADF photographs of the Cassinga massacre hide. This is explored in the following dialogues.

"I personally saw him killing wounded civilians!"

"Truth" is supposedly self-evident. Albeit, the telling of "truth" here is visibly eclipsed by the shadow that obscures others from seeing it as practical evidence, the essence of its meaning lies in the fact that it is procreated by actual circumstances. However, it is important to recognize that "truth" becomes immaterial when it does not relate to a practical experience of something. In the context of the Namibia political conflict, in the run-up to independence, certain events are regarded as "true" and others as "untrue" regardless of what historical facts they represent. Take a simple example: that the SADF carried out a systematic execution of Namibian refugees in Cassinga is undisputable "truth" for many Namibians, just as it is "untrue" for the SADF that it massacred innocent women and children in Cassinga. This is not to deny the fact that in the context of narrating (visually or orally) the Cassinga massacre, "truth" translates into the complete absence of the referent. As such, what is considered "true" by some is immaterial, "untrue" and contested by others, as a substitute for the obscured and missing actual world.

I am introducing the problematic question of "truth" as a way of trying to explore its limits and strengths in the context of the many conflicting "truths" told by different agencies of experiencing and reporting the Cassinga attack to the inexperienced other. I am referring to what individual survivors observed and witnessed in relation to the experiences and stories of the SADF photographs of the Cassinga attack. The following dialogues between Lazarus Cornelius and the photograph he detains in his hands explore this conflict.

In leading to the dialogues between Lazarus and the perpetrators detained in the image, Caroline Brothers writes in a different context that "by looking [at photographs], the [experienced] viewer is implicated in a highly structured pattern of vision and representation. Meaning inheres not in the photograph itself, but in the relationship between the photograph and the matrix of ... specific beliefs and assumptions to which it refers. The photo-graph is the site at which these 'invisible' beliefs ... manifest, the gaze of the photographer directing the gaze of the viewer, and it is in this constant dialogue between image and soci-ety that lays the photograph's greatest interest for the historian."[24] In examining the visual representation of the above photograph, the inexperienced viewer's gaze is manipulated in such a way that it encounters impenetrable hindrances, which prevent the viewer from see-ing the unacceptable things which surround the circumvented border of the photograph. The frontier that this photograph has created between the viewer and the inaccessible space prohibits the viewers' chance of seeing the "truth" of the deplorable scenes of damage to human lives and property, presumably, on all sides around where the two commanding of-ficers' stood.

Interestingly, the violence that this photograph renders us oblivious to is "precisely what is of interest" in this chapter. In this regard, the fact that this photograph is struc-tured in such a way that it prohibits the inexperienced viewer from seeing violence be-yond the confines of the photograph's parameters, encourages survivors to give testi-monies which rise beyond the confines of the photograph's staged "truth." As John Tagg put it in a different context, staging a certain genre of constructed "truth" for the public consumption is "infinitely vulnerable to qualification ... by a third variable."[25] In the context of this topic, the constructed "truth" represents this photograph whereas the "third variable" is suitably the witness of the Cassinga massacre. In this context, Lazarus in his capacity as a witness and survivor of the Cassinga massacre, his ability to investigate, explore and in-terpret this image according to his personal experience of individual paratroopers killings of civilians on the ground qualifies him for the "third variable." This is demonstrated in the following passage:

> This is the most wicked Boer that I spoken about earlier in the interview. He was so ruthless ... I strongly believe that this is him due to the following facts: Number one, he was the only Boer I saw carrying this brown shoulder bag. It resembled the Soviet made shoulder bags used by PLAN commissars and when I saw him carry-ing it, I immediately thought about Commissar Greenwell Matongo who often car-ried a similar bag with him – it should had been his – maybe he killed him and captured this bag from him – I thought that way, and that is how I became interested in this Boer ... I carefully observed this enemy as he walked alone. He was alone ... with a pistol, indiscriminately shooting to death people who were critically injured and fighting to stay alive: Tock! Tock! Tock! Tock! ... I can still hear the sound of his pistol in my ears. It was the most shocking experience of the Cassinga massacre ...

---

[24] Caroline Brothers, *War and photography*, p. 23

[25] John Tagg, *The burden of representation*. Cited in Caroline Brothers, *War and photography*, pp. 18–19.

that experience continues to bring much pain and sufferings whenever I remember this thing.[26]

Christopher Pinney tells us that photography "has no identity ... its history has no unity... It is a flickering across a field of institutional spaces. It is this field we must study, not photography as such."[27] I have pointed out that the SADF camera operators acted under political restrictions. They were instructed not to photograph things that disclosed deplorable pictures of human carnage in Cassinga. Hence, most of the SADF pictures of the Cassinga massacre, that are available to me, exclude scenes of bloodshed and civilian deaths. Nonetheless, since photographs are open to different viewers' interpretations, such as in the case demonstrated by Cornelius above, I argue that photographs defy the political and other orders that constructed them. In this way, photographs act indifferently to the rules of the apartheid state which regulated what photographs must show and what they must conceal. By breaking the state's attempt to control, destroy and silence acts of violence against civilians, the SADF photographs of the Cassinga attack become embedded with the notion of betrayal of those who staged particular realities before the eye of the camera. In this context, the SADF photographs of the Cassinga massacre can be understood as perfidious agents. This takes cognizance of the fact that individual survivors with experience and knowledge pertaining to the people and other aspects appearing in photographs can act as interlocutors. The way Cornelius is able to gather and explain those elements that this image conceals demonstrates the argument above..

Certainly survivors can use photographs as weapons against the perpetrators. That is, the same photographs that the perpetrators shot and staged with the purpose of concealing and keeping secret the unacceptable pictures of violence, can be used by survivors to implicate the perpetrators' unleashing of the indiscriminate and violent killing of civilians as demonstrated by Cornelius above. When survivors can transcend photographs' frontiers and disclose things beyond photographs' parameters, it can help historians and the public at large to acquire new knowledge, new ways of thinking and an understanding of the previously hidden secrets. Hence, since photographs are social objects without a formula to unlock meaning uniformly, what is "important is the way in which the links between the oral and the visual can counter and mesh with other forms in the contemporary, shifting the balance and allowing ... multiple forms of history transmission to operate."[28]

---

[26]   The author's interview with Lazarus Namutenya Cornelius, Etunda, 2008.
[27]   Christopher Pinney, *Camera Indica* p. 17.
[28]   Elizabeth Edwards, "Photographs and the sound of history," *Visual Anthropology Review*, Vol. 21/ 1 & 2 (Spring / Fall 2005), p. 38.

The way Cornelius explored and disclosed the unspeakable event that the photograph of du Plessis and Breytenbach is oblivious to, suggests that the act of staging photographs with the intent to disseminate a certain discourse is not efficient. This is in response to the fact that photographs are "read differently" in relation to personal experience and memory of seeing and remembering things in real life. These tangible realities and other distressing factors combine to construct meanings and effects beyond the staged and ambiguous realities that photographs bring to our sense of seeing. The fact that the meaning or interpretation of a photograph is not embedded in the content of a picture, but beyond the frame of it, is demonstrated in the following excerpt:

> Whenever the picture of civilians being shot dead at will ... it throws me back to Cassinga and I am grieved repeatedly. I tell you, memories of that pitiless soldier, moving alone and finishing the lives of the critically injured is emotionally and physically hurtful. Whenever I revisit it, I collapse emotionally and remain in my bedroom in fear and insecurity. People were killed indiscriminately, women and children, yet the perpetrator goes unpunished. How can I forgive a person like this one? ... Not at all, forgiveness is a façade, especially when there is continuing deniers of the massacre of innocent civilians ... such unending and deliberate piercing of the scars is inflammatory. The wound is reopened and starts to bleed repeatedly and profusely. Yah, I have forgiven them, at least, in words. However, the grief is deep inside me and I feel that I have not forgiven them, especially that Boer! Is he living a normal life when his hands are red with the blood of so many innocent people? Does he know that he has put many lives in trouble and robbed many families of their loved ones? What he did is very painful and a difficult experience to live with. Yes! It is reconciliation, but I fail to grab the context of this reconciliation. Where is justice? Where is it?[29]

As I have indicated earlier, a photograph may infer different meanings and interpretations from different agencies and forums that give it multiple voices and meanings beyond the restricted way that photographs contain and restrain. Thus, for the perpetrator, the photograph in this context may interpret a sense of "bravery for the mission well accomplished." It may represent the paratroopers as innocent of the crimes that they have been accused of committing against civilians in Cassinga. For survivors, as demonstrated in the excerpt above, the immaculate photograph is the associate of pervasive trauma: grief, anger and anxiety. In this relation, therefore, it appears evident that the perpetrators' photographs of the Cassinga operation can hide multiple acts of violence. They cannot, however, hide the anger and bitterness of the victims of that episode.

Generally, each survivor is deeply wounded when images fail to retrieve his \ her true picture of the Cassinga experience. This disturbing nature stems from the fact that sight is

---

[29] The author's interview with Lazarus Namutenya Cornelius, Etunda, 2008.

not used in isolation from other senses when survivors searched for scenes of violence in the different photographs of the Cassinga massacre. Other senses (hearing, seeing, feeling and smell) were collectively used as survivors tried to read photographs with the intention of discovering that which they had experienced in Cassinga. Indeed, as Elaine Scarry teaches us, "those attributes confirmed by both vision and touch tend to be felt to have a greater reality than those attributes experienced by only one of the two, or by one of the other senses without these two."[30]

Cornelius relied mostly on two senses: sight, the sense of seeing and touch, the sense of feeling as he attempted to trace and discover aspects inside and outside the boundary – the inclusions and exclusions in the picture of the things he experienced in Cassinga – of the image he confronted. He predominantly used his fingers or flat palm to name and map out positions in the camp, during the massacre, where he observed multiple scenes of brutality he attributed to Brigadier Du Plessis and others. In most cases, Cornelius pointed to structures or experiences in Cassinga beyond the boundary of the photograph with which he engaged. Consider the following examples: "I observed him killing the wounded people from this side ... the pit toilet which I avoided and which they later blew up, killing many people inside it was that side ... the river where many people drowned is located that side." The list of those features and experiences through which Cornelius tried to navigate the interviewer, but outside the borders of the photograph, is endless. This representation explains that this photograph conveys considerable exclusions of the events known to and experienced by survivors on that fateful and memorable day.

I construed that as the witness' finger runs over the photograph, it is a sign of ascertaining and discerning relationships between the photograph and memory. The more Cornelius recognized despicable things that the photograph ignores or excludes, the more he held firmly to the photograph. At this point, his voice often choked – it fell flat, as verbal dialogue became overwhelmed by the anger and rage in response to the fury of what he called the photograph's "untelling of truth." The "photograph's untelling of truth," that Cornelius bemoaned, points to the conflict between the actual experience of the violence and the visual misrepresentation and framing of the untainted picture of that violence which unfolded before survivors and witnesses.

In this context therefore, when Cornelius engaged Du Plessis' photograph for a considerable time, uttering words to the photograph (not to the interviewer), it can be interpreted as a way of interrogating the photograph's ambivalence and framing of the violence. Because to frame, as an embedded feature of photographs, is to enforce boundaries, to obscure see-

---

30 Elaine Scarry, *The body in pain: the making and unmaking of the world* (New York: Oxford University Press, 1985), p. 146.

ing violence beyond the staged realities of the photograph. It is a way of impairing human senses and of denying inexperienced people a chance to experience and comprehend deplorable pictures of the Cassinga massacre.

Nevertheless, as demonstrated in Cornelius' excerpt above, the victims of the Cassinga massacre are time after time reminded that the scourge of the Cassinga violence, which has brought endless suffering and sorrow, requires an intervention of justice, which has been long overdue. In this relation, the victims of this episode, dead and alive, can only forgive the perpetrators, if their untold suffering and degree of sorrow were to be recognized politically and economically, as I will later explain, and if justice were to take its course. A moment after Cornelius' dialogue with Du Plessis' photograph, he asked me if he could keep the photograph with him. He told me that he wants people in his constituency[31] to see these killers:

> A person like this one (du Plessis) should come here to see the deceased families. He should come here to face justice. He should come here to answer to questions about his role in Cassinga. His actions were inhuman ... instead of offering assistance to the wounded and helpless, he went amok slaughtering them. This is unacceptable. Can't they bring him and others here and face justice ... it would be fair enough to bring them here and face us while we are still alive. The public is eager to listen and hear what happened to their loved ones. I should keep this photograph to show it to my constituency when we commemorate the Cassinga massacre next year [2009].[32]

In the absence of survivors' justice, the victims find it unacceptable to forgive the perpetrators who remain unapologetic for the deplorable wrongs they committed. Indeed, issues of the victims' justice are the prerequisite for genuine forgiveness and "national reconciliation" and should be seriously kept in place if Namibia were to claim that it is certainly independent and sovereign. Survivors and affected families raise issues of reparations for the affected victims. Arguably, official acknowledgment or reparations for the victims of the Cassinga massacre may not equal the price of the suffering and the loss of the innocent lives, nor can they restore the violated human dignity of the victims. But, such approaches can be argued are the only ways of providing the victims with a sense of recognition for the injustices done to them, as seems to be the case with the Hereros of Namibia against the German government ongoing today.[33]

---

31 The author's interview with Lazarus Namutenya Cornelius, Etunda, 2008. Lazarus is a teacher by profession. He was the SWAPO Party councilor for the Ruacana constituency at the time of interviewing him. He retired at the end of 2010.
32 The author's interview with Lazarus Namutenya Cornelius, Etunda, 2008.
33 Jeremy Sarkin, *Colonial Genocide and reparations claims in the 21st Century: the socio-legal context of claims under international law by the Herero against German for Genocide in Namibia, 1904–1908* (Wesrport: Praeger Publishers, 2009).

In this context, Cornelius' intent to parade the accused perpetrator's photograph before the local population suggests the victims' aspiration for the long overdue justice. The victims demand a public apology and compensation that we might interpret as perceiving these ideals as fundamental forms of "reparation or recognition"[34] for colonial-apartheid violence against innocent Namibians, and as preconditions for reconciliation. It should be noted that, it is not only the victims of the Cassinga and Vietnam massacres who demand a public apology, but many other Namibians suffered collateral injuries and other human rights abuses in the years of South Africa's ruthless colonialism and apartheid rule in Namibia. Cornelius' initiative to parade the enemy's photograph before survivors and families of the dead in his community may disclose a quest for some form of dialogue with the perpetrators as a means to find some kind of healing and closure for both sides.

In reaching the end of this chapter, it is worth emphasizing that in confronting the SADF visual images of the Cassinga massacre, the inexperienced viewers' gaze is confined to the pigeonholed realities within the restricted boundary of photographs. For this reason, the inexperienced viewer cannot see deplorable situations of human suffering and carnage beyond the frontiers of such images. On the contrary, survivors of the Cassinga massacre view visual images of the Cassinga massacre differently. This implies two meanings: survivors approach the Cassinga visual images as sources of untold pain and suffering. This is because, when survivors come into contact with such images they are instigated to remember and explore multiple scenes of violence beyond the staged realities or exclusions of the visual, thereby getting irritated and wounded again. The second meaning infers that survivors find greater pain and discomfort in the SADF visual images of the Cassinga massacre than the inexperienced viewers: they find such images undermining the originality, authenticity, multiplicity and deplorability of the Cassinga experience.

Nonetheless, the SADF as well as individual paratroopers do not have the courage to distribute and disseminate horrific photographs of civilian casualties in Cassinga. As such, images of civilian casualties appear not to have formed part of the "group" of photographs donated to the SADF archives in Pretoria (as indicated at the beginning of the chapter). In particular, the emerging publications written by Colonel Jan Breytenbach and by Mike McWilliams (the official SADF photographer of the Cassinga massacre) appear to deliberately exclude photographs showing civilian casualties. Nevertheless, whilst such exclusions

---

[34] Compensation is argued to be better for the victims of political violence and affected families, rather than conceding simply that things were wrong. In 1992 when F. W. de Klerk attempted to apologize to South Africans for the apartheid wrongs, the ANC called the apology "inadequate," because it failed to acknowledge (in kind to the victims and bereaved families) apartheid wrongs and evils. See, "De Klerk apartheid apology was inadequate, ANC says." Online at http://www. deseretnews.com/article/252666/De-Klerk-apartheid -apology-was-inadequate-ANC-says.html.

explain that the SADF photographs cannot disclose or authenticate what actually happened in Cassinga, they convey another important reason to explain why the perpetrator holds back sensitive photographs of the Cassinga massacre: they find no pleasure in such photographs, because they valorize the deep scars which continue to interrogate and haunt them for the innocent lives they destroyed in Cassinga.

In this respect, it is important to note that both survivors and paratroopers emerged traumatized from Cassinga. Therefore, if postcolonial Namibia is interested in helping both victims to recover from shock, trauma, anger and grief, help must be given sensibly and in a human way. Not in the way that "the benefits [given] to the perpetrator ... outweigh the benefits [given] to the victim."[35] Thus, applauding the perpetrators with a number of privileges at the expense of the weak and the historically vulnerable populations is about maintaining and feeding the old apartheid culture regarding race, class and hierarchies of inferiority. Hence, this melancholic anomaly is not only discriminatory but it is, in essence, a repetition of violence: it exacerbates the sufferings that torture the civilian victims and families of the missing people in Cassinga who appear to bear the greatest burden of the Cassinga massacre for life, under an absolute silence that conforms to the prevailing political order. As long as this imbalance is not addressed, there can be no recovery and healing for all the victims (survivors, bereaved families and perpetrators).

---

[35] Pius Langa, "Apartheid bomber loses Concourt bid," Accessed from: http://www.dispatch.co.za/article.aspx?id=338529.

4 Memory of the Wounded Body, Oral Testimony and the Other

In the preceding chapters, I have explored how visual testimonies are not fully consonant with the practicality of the Cassinga violence as witnessed by survivors of the massacre. This chapter attempts to show how oral testimony fails to elicit the painful memories of the victims' wounded bodies. The violence perpetrated at Cassinga has clearly left scarring marks, openly evident, on some survivors' bodies. The chapter argues that the terrible memories incised into the victim's body as evident through the physical body scars lie far beyond the reach and understanding of the other, as no testimony is capable of transferring such memories.[1] The "other" here denotes the inexperienced viewers At this stage, it is evident from the position of this book that the majority of the victims of the Cassinga massacre were women. Moreover, the largest number of people who were physically maimed at Cassinga and who live today in dire need of medical and other assistance are women. In a brief description of the Cassinga massacre and the contestations that followed it, Martha Akawa's doctoral thesis made a significant point that Cassinga symbolizes "one of the incidents in which women were hailed as victims and heroines at the same time: ... women shared in death, defiance and victory."[2] As things turned out in post-war Namibia, "promises and pronouncements about equality have not been kept: 20 years after the end of the war, women's bodies remain battlefields."[3]

Whilst Akawa's argument attempts to register the suffering and the bravery of all Namibian women who contributed to the liberation struggle, particularly in exile, she has not addressed particular problems concerning survivors of the Cassinga massacre which this chapter attempts to explore. In particular, the woman's body as a "battlefield" is used as a crucial metaphor. It shows a few pictures of women's physically damaged bodies, resulting from the Cassinga attack, in order to emphasize women's endurance of the physical and emotional suffering since the attack. In particular, the chapter introduces the concept of internal violence. That is, the pervasive state of the endless suffering of the Cassinga victims, most of who are women, and which is not external or explicit to others. Therefore, although many survivors' bodies show terrible or visually unbelievable protrusions or damage, such sites should not be perceived as showing us survivors' actual endurance of suffer-

---

[1]   See Chapter 1 for the meaning of memory and testimony in the context of this study.
[2]   Martha Akawa, "The sexual politics of the Namibian liberation struggle," pp. 117–118.
[3]   *Ibid.*, pp. 117–118.

ing. Instead, the physically harrowing scars of the damaged body should be understood as concealing the actual sentient agony of the personal body that is not only damaged, but is also beyond repair and understanding of society at large.

When I interviewed the victims whose bodies are physically maimed as a result of the Cassinga attack, they told me that the sites of violence, evident on their disfigured bodies, may appear healed from the outside, but in reality such sites are gates (to which I return later) into profusely bleeding inside memories. The metaphor of "profusely bleeding" inner memories is analogous to the internally bleeding wounds of the victims since the Cassinga massacre. Notably, every single scar of violence protruding from survivors' bodies is not a lifeless effigy. Such scars or figures of violence, according to survivors, are sensitive areas and full of life because they are connected to the chronic injuries that are properly framed and beyond the reach of others and, most disappointingly, beyond the reach of the victims' own testimony.

Scars are visible, the pain is hidden

The pain of the wounded body, as Rauha Shitangi put it, is invisible as it is contained below the surface of the scars of damage that are clearly visible on the victim's body. Here, two important structures of the wound emerge. These are the physical and internal structures. It is the severity of the inside or open wound that survivors bemoan and describe as unleashing unhealing bitter memories of the Cassinga massacre and its aftermath. Shitangi explains:

> The picture of remembering Cassinga is like sustaining an injury on a sensitive area of the body ... Look at this terrible scar ... this deep cut at this sensitive area of my leg, omuthipa [which translates as the Achilles tendon] ... it appears healed – hasho – right? Of course not, because if I touch this area, even with a very soft touch, I can feel the pain deep inside ... the pain is inside ... it is chronic inside, permanent and untreatable.[4]

Cassinga is as sensitive as the Achilles tendon injury which when hurt may not mend and heal completely again. Its pain is alive inside, so painful that it hurts when tampered with. In this relation, the scars, effigies of violence on survivors' bodies, translate into lasting memories of pain and suffering. The use of the metaphor, omuthipa, a crucial and sensitive part of the body, suggests the sensitivity and the resistance of the wounded body to mend and heal properly. Evasively, the "body in pain" appears healed when looking at it externally and seeing the external scars, but it is throbbing inside. And, without communicating their

---

4   Author's interview with Rauha Shitangi, Okadhila, 2007.

pains and sufferings, survivors might live amidst us and we might unknowingly take it for granted that all is well with them. The point is that survivors are constantly waging a protracted struggle with their emotional memories. This struggle is endless because memories of the Cassinga massacre switch on, uncontrollably, now and again. Martha Mwatilifange explains:

> That scene near the Cassinga garage sickens me. That place, where some of us reassembled after the massacre ... It is such a horrendous scene, so traumatic that it is beyond my words ... such a shocking horror that no one can describe. ... people roasted to death ... the smell of roasted human flesh remains unbearable ... Whenever I remember and recount that horror ... the already open wounds start to bleed profusely ... It was horrible, seeing dozens of people roasted and beyond recognition is hurting ... it is something I do not want to remember and talk about it ... it opens the wounds.[5]

For the physically wounded victims of the Cassinga massacre, the remembrance of that event and its deplorable aftermath is a frequent experience, so awful and unavoidable due to the permanence of disability on the victim's body. In fact, even with successful medical treatment and recovery from the pain of the external damage, the inside damage is nevertheless permanent. It is this incurable injury that the victims decry and want the public to understand as Hendrina Kiiyala explains:

> I was seventeen when this terrible violence damaged my life. I was a child, separated from my parents by the war and violence inside Namibia. I went into exile hoping to escape violence and receive education for a better future. The unfortunate happened a few months after arriving in Cassinga ... Many people died on that day and survivors were left in very difficult situations, emotionally and physically. In the immediate aftermath of the massacre, I had this thought it was better to have died than surviving the killings. The pain was so unbearable. We did not receive any treatment on the day of the attack. The second day also passed without any treatment ... From Cassinga, those of us who were seriously wounded were transported to the Cuban military clinic at Techamutete, about 25km from Cassinga. The group consisted of Namibians, Cubans and Angolans who needed emergency treatments. Unfortunately, we only received painkiller tablets there. On May 6, a helicopter flew sixteen of us, all Namibians to a hospital in Huambo. Others went to Luanda and so on. We had horrible experiences in Huambo. Each one of us, except one little girl, had a limb amputated ... my arm was surgically removed there, in Huambo. This happened because I did not receive treatment on time. We spent three days without treatment after the massacre. Sometime in June 1978, we arrived in Luanda en-route to East Germany (GDR) for further treatment and to receive artificial limbs. My initial stay in the GDR was discomforting and traumatic. Remember that, it was all whites who did all these bad things to us in Cassinga. Emerging from that terrible experience of

---

5   Author's interview with Martha Mwatilifange, *Oshakati*, 2007.

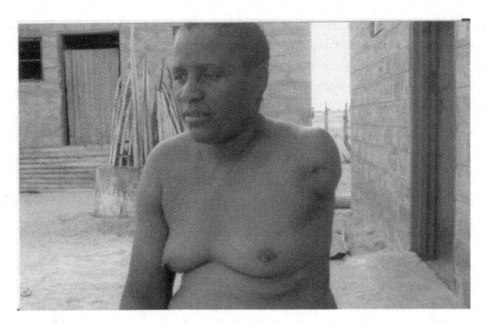

Fig. 4: Hendrina Kiiyala photographed inside her homestead at Oshiku sha Shipya, north central Namibia, 11 June 2009. She opted for her photograph to look this way.

racial killings, I could trust no white person... In Germany, therefore, it took very long to accept that they [Germans] would do no harm to me. How different were they from the Boers who brutalized us for no wrongs? I harbored that anxiety for very long. ... We received treatment at a clinic called Berlin-Buch. There was a nurse called Ellen (sic) who was so friendly to me and treated me like her own child, but I only realized her mother-like approach after some time: the thing was, I lost appetite for most of the period I spent in the hospital. She was concerned about my poor appetite. She frequently told me that she would send me back to Cassinga if I did not eat and finish my food. That was her way of trying to encourage me to eat and stay alive. I did not take her words lightly ... The more she mentioned Cassinga, the more I felt a tumble in my stomach and the more I lost appetite for food ... Of course, she was aware of the physical injuries on my body, but she was unaware about the emotional damage such deplorable experience created in me, the heavy load of traumatic memories inside me, mistrust, fear and feelings of insecurity that the terrible Cassinga experience planted inside me. If I had a way of explaining and unpacking the pain, trauma and shock inside me, she would not have made such remarks.[6]

In following Lawrence Langer's presentation of Holocaust testimonies, "the body can be maimed in many ways, not only through mutilation,"[7] thereby making it an "active agent" of

---

[6] Author's interview with Hendrina Kiiyala at Oshikuku (place of work) on 11 June 2009 and at Oshiku sha Shipya (homestead), 21 December 2009.

[7] Lawrence Langer L., *Holocaust testimonies: the ruins of memory* (New Haven and London: Yale University Press, 1991), p. 101.

pain.[8] By looking on the surface of Kiiyala's amputated arm and, indeed, her mutilated body as a whole (the emphasis here is on the internal damage rather than the external damage), it is certainly plausible to imagine that the injuries and the pain she sustained and suffered were terrible, as she described it in the interview. But, like photographs, scars of violence, which seal violence beneath them, are not anything that survivors can rely on when hoping for their living painful experiences to reach, in the pragmatic nature of the never-healing wounds, the broadest possible public audience and understanding. Of course, there is a relationship between the physical damage of the body and the violent penetration of the pain into the victim's body. But, the physically harrowing scars of the damaged body should, instead, be interpreted and understood as concealing the underlying agony which is hidden and self-evident of the injured body that is not only damaged but also beyond repair.

As Elaine Scarry writes, "physical pain has no voice, but when it last finds a voice, it begins to tell a story, and the story that it tells is about"[9] the physical scars' inability to elicit the innermost pain and suffering of its victim. In this relation, Kiiyala's stump of her amputated arm elucidates the argument I am constructing. It is unambiguous that the physical site of damage on her body is transparent in the photograph, but the pain, disability and suffering which emanate from it are implicitly and exclusively personal experiences. This is particularly so when the intent to communicate the victims' "pervasive and enduring" distress becomes difficult through the visual or "verbal expressibility."

It is also clear that Kiiyala's picture of the amputated arm reveals a 'heartrending site.' Indeed such poignant and distressing images of her damaged body emit shocking and hurtful emotions for the concerned and sensitive viewers. Nonetheless, the external pathos that this photograph flashes into view confines the experience of violence to a particular area of the victim's body. This implies that such external scars on the victim's body are not as complex and damaging as the innermost violence that invasively sits beneath the surface of the protruding scars or amputated body parts. Equally so, permanent scars of violence on the victims' bodies are not as disturbing as when listening to the victims' stories of violence. For example, listening to the victims' traumatic stories during the interviews was quite emotionally charged when compared to the representation of such experiences through photographs. This is not to claim that by spending time with survivors during the interviews or personal communication with them, it was possible to understand their implicit memories and suffering. However, the tangible presence of the victims' physical injuries and the trauma embedded in the stories they told presented me with a more complex picture about their unending suffering.

---

[8]   Elaine Scarry, *The body in pain*, p. 47.
[9]   *Ibid.*, p. 3.

Damaged bodies, long suffering and passive victimhood

According to survivors, long suffering is as a result of a process that involves two types of violence, but which are nevertheless jointly connected. These are the transitory and permanent categories of violence. The first category of violence is associated with the actual occurrence of the massacre. Survivors recognize this experience as the process when violence entered the victim's body: it involves the actual individual recording and memorization of the painful things experienced (physically and emotionally) as the violence unfolded. The permanent category sets in the moment the transitory phase is completed. It is the replay of the assault pictures or scenes of violence recorded during the period of witnessing the massacre. This category transcends the actual period and space when and where violence was initially experienced. It is specifically associated with the individual victim's endless struggle against the recurring traumatic flashbacks and nightmares. As such, this phase represents the gruesomeness of carrying the burden of the relentless returns of the Cassinga traumatic scenes, combined with the excruciatingly endless and personal suffering.

As a consequence of enduring the pervasive suffering in isolation, the victim may become vocally wounded and repressed into "passive victimhood." This implies "collusion" between the wounded body and "silence."[10] This collusion may partly explain why the victims

Fig. 5: Helena Shixuadu Ipinge, Oshakati, 2009.

---

[10] Helena Pohlandt – McCormick, "I saw a nightmare' ... Doing violence to memory: The Soweto uprising, June 16, 1976," in *History and Theory*, Vol. 39, No. 4, Theme Issue 39: "Not Telling": Secrecy, Lies, and History (Dec., 2000), p. 23.

of the Cassinga massacre are enduring so much pain and suffering in silence for so long. This does not mean that they do not want to communicate their miseries. Nor is this failure entirely inherent in the fact that physical violence "resists verbal objectification," or because there is an absence of language for pain. Its meaning is closer to suggesting that the victims feel isolated, they feel repressed and condemned to "contain" and deal with their sufferings individually and in silence as nobody appears prepared to empower them to speak for their rights as persons who need justice on their side.

In this light above, it important to explore passive victimhood in the context of its extremely harsh victimization as represented in the following visual and oral testimonies of some of the victims whose bodies are permanently damaged following the Cassinga massacre.

Passive victimhood, to concur with Helena Shixuandu Ipinge, nourishes the aggressive nature of the permanent stage of the Cassinga violence into an on and off living experience. She explains:

> Sometimes I am disconnected from it, but whenever I see my face like this in the mirror, it is like pressing the button that switches on the screen of the Cassinga violence ... In the mirror, my real face is invisible ... I see the bitterness and anger instead ... I am very angry with those who caused this terrible damage, those who stole my natural features ... why did they do it? Why did they cause all these endless pain? Why are they not accountable for all these endless sufferings? How can I forgive them?[11]

The "on and off" violence that Ipinge describes concurs with what Cathy Caruth, in the context of the Holocaust trauma, identified as "second wounding" or "double wounding."[12] In the case of the victims of the Cassinga massacre, the "double wounding" calls to mind the understanding that the Cassinga violence finds no resolution within the victims' individual space. This is particularly so when society appears to ignore the victims' ongoing suffering and trauma. Certainly, Ipinge experiences many returns of very sad moments of the massacre, which have left a permanent and unpleasant brand on her face. Looking at her face in the mirror is a way of reflecting on the terrible experience in Cassinga, and connecting it to her bodily and emotional sufferings since that fateful day of catastrophe, human suffering and wretchedness. In other words, her damaged face is the agency that generates an "anguished memory" embedded in the irreplaceable beauty stolen from a young girl without compensation: it refers to the victims' anger, sadness and frustration when the perpetrators

---

[11]   Author's interview with Helena Shixuandu Iipinge, Oshakati, 2009.
[12]   Cathy Caruth, *Unclaimed experience: trauma, narrative and history* (Baltimore: Johns Hopkins University Press, 1996), p. 8.

escape taking responsibility for the Cassinga massacre. This is all under the watchful eye of the justice system which ought to speak for and protect the victims of apartheid-colonial violence against innocent civilians, particularly women and young girls. Ipinge's expression of shock and anger is therefore a way of interrogating the unfairness of the justice system since Namibia became a democracy in 1990.

Indeed, the continuity of the unhealing permanent memories stem from a number of causes. For example, both Namibia and South Africa did not honour the expectations, prior to democratization, of the victims of colonial and apartheid atrocities. Paradoxically, democracy turned out to benefit the perpetrators at the expense of the victims of political violence under apartheid and colonial rule in Namibia. The victims are under the state obligation to forgive the perpetrators whom the state shields from prosecution. Indeed, in the eyes of the formerly oppressed, democracy has unquestionably added more misery to the victims' experience of the pathos of colonialism. Certainly, the victims of the Cassinga massacre and other related violence in Namibia are unhappy about the enforced "reconciliation without justice" (which I have explored in Chapter 6) for the victims of apartheid-colonialism in Namibia.

It is apparent that survivors demand justice and nothing else. They feel strongly that the perpetrators of the Cassinga massacre should apologize, take responsibility and compensate the victims for the damage incurred. In the absence of social justice, the bleak cycle of traumatic violence continues to recharge repeatedly and adds more layers of pain and suffering felt by the victims of the Cassinga massacre, the survivors and affected families. Therefore, it is not surprising that survivors voice a concern that their sufferings, grievances and nightmares have reached a level that is no longer easy to contain, at least emotionally. I am not saying that an initiation of victims' justice can repair and remedy emotional suffering. What I am saying is that it is possible to interrupt and reduce the layers of the injurious but "tainted (implicit or obscured) memories," if steps were taken to listen to the demands and aspirations of the victims.

The misery of Lonia Vatileni alias "Ndjeimo," whose images of unacceptable body damage appear below, indicate the intensity of the physical damage as well as the emotional and health related issues that this damage generates. Vatileni explains:

My health has been considerably compromised ... My amputated feet are never healing ... they itch terribly, especially when it is cloudy and wet ... Those who did these terrible things to us are not accountable to our unending sufferings. The Boers are untouchable, if they were approachable and able to listen, we would want to ask them to repair and fix the damage they created. The government preaches national reconciliation. What reconciliation? Who benefit from it? With my physical disabilities, endless emotional pain and suffering, the coercion to forgive the Boers is an-

Fig. 6: Lonia Vatileni alias Ndjeimo, photographed at Ongwediva, north central Namibia, 21 February 2009.

other nightmare. Forgiving them for what? Have we done them any wrongs? And, how can I forgive them when they have not acknowledged responsibilities for our innocence, permanent disability and endless suffering? They have made my life miserable, yet I must forgive them? Must I condone violence and unhealed wounds? ... I am a cleaner and my wage is not enough to help me deal with my disability-related problems, such as getting proper medical assistance. I am also a single mother, with five children and I do not have a proper house. Two of my children have completed schooling but they are unemployed. Their father was a SWAPO combatant. He was killed in the war. I need support to assist these children, to finish their studies and maybe help me tomorrow.[13]

The burden of forgiveness as politically promoted since Namibia became independent is in conflict with survivors' "anguished memories." In view of this distressing situation, it becomes certain that survivors' actual experience of the Cassinga massacre and their ongoing suffering are intertwined. Certainly, Vatileni's statement suggests that the traumatic effect of the actual physical moment of the violence combines with the traumatic aftermath of the massacre and subscribes to life-long suffering and fathomless agony. The prolonged survivors' suffering and disappointment echo the dominant presence of inequalities in society:

---

[13]   Authors's interview with Lonia "Ndjeimo" Vatileni, Ongwediva, 2007.

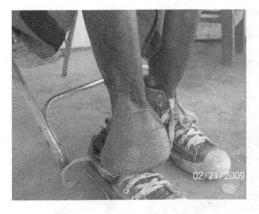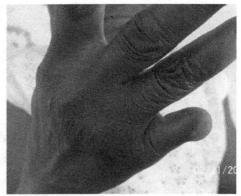

Figs. 7 and 8: Lonia Vatileni's amputated foot and fingers, photographed at Ongwediva, north central Namibia, 21 February 2009.

race, class, gender and economic disparities between the rich and poor, which characterize a society emerging from apartheid, colonialism and racial rule.

The way survivors chronicle their anguished stories suggests one other crucial issue. That is, survivors' reflective traumatic memories aim to stir and direct public attention, not to the actual moment of the Cassinga massacre as it is politically remembered. The victims intend making the public aware of the contemporary problematic issues of humanitarian concerns which continue to affect them since the Cassinga massacre. These are the issues which survivors are particularly concerned with and want addressed if they were to meaningfully accept and forgive their former enemies.

When I paid Sabina Uupindi a visit at her homestead in Ombafi, Ombalantu, it transpired that the severity of the survivors' suffering (emotionally and physically) is indeed a combination of the actual experience of the massacre exacerbated by individual survivors' socio-economic challenges that they face on a daily basis. Uupindi who lives with a number of dependent children under her care is a single mother with little or no income to sustain the little ones under her custodianship. The point is, unlike survivors with access to decent employment and living, those of them who live below the poverty line, in generally poor socio-economic environments, appear more severely affected by the recurring traumatic memories of the Cassinga massacre.

It is important to recognize that the degree of suffering and the enduring severe traumatic memories relate to a number of other factors. Individual survivors told me that the higher the intensity of the physical and emotional violence the victim experienced and recorded, or the severity of the injuries and disability the victim sustained during the massacre, the more excruciating the physical and emotional suffering as Uupindi explains:

Each survivor accumulated personal experiences of the massacre and of surviving the horror. Some people were lucky to have escaped from the camp before the foot-soldiers moved in. In my case, I was unfortunate to have fallen in the hands of the enemy. My friend, Loide Amwaama and I were found hiding ... both of us were by then wounded ... Our captors did not do any physical harm to us, but they took us to traumatic scenes around the camp, where people were horribly killed in mass numbers. One shocking experience is when they took us to a dead person body wearing a military uniform ... his body was badly mutilated and his intestines were on the floor ... we were terribly shaken ... but they were pitiless ... they ordered us to sit at the sides of the mutilated body ... placing the corpse between us. Loide sat on the right and I sat on the left side of the corpse. They told us that we must not look away from the corpse ... I had never been that close to a dead person, and worst of all, the body was badly violated ... it was horrible – horrible. From that scene, they took us to other horrible, horrible scenes where we found many other people dead, most of them lying in pools of blood. We were under the escort of four Boers for most of the time ... at the end of it they took us to the clinic where we found another group of our comrades rounded up.[14]

Uupindi's preoccupation with the sites of the physical and emotional memories implies that violence is rationally dynamic and transferable. It moves and transcends, as I have indicated earlier, the shared physical space and specific moments into the private and internal space of the victim. The degree of survivors' obsessiveness with violence in the distant present of the Cassinga massacre suggests the level of the psychological damage that survivors have suffered for a very long time. This detrimental effect becomes a concern, especially in considering that the victims exposed to such traumatic experiences were children at the time. And for most of them, it was their first experience of seeing dead people, pools of human blood and other horrible pictures of human catastrophe. This scenario takes into account the fact that in some customs, such as those of Aawambo, children were not allowed to view dead bodies. And, should that happen, the victim was to be cleansed, a practice which survivors of the Cassinga massacre side-stepped in the immediate aftermath of the massacre. Cleansing is a customary practice where the victim is psychologically prepared to manage the shock, distress and nightmares.

The following description attempts to explain the unacceptability of the violence and the need for counseling of those who witnessed such acts of violence:

The disoriented and confused children including a number of babies who were in search of their mothers and crying for help were neglected ... It is regrettable and traumatic for those of us who survived and continue to recall such distressful memories. Counting on the intensive attacks from the air which lasted for about an hour, I can say that there was no time to attend to the wounded and all those who needed

---

14 Author's interview with Sabina Uupindi, Ombafi, 2007.

73

help such as women and children. It was all about saving own life. At first, people were running together in small groups. But afterwards, people realized that it was risky running in clusters. Women especially sought the company of their male folk. They hoped to receive protection from them, but men were dodging and avoiding them. There was also a sense of avoiding people wearing white or red, target clothes, which the enemy could easily detect.[15]

Other survivors narrated similar horrific testimonies that suggest that counseling is needed for the Cassinga victims. Darius Mbolondondo Shikongo, one of the few rescuers of civilians in Cassinga, told me how he continues to suffer from emotional distress which is attributable to his failure to rescue the victims who were critically wounded and unable to walk:

In fact, I whisked many children across the river before the Boers came inside the camp. But, it was difficult to help other people who were critically wounded and could not walk. I did not pay attention to them during the rescuing exercise, as it required more than one person to carry each of them to places of safety. Pictures of those distressful moments are pervasive. They keep on returning, seriously wounding me and making closure and healing impossible.[16]

Rauha Shitangi narrated living a life of nightmares since the unacceptable violence she experienced in Cassinga:

I cannot remember the name of that young girl, but she was one of the students from the St. Mary's Odibo High School.[17] I found her deep in the bush, critically wounded. The place where I found her was relatively safer and I decided to stay there with her. Regrettably, she died, as I watched on. She was a courageous young girl. In spite of the awful pain she experienced, she was very brave to tell me her full name and her address in Namibia ... Regrettably, I have not been able to remember her name and her parents' address when things returned to normal. She died shortly after passing that information to me. I had deep cuts on my leg and buttock and stayed at that spot, rescuers, the Cubans found me there. We left her dead body there ... what happened to it I do not know ... but, it is so painful and troublesome ... I feel guilty that I failed to convey her death to her family as she entrusted me to do before she died.[18]

The late Rev. Michael Amukoto echoed Shitangi's dilemma in that he is continuously haunted by an enduring shadow of guilt. This pertains to his inability to explain what happened

---

[15] Author's interview with Michael Amukoto, Onaniki, 2002.

[16] Author's interview with Darius "Mbolondondo" Shikongo, Ondangwa, 2007.

[17] Odibo is an Anglican Mission school at Odibo, a rural area located about 1 km south of the Angolan border. According to Lena Kamati, a former Odibo student and Cassinga survivor, "early in 1978 a group of more than two hundred students left the school for Angola under the escort of SWAPO fighters. Some of them arrived in Cassinga a few days before the attack.

[18] Author's interview with Rauha Shitangi, Okadhila, 2007.

to his family members whom he lost in Cassinga. He tried to explain his ordeal to me as highlighted in the following excerpt:

> I lived with my wife and four children in Cassinga. After the massacre, I did not see my wife and my eldest daughter, Nuusiku Lengomwenyo Amukoto. I still do not know what happened to them. The uncertainty about what happened to my people is very hurtful and keeps on returning since the Cassinga massacre ... this situation always demands explanations which I ought to have, but which I do not have and I do not think I will ever find ... such as whether my people are really dead. If they died in Cassinga where are they buried – in the mass graves? These nightmares and those of my other two sons Gabriel and Otto Amukoto, who also died in exile during the successive years of the Namibian liberation struggle and whose remains are unaccounted for, also bring much suffering and endless grief every day. The shadow about what happened to my people is unacceptable.[19]

The "shadow" that Amukoto bemoans is a painful metaphor for the neglected world of the dead or, as Amukoto repeatedly put it in the interview, my people, "aantu yandje." When there is an inability to see, know, understand and find answers when situations are shrouded in absolute darkness and silence, such disturbing realities translate into Amukoto's single-handed and directionless search for "answers" and explanations about how his wife and daughter possibly died at Cassinga.[20] And, if they were killed, what exactly happened to their bodies? From this deplorable event, the aftermath of the Cassinga massacre translates into an impenetrable frontier that disconnects the living from the dead. This barrier is so hostile and impassable that it prohibits the bereaved families from practicing acceptable norms in line with respective individuals or communities' performances of rituals and rites for the dead. This is one other adversity that propels survivors' sense of guilt and suffering in the face of the violated and unfulfilled individual clan and societal practices.

In the confines of this insurmountable quagmire, survivors and affected families of people who are the unconfirmed dead, or whose burial grounds are not yet confirmed, have been trapped in the traumatic moments which never end. When violence involving the mass killings or disappearance of people is shrouded in the absence of identified human remains or graves, it creates further injury. The bitterness for the unconfirmed losses of the loved ones crystallizes into a cycle of relentless traumatic violence that continuously brings around lasting painful processes of rumination or the recurrence of undiluted violence.[21]

---

[19] Author's interview with Michael Amukoto, Onaniki, 2002.
[20] Two of Amukoto's children died in separate incidents, one presumably in combat, in the years following the Cassinga massacre.
[21] Rumination is discussed in Chapter 7.

Political recognition, especially for individuals, whom survivors credit with the rescue and saving of many lives in Cassinga, would serve as a form of counselling and maybe healing. Contrarily, lack of recognition for such exceptional roles may generate painful memories and individual suffering:

> I still believe that I am yet to receive recognition like other heroes who have received special recognition since independence ... only if my role during the Cassinga massacre is anything to be remembered ... but who is a hero, a politician? I think it is genuine that we all get official recognition and rewards while we are still alive.[22]

Namibia's lack of recognition of persons, other than prominent politicians, for their bravery and selflessness in saving others' lives in conflict situations, or other contributions made during the liberation struggle, might well trigger emotional pain, hopelessness and frustration of those people. In this context, the absence of attributing official recognition to individuals known and accredited by oral sources for their selfless roles of saving civilian lives can result in tensions and disappointments. Important to note is that such frustrations and disappointments concern the survivors who were saved by rescuers like "Mbolondondo," more than it concerns the rescuers themselves.[23] In this way, by registering the unhappiness regarding the unrecognized role one has played in rescuing the lives of others is not, necessarily, about expectations of some sort of material reward, though this is crucial it is, primarily, a societal norm. As human beings, we owe recognition to such exceptional men and women of integrity. Nothing dilutes their unique contribution, their bravery, selflessness and exemplary deeds under extreme and difficult circumstances during the trying times of Namibia's protracted walk to freedom. In fact, this situation is tantamount to forging a culture of forgetfulness, which remembers and commemorates a few at the expense of many unrecognized histories. Amukoto explains:

> It hurts, it is really painful and discomforting. Our people are not committed to preserving the histories of what Namibians paid for independence. It is so disappointing to watch our valuable heritage disappearing. It is a betrayal to our loved ones whose

---

22 Author's interview with Darius "Mbolondondo" Shikongo, Ondangwa, 2007. Mbolondondo is currently the SWAPO council for the Olukonda constituency, following the 2010 regional and local elections in Namibia.

23 Every Cassinga survivor whom I have interviewed pays tribute to the brave men, such as "Mbolondondo," "Nakatana," Paavo Max and David Kamakondo (at least to mention individuals whose names were provided in my interviews), who saved many lives in Cassinga. Survivors told me that they would not have survived if it were not for the bravery and humanitarian efforts provided by individual SWAPO combatants who in lieu of escaping through various exits known to them, as trained guerilla fighters, chose to volunteer and save the lives of vulnerable civilians. These men whisked away a number of civilians from the camp, across the brimming Cubango River, before the paratroopers moved into the camp.

blood we say "waters our freedom." Our people tend to forget too soon. Imagine, our children are not even taught these things (such as the Cassinga heroes and heroines) in schools. Namibia has traveled a long and protracted journey to get where we are today.[24]

Indeed, as Hendrina Kiiyala adds:

Those of us who went into exile lost many people, not only in Cassinga. We left many people at every place we settled, Lubango, Vietnam, Kwanza-sul, Vienna, Ndalatando, Omatala, in the bush where our soldiers fell fighting the enemy and many other places. We buried so many people and lost many others, whose graves are unknown ... these are some of the histories that we must preserve, teach, explore and research as a nation.[25]

To this end there is fear that:

The generation that fought against the South African colonial rule is dwindling. Take, for example, our group of 1976. Five hundred of us, including fifty women, left Zambia to Kongwa in Tanzania for military training. But, look at things today. How many of us are still alive? Of course, many of our colleagues died in the war. But, those of us who survived the conflict have tried nothing to document and preserve our important histories.[26]

And, as Martha Ndamona Mwatilifange-Uusiku observes:

Survivors as the eyewitnesses of the Cassinga massacre are the primary materials and sources of what Cassinga means. If we die with our testimonies, the generations to come will never know and understand. They will never be able to retrieve our stories from the graves ... our generation will be blamed for sitting idle and watching these precious histories die with us. We are still alive today for a purpose. We are the living testimonies of the Cassinga massacre and what happened thereafter.[27]

Nevertheless, survivors are worried that the inexperienced people are complacent and appear not to take survivors' stories seriously. This is the view expressed in the following extract:

The Cassinga massacre appears like a joke to non-survivors, but to us [the survivors] it is endless suffering. Many times, I have tried to tell what happened and continues to happen to me since then, but none appears to believe me, share with me the painful moments ... no one is interested in offering alternative which could help me deal with my difficult situations. Many could not pay attention because what I tell them

---

[24] Author's interview with Michael Amukoto, Onaniki, 2002.
[25] Author's interview with Hendrina Kiiyala, Oshikuku, 2007.
[26] Author's interview with Paavo Max, Efindi, 2008.
[27] Author's interview with Martha Mwatilifange, Oshakati, 2007.

appears unreal, but Cassinga left me permanently wounded and continues to incur wounds in the present. This situation becomes worse, especially, when a comrade dies ... it reminds me of those other comrades I lost in Cassinga.[28]

Martha Mwatilifange adds the following:

Whenever I receive a news of death of a Cassinga survivor, it scratches on the wounded part of my memory. And you know, many of them just died like that, without their stories being told, recorded and preserved.[29]

This unwelcome situation may prevail, because the tangibly wounded memory remains implicit, hidden from the intended public audience. As a result, it is difficult to recognize as real when survivors communicate their suffering to the inexperienced audience in forms of testimony other than disclosing the damage inside them. However, to conclude, it should be understood that when the public shows no interest in listening to survivors' traumatic experiences and emotional sufferings it generates negative consequences that prolong the pain and suffering of the Cassinga victims. I have problematized survivors permanent injuries as an acidic substance that do not virtually exist as tangible evidence on the surface as scars on the wounded victims' bodies, but reside below obscured from others' experience and understanding. I have argued that while permanent injuries are empirically tangible and violent inside the body of the beholder, these are not visible for the other people to see and offer assistance to the sufferer. In addition, the victims whose bodies are maimed and offer disturbing evidence of violence do not have a language to express their suffering and unending pain other than telling us stories about the atrocious Cassinga massacre and its excruciating aftermath. Regrettably, such testimonial accounts are entangled in the insuffiency of language that conveys the absence of the tangible violence. In this context, it is problematic if survivors' testimonies were to be embraced as authenticating the dynamic of the actual violence implanted in their bodies. Of course, the victims' disclosure of the physical damage on their bodies such as in the case of Vataleni, Kiiyala, Ipinge and many others, symbolizes the survivors' struggle to find appropriate techniques to communicate their sufferings to the public and invite a response that may serve as a remedy for counselling and healing.

---

[28] Author's interview with Ignatius Vahongaifa Mwanyekange, Windhoek, 2009.
[29] Author's interview with Martha Mwatilifange, Oshakati, 2007.

5 The Aftermath of Cassinga and the Unapologetic Perpetrators: Guilty or Innocent?

As a matter of fact, apartheid South Africa needed to repress and wage indiscriminate war against unarmed Namibian population groups to sustain its illegal and forcible hold on power in Namibia. In particular,

> In the opening months of 1981 ... the number of South African troops in the territory had reached 100 000 – approximately one soldier to every 12 members of the Namibian population. ... The actual number of troops in Namibia fluctuates considerably, depending on preparations for attacks into neighbouring Angola. Before each of these attacks, additional troops are mobilized and moved to Namibia. This makes it difficult to reach an exact figure for any particular time. South Africa's military build-up in Namibia has been accompanied by the enforcement of increasingly harsh and authoritarian security measures, to the extent that, by 1981, more than 80 per cent of the population were living under de facto martial law.[1]

The greater the South African military presence in Namibia and the greater "de facto martial law," the higher the rate of violence committed, with more people forced to leave Namibia and greater loss of support for the SADF among the affected Namibian populations. The SADF and other South African security forces in Namibia were unpopular with many Namibians. It is evident that the SADF, as a collective, was unpopular among many white South Africans. This could be explained by the fact that apartheid establishment was largely sustained by military conscripts who served a compulsory period of military service, including going to the border of Namibia and Angola to fight SWAPO combatants. The SADF maintained a force of military reservists who had served a two-year compulsory military service, after which they returned to civilian life and waited to be called up at any time for military service. The SADF appeared to have some trust in the military reservists who were individually called up for special operations such as the Cassinga operation.

> It therefore appears that most of the SADF paratroopers who participated in the Cassinga massacre were individuals drawn from the Citizen Force, which was made up of volunteers serving an initial period of training and active duty, followed by several years of reserve status. They rotated into active duty when called upon. According to Breytenbach, a battalion of 370 men who were involved in the Cassinga operation was referred to as a "composite battalion," that is, the reservists were taken from two separate battalions, namely 2 Parachute Battalion and 3 Parachute Battalion.

---

[1] International Defence & Aid Fund, "Apartheid's army in Namibia: South Africa's illegal military occupation." *Fact Papers on Southern Africa, No. 10* (London: Canon Collins House, 1982), p. 3.

Parachute Battalions 2 and 3 were reserve units of the Citizen Force with all the officers, non-commissioned officers and men having completed either nine months, 12 months or 15 months of full-time military training, during which time they served with 1 Parachute Battalion.[2] Breytenbach claims to have listed, in his recent publication, the names of all the paratroopers who participated in the Cassinga attack.[3] Regardless of who these individuals were, it is common sense that while soldiers are compelled to act collectively when in combat operation, the fact that each soldier is an individual, with unique personalities, etc., cannot be underestimated. In fact, in any armed violence that ends in humiliation, the individual soldier is the great loser and sufferer in the aftermath of the war. Thus, the paratroopers left Cassinga as individuals, some of them indeed inflamed with anger and embarrassed by their collective actions against the innocent lives of civilians whom they were told, prior to landing in Cassinga, were armed terrorists. So, as a former SADF conscript confided to me in an interview, "several senior officers left the army after Cassinga ... disenchanted with the army over the SADF actions in Cassinga."[4]

The senior officers' disillusionment with the army suggests that many paratroopers returned from Cassinga psychologically damaged, muted, some of them so embarrassed that they decided not to tell anyone about Cassinga, not even their spouses. Consider the following statement by the wife of the commander of the Cassinga massacre:

> Eventually my husband came home [from Cassinga] ... Then twenty five years later I learnt about that day [the day of the Cassinga attack] when I typed the manuscript of this book [Jan Breytenbach's book, *The Eagle strike*]. I read the individual stories ... sometimes I cried as I read, because on that day, so long ago, I had been praying not knowing what they were going through ... My tears were because I didn't know. I didn't know what my husband went through when he came home because he never told me.[5]

This revelation discloses how the experience of the Cassinga massacre was so gruesome and inhuman to the extent that paratroopers shied away from disclosing, even to their loved ones, the indiscriminate killing of innocent civilians. Indeed, most people would have the view that all paratroopers jointly agree with the SADF official telling of the Cassinga episode. The fact is, Cassinga paratroopers' testimonies of the Cassinga episode are much more diverse than what many people would have expected. It is also unambiguous that the SADF silence over or denial of the indiscriminate mass killings of civilians in Cassinga has divided and put the former paratroopers at odds with one another. This is primarily noticeable between the former senior commanders, the so-called professional soldiers of the operation,

---

[2]   Edward Alexander, "The Cassinga raid," Appendix C to Chapter 4.
[3]   See Jan Breytenbach, *Eagle strike*, pp. 446–451.
[4]   Email received by the author from an anonymous former SADF conscript, 13 November 2010.
[5]   Statement by Jan Breytenabach's wife. In Jan Breytenbach, *Eagle Strike*, pp. 386–387.

and their former junior officers.[6] This conflict surfaces in the way different paratroopers unleash personal accounts that contradict the SADF official version of the Cassinga episode (see below).

As pointed out earlier, in the run-up to the Cassinga massacre, the SADF was prepared to ensure that "credible coverage and immediate release [of the SADF storyline of the Cassinga attack] is essential to counter claims of SADF operations against and mass killings of civilians, especially women and children."[7] From this statement it appears obvious that the Cassinga violence was in all instances foreseeable, and anticipated to unfold into two very distinctive but connected phases. This translates into the short- and long-term "resulting injuries,"[8] comprising the physical violence (short term) and the rhetorical or emotional violence (long or indefinite violence). My task here is to grapple with the later, emotional violence, which is overtly promoted by the paratroopers who remain adamant that Cassinga was not a civilian camp.

In a move to "improve own credibility regarding" the massacre of Namibian refugees at Cassinga, the SADF entered a "critical period" of "media feeding," in attempts to "clinically" repair the damage done to the SADF "credibility."[9] This move marked the beginning of the SADF public denial of the Cassinga massacre. In fact, it initiated the birth of those who are the deniers of the Cassinga massacre. This category of paratroopers can be best described as politically poisoned: For the better or worse, these proponents of apartheid killing machines are resolutely committed to perpetuating verbal, print media and photographic imagery, which advocate the absence of any Cassinga massacre. They are belligerent, publicly adamant that there was no mass killing and maiming of innocent civilians in Cassinga.

The belligerent Breytenbach is one of the Cassinga paratroopers who is publicly obstinate and adamant that paratroopers did not carry out the senseless killings and maiming of defenceless civilians.[10] For instance, in the foreword to Graham Gillmore's book, *Pathfinder Company: 44 Parachute Brigade The Philistines,* Breytenbach wrote:

> On Ascension Day, 1978, a composite South African parachute battalion jumped onto the tactical HQ of SWAPO's PLAN army, based at Cassinga, 250 kilometres north of the Angolan border to destroy the facility, their logistics, and to wipe out a

---

6   Visit: http://www.sainfantry.co.za/e107_plugins/forum/forum_viewtopic.php?16
7   Chief of the SADF, "PSYAC Planning Directive No. 3 \ 78, Operation Reindeer (Top Secret): Phase Three (media coverage). " Source: SANDF Archive, Pretoria.
8   Elaine Scarry, *The body in pain,* p. 75.
9   Media Analysis: Operation Reindeer (Top Secret). Ref. No. HS OPS 310 \ 4 \ Reindeer, Dated 8 August, 78, based on CSI'S Media Analysis document MI \ 205\13\1\1. Source: SANDF Archive, Pretoria.
10   See Appendix G of this book. Also visit: "Cassinga string"/ facebook. Online at http://et-ee.facebook.com/topic.php?uid=40615219623&topic=15512, Accessed on 29 June 2011.

strong concentration of SWAPO guerrillas. The airborne assault, part of Operation Reindeer, was an unqualified success; the whole base was destroyed. 608 PLAN fighters were killed, with many more wounded which pushed the final SWAPO death toll to well over a thousand. We lost only four paratroopers killed in action plus a dozen or so wounded. According to airborne experts in Britain and Australia, this was the most audacious parachute assault since the Second World War; the mounting airfield was well over 1,000 nautical miles away. I was the commander of that airborne assault, which although successful above all expectations, also highlighted many shortcomings, some of which nearly led to a disastrous outcome.[11]

On a similar note, the then Right-wing Freedom Front Senator Tienie Groenewald, who was the military Chief of Staff of Intelligence at the time of the Cassinga massacre, defended the assault: "There was no massacre at Cassinga ...it was the finest military operation conducted by the SADF."[12] And, during a special meeting of Parliament's Defence Committee called to investigate the unauthorised parade held by 44 Parachute Brigade in Bloemfontein on 4 May 1996, the former National Party Senator Mark Wiley who had been "at Cassinga" was quoted to have said that the remarks that Cassinga was a refugee camp are "nonsense."[13] In line with such representations, the Cassinga deniers include individual ex-paratroopers calling themselves "proud warriors," who continue to claim that the Cassinga massacre is a deed of pride and heroism.[14] They are proponents of violence that unnecessarily continues to harm and exacerbate the suffering and pain of others, namely the Cassinga survivors and affected families of the dead and missing Namibians. This is eminently the case with their unrepentant and provocative statements, for example, arguing that apartheid-colonial violence in both South Africa and Namibia was "all worth effort ... the proud attainment of all those in the South African uniform – those who won... that is why Namibia and South Africa bore almost no scars of war when their respective movements towards political settlement began."[15]

Writing about Argentina's "Dirty War" junta (1976–1983), Marguerite Feitlowitz asks: "when known torturers are said to be heroes, what happens to the minds of those they injured?"[16] In this relation, this work considers the SADF rhetorical violence as not only

---

[11] Jan Breytenbach's foreword to Graham Gillmore's book, *Pathfinder Company: 44 Parachute Brigade The Philistines* (Johannesburg: 30 Degrees South Publishers, 2010), Foreword.

[12] Minister to apologize to Namibia for military parade, online at http://saf.romandie.com/post/11652/94803.

[13] "ANC Daily News Briefing." Online at http://www.e-tools.co.za/newsbrief/1996/news0606.

[14] Jan Breytenbach, *Eagle strike*, p. 561.

[15] Jannie Geldenhuys. *At the Front: A General's account of South Africa's border war* (Johannesburg: Jonathan Ball Publishers, 2009), p. xv.

[16] Marguerite Feitlowitz, *A Lexicon of Terror: Argentina and the Legacies of Torture* (New York and Oxford: Oxford University Press, 1998), p. xi. Cited in Helena Pohlandt-McCormick, "I saw a nightmare ..." p. 24.

hurtful to the victims of apartheid's uncivilized law and order, but as generally degrading to the dignity and integrity of all the victims of apartheid and colonialism in Namibia as well as in South Africa. It is indeed worrisome and disreputable of some human beings to entertain a sense of being more human than others. The deniers' continuing rhetorical praise song of brutal violence beyond the fall of apartheid-colonial rule, indicates a strategic shift of torture. Torture is a long-term strategy premeditated by the SADF before attacking Cassinga. In essence, in the wake of the collapse or the "breakdown" of the SADF military supremacy,[17] proponents of the old order resort to emotional or rhetorical violence as a way of revenging, in part, their military capitulation. This sort of vengeance invokes the continuation of the physical and emotional violence, to wound the victims by using a different approach. Thus, rhetorical torture is the continuation of the military violence by other means, to adapt Carl Von Clausewitz's assertion that "war is the continuation of politics by other means."[18]

This form of long-term torture is, arguably, a strategy that indicates the SADF passion to increase and transfer the pain and suffering of the victims "beyond the physical to the moral"[19] realm of damage. This could be translated in terms of Elaine Scarry's observation that "torture" is "a parallel act of deconstruction. It imitates the destructive power of war... whereas the object of war is to kill people, torture usually mimes the killing of people by inflicting pain, the sensory equivalent of death, substituting prolonged mock execution for execution."[20]

Certainly, the essence of this SADF rhetorical torture is a malevolent act against people already victimized, particularly the survivors and affected families whose lucky escape from Cassinga extinguishes the deniers of the Cassinga massacre's joy and nourishes their unease over the lives that were not destroyed. Certainly, emotional torture is unlimited and therefore worse than the physical violence: it is the extension of the unfinished violence, its project is to inflict heavier and prolonged human misery, to alter and misrepresent the voice, pain and suffering of the victims and those that express sympathy for their ongoing ordeals. Consider the following version:

> I read your article on Cassinga today, somewhat belatedly, while surfing the internet. I am undecided as to whether you are another Namibian who perpetrates the lies SWAPO originated about Cassinga, or whether you are simply ill-informed as to

---

[17] Elaine Scarry, *The body in pain,* p.78.
[18] Carl von Clausewitz, *On War,* edited and translated by Michael Howard and Peter Paret, commentary by Bernard Brodie (Princeton: Prinston University Press, 1976), pp. 91–93. Cited in Elaine Scarry, *The body in Pain,* pp. 77 & 334.
[19] *Ibid.,* pp. 91–93.
[20] Elaine Scarry, *The body in pain,* p. 61.

the truth of the situation. In either case, I suggest you read my recently published book, The Battle for Cassinga, by Mike McWilliams. You can get it from Amazon or order it from 30degreessouth.co.uk. In the book, you will find the truth about Cassinga. That it was SWAPOs Southern Military Head Quarters and that SWAPO disguised it as a refugee camp in order to fool the UN into supplying food, medicines and aid to the base. In order to complete the ruse, SWAPO kidnapped a bus load of children from SWA a couple of weeks before the UN inspection tour so that the base could show that children were a part of the population. If you are in any doubt as to whether Cassinga was a military base, read Comrade Timothy's notebook found at Cassinga. In it, he writes about the military force of brigade strength garrisoned there. He names all important officers and their functions and reporting structures. You will be surprised at how SWAPO has fooled both you and their sympathetic friends into believing their lies all these years. Naturally, if you are one of SWAPOs propagandists, you won't be surprised, but in any case, with the discovery of Comrade Timothys notebook, SWAPO has been revealed as the cold blooded murderers they were.[21]

The author's dialogues with McWilliams continued as follows:

My sincere apology for responding to your mail very late. Nevertheless, I am glad to come back to you, albeit late, and communicate with you again. Thank you for the interest you have shown in my article, "the undisclosed of Cassinga," published in the *Mail and Guardian* in May 2012. I had been waiting for the delivery of your book, *The battle for Cassinga,* which I received a few days ago from the Exclusive books in Cape Town. I read your book with keen interest and I understand your position. However, as an academic, I am more interested in the aftermath of the Cassinga attack other than the ongoing stalemate between the hostile politics. I should remind you that my article, in *The Mail and Guardian,* wished to explore the whereabouts of the documents that the SADF allegedly captured in Cassinga as "evidence" that Cassinga was a SWAPO military facility.

I find it most unfortunate that you did not provide any information about the whereabouts of the crucial Cassinga documents or materials "captured" during the attack. For example, the pictures that you (as the accredited photographer for the Cassinga attack) photographed as "evidence" that Cassinga was indeed a sophisticated military base. Interested academic historians, on the subject of Cassinga, would be curious, for example, to access "Timothy's notebook" and other documents for a close examination and to debate things comprehensively. How can one access such crucial documents? I must say that I found many gaps in your book. This is attributable to a number of subtly explained issues. For example, you unsubstantiatively wrote that a helicopter left Cassinga "loaded with four bulging trunks of documentation taken from Hamaambo's offices" in Cassinga. I think, it would have been better if you were to explain what happened to such crucial documents or where they can be located. You also wrote that at Ondangwa, paratroopers were searched and anything

---

21 "The battle for Cassinga," email received by the author from Mike McWilliams, Monday 31 May 2012.

that was picked up at Cassinga was confiscated from individual paratroopers. You, in particular, as the SADF accredited photographer for the Cassinga attack, "handed all the exposed army films for both the 35mm and movie cameras" to the SADF ... luckily, films from your private camera survived the search. Of course, some accounts in your book would provide first-hand information for many people. Nevertheless, I strongly believe that, in the absence of solid evidence to support your narrative, it's almost unworkable for your side of the story to persuade the public that Cassinga was, indeed, a sophisticated military stronghold for the SWAPO guerrillas. As I have argued in my article, many people would reason that the SADF reluctance to disclose weapons, military documents and photographs confiscated or recorded during the Cassinga attack encourages the public scepticism. Likewise, should the SADF confidently disclose the undisclosed of Cassinga, the ongoing claims that the SADF paratroopers (as a collective) massacred innocent civilians in Cassinga would proof ineffective.[22]

In response, McWilliams wrote:

You will believe what you want to believe and there is nothing I can do about that. I was there, so I know the truth. SWAPO provided absolutely no evidence that Cassinga was NOT a military base, yet you wish to believe them instead of the SADF version. Even the TRC could find no proof of a massacre of civilians. Be that as it may. With regard to the collected documents from Cassinga. I have no idea where these may be. The SADF archives had the photos I took. These are all black and white. Mine were all colour, but the publisher of my book did not reproduce all of my personal pictures in full colour, I suppose for cost reasons. The 16mm movie film I shot is missing, although it was shown on SATV a day or two after the battle, but has never been seen again. You of course must understand that the present government and SANDF have no interest in supplying any documentation which would show Cassinga to be what it was, the main training and supply base for SWAPO in Angola, so it is debatable as to who actually destroyed or hid those records. With regard to Timothy's Soldiers Notebook, it is in the safe keeping of Jan Volschenk of Port Elizabeth and if you wish to inspect it, I will put you onto him to see if he will agree. Failing that, I can send you PDF scans of every page of the Notebook. This would show you exactly what it looked like and every word written, including the section in Oshiwambo that I had translated for my book. I am afraid that finding the missing Cassinga documents may be an impossible task as even Gen. Mac Alexander, someone quite sympathetic to the SWAPO version of the story was unable to find much more than my photos in the SANDF archives when he wrote his MA thesis on the battle. Let me know if you would like the scans of the Soldiers Notebook and I will email them to you.[23]

---

[22] Author's email response to Mike McWilliams, Monday 20 August 2012
[23] Email response from Mike McWilliams, Monday 20 August 2012.

The day of parading and medals

This correspondence emphasizes that the Cassinga event remains divisive and polarized as ever. This may introduce the fact that on the SADF calendar, the Cassinga anniversary marks a spectacularly impressive and award-winning day in honour of the soldiers who participated in the Cassinga attack. This is while in Namibia, the Cassinga anniversary is officially remembered and commemorated every year as a day of mourning and loss of the innocent lives of irreplaceable loved ones.[24] Thus, in the years that followed the Cassinga massacre, prior to South Africa democratization, the SADF adorned 4 May, each year, as a public day of admiration, excitement, jubilation and celebration. It was possibly a regular practice in Namibia, because on 4 May 1988, the SADF celebrated the tenth anniversary of the Cassinga massacre with a military parade in the northern Namibian town of Oshakati. During that occasion, "General Ian Gleeson, the chief of staff of the SADF at the time, boasted that the raid had been the most successful paratrooper operation of its kind anywhere in the world since World War Two."[25]

Therefore, on this day of "great jubilations and excitement" for the SADF, individual paratroopers are honoured with medals and their names pronounced in due respect for their participation in the violence at Cassinga. Namibia's transition to independence in 1990 pushed such open celebrations into retreat and silence. However, in South Africa, the SADF kept such celebratory parades alive, conducted publicly every year. This practice came to a halt, at least explicitly, when in 1996, Joe Modise, by then the Minister of the new South African National Defence Force (SANDF) declared it "an insensitive act"[26] and ordered that

---

[24] The Cassinga anniversary, 4 May, is a national public holiday in Namibia. The day has been commemorated by SWAPO since the Cassinga massacre. Giorgio Miescher, Lorena Rizzo & Jeremy Silvester, *Posters in action: visuality in the making of an African nation* (Basel & Windhoek: Basler Afrika Bibliographien & National Archives Namibia, 2009) pp. 140–150.

[25] The SADF celebration of the Cassinga massacre in 1988 was reported in *The Star*, 5 May1988, p. 3; *The Namibian*, 6 May 1988, p. 5. Also see Piero Gleijeses, "The massacre of Cassinga." Online at http://emba.cubaminrex.cu/Default.aspx?tabid=6027; Jannie Geldenhuys, *At the Front: a General's Account of South Africa's Border War*, p. 381. General Ian Gleeson was the overall commander of the Cassinga attack. He flew to Cassinga in the late morning of the Cassinga massacre.

[26] "SA to say sorry for celebrating Defence Force raid," *The Star*, 4 June 1996. Also, see "SANDF Chief called to account for controversial parade," *SAPA*, 3 June 1996. The story reads: "The SANDF Chief called to account for controversial parade: SA National Defence Force chief, Georg Meiring, has been summoned by Parliament's joint defence committee to account for a parade in Bloemfontein last month commemorating a controversial airborne assault in Angola in 1978." Defence committee chairman, Tony Yengeni, said he had called the meeting so that Meiring could explain "how on earth they (the Defence Force) can continue to observe apartheid era crimes in the new South Africa." On 4 May 1978, South Africa launched an airborne raid codenamed "Operation Reindeer" on what it claimed was a SWAPO training base in Cassinga, Angola. "But it was a very brutal massacre of women and children in a Swapo refugee camp in which hundreds of people were killed," Yengeni said. Describing it as the Namibian people's equivalent to South Africa's

"steps should be taken to ensure that no similar event"[27] ever takes place in the future. However, according to reliable sources connected to the former SADF soldiers, the celebrations of the Cassinga massacre as "a jewel of military craftsmanship" still take place in silence. In the following statement, Jan Breytenbach acknowledges that "the majority of the Cassinga paratroopers" still celebrate the Cassinga massacre as a victory for the SADF: "this order [the ANC decision stopping the former SADF public celebrations of the Cassinga massacre] is slavishly obeyed by some of our PC [politically correct], former comrades but certainly not by the majority and most definitely not by the paratroopers who were there."[28]

The way the proponents of the old order continue to pronounce derogatory public rhetoric such as referring to the Cassinga day as "SWAPO's day of shame,"[29] and other provocations, which are currently flowing in the "Cassinga string" or social media provide ingredients for the argument I am making.[30] This "renewed interest" in the Cassinga event mainly receives contributions from the former Cassinga paratroopers. The Cassinga string website intents to silence the SADF role in the violence against Namibian civilians, its less obvious aim is possibly to propel a certain distress: to infuriate and prolong individual victim's longsuffering and unhealed emotional injuries. This is, for example, demonstrated by Ellen Namhila's response to Jan Breytenbach's article published in the *Sunday Independent* (see Appendix H and I for correspondence between Namhila and Breytenbach). Nevertheless, the Cassinga victims' ordeal is not anything to make proponents of the Cassinga killings regret and apologise for their unacceptable violent actions on civilians. Consider the following version:

> Thank you for the opportunity to reply to Dr Louis Bothma's review of my book, The Battle for Cassinga in Books Live.I apologise for not writing in Afrikaans, but my military version of the language would upset the sensibilities of your lady and child readers, and that would be unforgivable in a family website.While Dr Bothma has many kind things to say about the book, he also has some criticisms, which I would

---

Sharpeville massacre, Yengeni said Meiring should apologise to Namibians and South Africans as the 44 Parachute Brigade in Bloemfontein had "celebrated" the event by holding an anniversary parade on 4 May this year. The Ministry of Defence had been unaware of the parade, which was not "in keeping with the department's policy." The committee wanted to know whether Meiring was aware of the parade, and "we want him to assure us that nothing of this kind will ever happen again."

27 See, "Minister to apologize to Namibia for military parade," *Mon Sejour en Afrique du Sud*, (Cape Town), June 1996: Availanble at: http://saf.romandie.com/post/11652/94803. Also in, "NZO to apologize to Namibia over Cassinga parade," *ANC Daily News Briefing*, Thursday, 6 June 1996. Online at *http://www.e-tools.co.za/~etools/newsbrief/1996/news0606*.

28 Jan Breytenbach, *Eagle strike*, p. xvi.

29 *Ibid.*, p. xvi.

30 "Cassinga string"/ facebook. Online at http://et-ee.facebook.com/topicphp?uid=40615219623&topic=15512

like to address here. The Title of his review, "Navorsing Ontbreek in Strydige Cassinga Blik." I make no pretence that my book is an exhaustive or complete history of the battle. Colonel Jan Breytenbach wrote the definitive book, *Eagle Strike* in 2008 which is detailed and exceptionally well researched by himself, the officer commanding and planner of the attack. It would be futile and foolish of me to attempt to surpass the un-surpassable and produce a better researched book than the Colonels. Instead, I have written from the viewpoint of an ordinary troop at the battle, trying to get some points across that have so far eluded us because of insufficient documentary evidence being available. Namely, Cassinga was a SWAPO/PLAN military base, and not a refugee camp and SWAPO had lied about this to protect their reputation with the United Nations, having kidnapped young children to persuade a visiting UN delegation that SWAPO was running a refugee camp instead of a military base, in order to get money, food and medicine from the UN for their troops. This was against UN regulation regarding aiding and abetting warring factions. Furthermore, Helion, the London based publisher, in conjunction with 30 Degrees South, the South African publisher, had some stipulations that Dr Bothma, being a self-published author, does not have to deal with. Notably, the length of the book was restricted to 40 000 words and no Foreword or Index was catered to. These restrictions, made for marketing and commercial reasons, naturally limit the amount of research that can be included, if one is still to describe the battle fully. Dr Bothma asks why the four "trommels" full of documents were not researched. Those documents were not even made available to a General writing an MA thesis on the battle, so they were very unlikely to be shown to a Rifleman trying to prove the opposite to what the present day army would wish to be revealed. With regards to Brig. Du Plessis being interviewed? I was actually at the battle, so wrote what I experienced. Brig. Du Plessis has had an opportunity to make his side of the story known, which he did in a tape recorded interview, the transcript of which was published in Sept 2005. Dr. Bothma is well aware of this interview as it was conducted under his auspices. I could not rely upon this , as it was filled with inaccuracies and untruths, both about the roles played by people on the ground as well as factual errors as to what type of aircraft were used, where the relevant bases in SWA were and what part they played in the operation. Practically every "fact" on the tape was wrong as presented by the Brigadier, so the interview was without any value. Dr Bothma has a problem with the anonymous letter sent to a Namibian newspaper by a self-confessed ex-SWAPO soldier which tells of the Shipanga faction and talks about Koevoet type camouflage. He intimates that because Koevoet only operated after Cassinga, the letter was unreliable. This despite the fact that SAP were wearing camouflage in SWA at that time, and the writers linking it to Koevoet is an easy explanation. Dr Bothma knows that documentary evidence from Namibia on the border war is very hard to come by as his own books clearly show. Why this should be any different for my book is difficult to see. The story about the spy Dieter Gerhardt was relayed to me by an ex-Military Intelligence officer who now lives in North America. His residence status would be in jeopardy were his name to be revealed, so should this vital piece of information be excluded because of this? One of the main reasons why Helion, the highly respected overseas military publishing house asked me to write the book was the fact that I had impeccable first hand evidence, both photographic, documentary and eye-witness testimony to prove that

SWAPOs version of events was a long-running lie. This, to my knowledge, was the first time the outside world showed an interest in what really transpired in our propaganda-beset conflict. The captured SWAPO soldiers notebook showed that Cassinga was a Brigade strength military base, and it revealed the names of all the officers and key persons manning it as well as their tasks and duties. This note book, together with the TRC evidence and United Nation Reports, showed that SWAPO disguised Cassinga as a refugee camp by kidnapping children from SWA immediately before a UN inspection of the base so as to fool the UN into supplying SWAPO combatants with money, food and medicines in contravention of UN regulations regarding aid to combatants (See Appendix F, for the UNICEF report on their visit to Namibian refugees camp at Cassinga before the attack). In closing, most of those who have read the book, both here and abroad, have called it a Revelation, rather than lacking in research. So, while Dr Bothma's review is much appreciated, his academic nit-picking is perhaps a little out of place regarding a book that makes no pretence to be an academic exercise and perhaps the fact that it is in its second edition within five months shows that it has some merit beyond those of Dr Bothma's narrow interests. It may also be of interest that Colonel Jan Breytenbach wrote, "I just browsed through the rest of the article very quickly and I picked up that they claim that Koevoet and 32' recce wing were established after Cassinga. Well I was commander of 32 before Cassinga and I established the 32 Bn Recce Wing before I left to do the Staff course and thus at least 18 months before the Cassinga battle. I can not recall when precisely Koevoet was established but it was before I left 32 to attend the Staff course because I already had some interaction with Koevoet at the time – thus some time before Cassinga." On the face of it, I would venture that Dr. Bothma's review is not a scientific work and that throwing stones, like throwing boomerangs, while living in a glass house, is counterproductive.[31]

This sort of unapologetic statement presents the public with a conceptual picture to think about such violent rhetoric as a reflection of the former SADF's brutal actions which have been internalized by individual ex-soldiers who refuse to yield to change or accept that apartheid was evil and unpopular. This unpopularity, of course, resulted in its political demise. It is, however, of much concern that such provocations continue to unfold, unnecessarily, many years after the fall of apartheid in South Africa and colonialism in Namibia. Nevertheless, the rising tide of the spoken and printed violence suggests, firstly, that the deniers are taking this stand in response to the absence, in both Namibia and South Africa, of a law or an act of parliament outlawing and making it criminal to deny the SADF mass killing of Namibia civilians in Cassinga and elsewhere. Secondly, the deniers are seemingly embarrassed by their brutal conduct in Cassinga. Hence, they seem to create stories in the way they do, in an attempt to repair their damaged reputation. Thirdly, their attitudes are inherent in the SADF histories of habitual denial, its notorious projection and casting of acts

---

[31] Mike McWilliams, April 30th, 2012. Available at: http://bookslive.co.za/blog/2012/04/17/louis-bothma-resenseer-battle-for-cassinga-deur-mike-mcwilliams/ (Accessed 2013).

of brutal violence onto others. During the war, the SADF projected the notion that SWAPO terrorized its own people. For example, they argued that one of the reasons for attacking Cassinga was "to maintain law and order and to protect the Owambo people from SWAPO intimidation."[32]

Interestingly, the conduct of war for the 'protection of civilians' provides further proof of how war makes no sense even when executed with the best intentions in mind."[33] In fact, the "oxymoron" or absurdity of killing civilians to protect civilian lives "calls for questioning the context" of the SADF illegal occupation of Namibia and cross-border violations of independent and sovereign states, such as Angola. In terms of the political propaganda that circulated in the SADF, SWAPO was labelled a terrorist organization, and its followers, particularly those who were in exile, regardless of age, gender, career, disabilities, etc. were all classified as 'terrorists'. The irony, however, is that the Owambo people whom the SADF claimed to protect from SWAPO intimidation formed the backbone of SWAPO at home and in exile. However, the significance of this scenario lies in helping us to think that the SADF motive of attacking Cassinga was not to protect Namibian civilians, at home and in exile, but simply to cause general damage[34] and intimidate the civilian populace, the source of SWAPO's strength and existence.

Be that as it may, the deeply saddened and non-provocative victims, some of them living with physical disabilities from Cassinga and all of them with different levels of rage and despair, feel undignified when their sense of suffering, trauma and loss of loved ones continue to be exacerbated. Such systematic provocations unfold under the watchful eyes of the two postcolonial-apartheid states, Namibia and South Africa, and under the ambiguities of national reconciliation. The perpetrators enjoy state amnesty, devoid of any compulsion to acknowledge the unacceptable brutal violence against the Namibian civilian population. In spite of the general amnesty granted to them, proponents of the Cassinga killings do not only remain unrepentant of killing untold numbers of Namibian civilians, maiming and causing incalculable destruction to property and livelihood, but they continue, unceasingly, with disrespectful and injurious public rhetoric.

It is disconcerting for survivors when the deniers dismiss claims that they used bayonets to slaughter civilians. In fact, it is almost senseless to prepare for a battle without all the necessary ammunition for the unexpected eventualities in combat. In considering that the camp was an easy operation for the paratroopers, one discerns with near-certainty that Cas-

---

[32]   Chief of SADF, "PSYAC Planning Directive No. 2 \ 1978, Operation Bruilof (top secret): Phase Four. Source: SANDF Archive, Pretoria.

[33]   Larbi Sadiki, "To bomb and protect." Online at http://english.aljazeera.net/indepth/opinion/2011/03/2011329125911441807.html

[34]   Elaine Scarry, The body in pain, p. 65.

singa was not what the unremorseful perpetrators describe it to be. There are several hints even within their own discourse to corroborate arguments that Cassinga was a noncombatant facility. Namely, if Cassinga were not a soft target, the SADF would not have decided to drop paratroopers deep into enemy territory where the population in the camp outnumbers the paratroopers' number by far. For example, Operation Reindeer as it was officially code-named consisted of 370 combatants,[35] though in some other sources this figure is higher. In this context therefore, it is almost unthinkable for this small number to parachute into a "fortress" of more than "4000 armed fighters" and miraculously get away without incurring significant casualties, except losing less than five men.[36] The crisis in this case is not that the organic picture of the Cassinga massacre remains mysterious, it is a new zone of mystery that unfolds when deniers dismiss other Cassinga narratives as untrue. In fact, the "truth" of the Cassinga massacre is what the deniers attempt to conceal and try to obliterate, as previously discussed.

As I have put it earlier, some of the Cassinga deniers have resorted to the social media and other social network spaces to package and frame the SADF version of that event without thinking of the effects on the victims of that episode. In fact, it can be argued that for this category of former soldiers, the victims of the Cassinga massacre do not matter, as they do not exist as people for them. Whatever importance this category of paratroopers attach to the text as the absolute "truth" of the Cassinga massacre, this is indeed inconsequential and incompatible with the ordeals experienced by the victims of the massacre and which continue to torment the lives of many people in Namibia today. In other words, for the deniers of Cassinga, the concept of telling the "truth" means the untelling, reconfiguring or unravelling what is virtually unrepresentable. In every text or spoken language the "truth" falls flat, it is suppressed and obliterated. Nonetheless, with or without bayonets, it is an undeniable fact that maximum damage was inflicted on civilians, people who possessed no means of self-defence and were not trained to act that way:

> I, and many of my friends whom I lost in the bombing were not military people. We did not study military matters and did not have guns to fight anyone. I can state categorically that Cassinga was not a military base.[37]

When reading Namhila's version against the SADF planning of the Cassinga attack, the perpetrator's claim that Cassinga was a military camp appears to be a fabrication of truth about the Cassinga camp. Consider, for example, the fact that , even before the massacre

---

[35]   Jan D. Breytenbach, "Airborne assault on Cassinga base, 4 May 1978," p. 147.

[36]   Edward Alexander, "The Cassinga Raid," p. 139.

[37]   Ellen Namhila, "I was at Cassinga and it was not a military base." In *Sunday Independent*, March 9, 2008.

took place (as I have pointed out earlier), the South African government had already meticulously designed and put on paper deceitful ways of informing the public about the outcome of the Cassinga attack.

So, to suggest that the world subscribes to a singular version of the "truth" of the Cassinga massacre, as the SADF suggests, is to obscure the multiple realities of that event. Therefore, it is crucial to think of such version of "truth" as embedded in the practice of "deceit and concealment" but which, as in the case of other violence perpetuated by apartheid South Africa, also conveys a sheer "violent assault on the dignity of (the) victims."[38] As a "fundamental fact" of any violence, the SADF attacked refugees in Cassinga to finish them off. This is self-evident in the SADF central objective of attacking the camp: to "break the backbone of SWAPO"[39] by killing as many civilians as possible. And indeed, this metaphor, "the backbone of SWAPO," suggests young people, particularly children who were leaving Namibia in a huge and unstoppable exodus to Angola. South Africa perceived the increased number of young Namibians leaving the country a serious threat to the future political stability and the maintenance of apartheid hegemony and colonial rule in Namibia and South Africa as well.

It is particularly important to think about the denial of the Cassinga massacre, that appears more intense than before, in the context of the fact that the war for the independence of Namibia and the end of apartheid rule in South Africa ended with distinctive "winners and losers" on the political front. As pointed out earlier, this political turn around disparaged the hard-nosed ex-soldiers in the SADF. In fact, this category of soldiers had "their array of stresses" emanating from the unpopular war which ended in complete humiliation. This is unambiguous in considering that some of the hard-nosed ex-soldiers of the vanquished army continued with euphoric military parades celebrating "historic victories" of the SADF such as that of the Cassinga massacre.[40] Yet, it is also evident that for some soldiers the "defeat" of the apartheid army by SWAPO, ANC and their allies, predominantly the Cuban international forces, marked the beginning of the end of most soldiers' service, most of whom were conscripted into the unpopular apartheid security forces.[41]

It is equally important to think about the denial of the Cassinga massacre in the context of the early 1990s political turnaround and transformation in South Africa. This political

---

[38] Helena Pohlandt-McCormick, "I saw a nightmare …" p. 29.
[39] Chief of the SADF, "PSYAC Planning Directive No. 3 \ 78, Operation Reindeer (top secret): Phase Three (Media coverage)." Source: SANDF Archive, Pretoria.
[40] "SA to say sorry for celebrating Defence Force raid," *The Star*, 4 June 1996. Also see the "SANDF Chief called to account for controversial parade," SAPA, 3 June 1996.
[41] Thompson, J. H., *An unpopular war, from afkak to bosbefok: voices of South African national servicemen* (Cape Town: Zebra Press, 2006).

shift appears to have placed the inflexible former servicemen further away from acknowledging responsibility for the violence committed against civilians during the period of South African colonial rule of Namibia. In fact, it is humiliating to them when the violence that apartheid exported outside the state of South Africa and the quasi-defeat they suffered at the end of the conflict is said to be "akin to the Vietnam war experience." This is based on the public perception that the war was unjustifiable and caused unnecessary, and even catastrophic, conditions for many innocent lives and property, especially in northern Namibia. Arguably, those who committed violence and acted as the tools of apartheid's cross-border aggression benefited nothing from the violence. Instead, their service only earned them an undesirable public reputation. It is this undesirable publicity that instills embarrassment and uneasiness in such a way that perpetrators of apartheid violence find it extremely unacceptable to publicly acknowledge responsibility for the multiple deeds they committed during the course of the conflict, especially the indiscriminate killings of civilians, inside Namibia and outside its borders.

Jan Breytenbach is perhaps the greatest proponent of the SADF version of the Cassinga event in the present time. However, as a matter of trying to dislodge and fabricate facts about the Cassinga massacre, it is uncommon to find his account contradicting the SADF official version of the Cassinga attack. In the preface to *Eagle strike!* Breytenbach noted the following:

> It certainly was a day of violent death, a day when eagles descended from the sky above Cassinga to wreak terrible vengeance on the occupants of what was considered to be a major SWAPO base by the SADF and a refugee camp by SWAPO.[42]

This statement sets out a number of pertinent issues. The first issue is the narrator's retreat from the militaristic terms that Cassinga is associated with by the SADF. Arguably, the escape from the usual singular SADF rhetoric of referring to Cassinga as a "military base" into a personal account of the event might appear to legitimize Breytenbach's personal experience of the events at Cassinga. Secondly, this statement points to something important with the term "considered." In other words, the decision to destroy Cassinga was based on a perception, which translates into a semi-acknowledgement that it was not yet a military camp. Hence, the Cassinga massacre was not aimed at destroying a military facility, rather the attack on Cassinga was embedded in the SADF fear that the majority of the young people in the camp were potential SWAPO fighters. Ironically, most of the children who were in Cassinga did not make it to military training. Instead, many were sent to non-military schools in different countries around the globe, in particular to Cuba. However, it is interesting to

---

[42] Jan Breytenbach, *Eagle strike,* p. xi.

note that at times or when examined closely, the SADF's reports of the Cassinga massacre unleashes, as I will explore below, personal accounts which deviate from the SADF framed picture of the Cassinga attack.

In an article entitled "Airborne assault on Cassinga," Breytenbach retreated from the SADF framed description of the Cassinga trenches as the "defensive facilities" from where SWAPO combatants launched defensive attacks against the advancing paratroopers. Consider the following statement: The trenches constituted a space where the SADF performed the most sinister, "horrific slaughter ... horrendous death toll"[43] of unarmed civilians. He further stated that, the trenches were "filled to the brim with escaping SWAPOs."[44] *These acknowledgments are important for three reasons. Firstly, they corroborate survivors' testimonies that* women and children clogged *the trenches where they were ordered to seek protection from the aerial bombardments. The paratroopers caught up with civilians in the trenches where they* bayoneted and shot them at point-blank range.[45] *Secondly,* the "escaping SWAPOs" corroborates survivors' arguments that the victims were unarmed and posed no threat to the paratroopers, nor did they intend confronting the paratroopers as they had no weapons. What is then particularly disturbing is the order that Breytenbach needlessly issued for the brutal massacre of the harmless and defenceless SWAPOs in the trenches.

In the following statement, Breytenbach discloses the command he gave for the indiscriminate killings of civilians in the trenches:

> Johan Blaauw had requested my permission to clear the trenches – facing him – immediately ... [because as] the AA [anti-aircraft] guns were put out of action for good – the clearing parties – moved with more freedom to clear the trenches still occupied by SWAPO. The two clearing parties (Johan Blaauw and Tommy Lamprecht platoons) met in the middle ... the subsequent slaughter was horrific ...[46]

Breytenbach's indirect acknowledgment that he issued the indiscriminate order to slaughter unprotected civilians suggests that he knowingly killed defenceless civilians. The two adverbs "willfully and "wantonly" infer acts of knowability and reckless action intended to cause greatest loss to lives and property. Therefore, the authorization to use "deadly force against" helpless civilians clogging the trenches as their last hope of surviving the killings put the SADF official discourse of the Cassinga attack to a litmus test. Indeed, such conduct "amounted to a criminal culpability."

---

[43] Jan Breytenbach, "Airborne assault on Cassinga base, 4 May 1978," pp. 154–155.

[44] *Ibid.*, p. 154

[45] The bayonetting and the shooting of civilians at close range cropped up almost in every interview with survivors.

[46] Jan Breytenbach, "Airborne assault on Cassinga base, 4 May 1978," pp. 154–155

It would seem, in fact, that the deplorable things that the paratroopers committed against civilians in Cassinga are so colossal that attempts to contain and hide everything become almost impossible. Arguably, the more the deniers of the Cassinga massacre attempt to deny the unnecessary killing of civilians, the more their statements fall flat or become contradictory, thereby making concessions to the events they attempt to obliterate and conceal. The following statement corroborates the argument I am making:

> There was a massacre ... I was the one who led my paratroopers through an orgy of killing women and children.[47]

Since the experience of individual paratroopers in Cassinga enters the public space through the SADF-constructed and packaged version of what it wants the public to know and believe about the Cassinga attack, it is possible to hide many realities of the Cassinga massacre. It also means that irrespective of their attempts to conceal the unacceptable horror of the Cassinga massacre, it is almost impossible to "hide everything." Instead, the perpetrators' persistence in trying to conceal unacceptable violence is a way of leaking and disclosing conflicting narratives. These contradictions are important indicators. They suggest a presence, yet subtle, of multiple and terrible undisclosed realities of the Cassinga massacre. Nevertheless, the "real" witnesses of the Cassinga massacre were the paratroopers, not the survivors who were beleaguered with fear, panic, shock and confusion. Likewise, "the best source of evidence on the scene of any crime is always the perpetrator himself ... who almost always wants to confess"[48] in ways and means that are subtle. Therefore, it is common that when reading the deniers' accounts against the grain, one can be almost certain to spot aporias and ambiguities: because, when writing or speaking about the Cassinga massacre, which was so deplorable, it becomes almost impossible to forge a language that can completely hide and silence everything that the perpetrator intends to suppress and conceal. Such residues of the untold practicalities should be considered as important indicators of the missing realities. Importantly, since such aporias testify to these missing realities, they help navigate social science researchers towards exploring and closely examining the complexities and difficult issues that deniers attempt to hide and destroy.

---

[47] Jan Breytenbach, *The eagle strike*, p. 553.

[48] Forensic psychiatrist Andrew Hodges utilizes a pioneering method of "thought print decoding" technique, based on the unconscious mind's universal urge to tell the truth. Hodges shows how suspects unconsciously confess between the lines (in both written and oral communications). He spotted valuable forensic documents, such as emails, that analysts or readers overlook when critical readings or careful attention to the perpetrators rhetoric is ignored. By decoding the hidden messages scene by scene, Hodges was, for example, able to unlock a "Pandora's Box of deceit." etc. In Andrew Hodges, *into the deep – the hidden confessions of Natalee's killer* (Birmingham: Village house publishers, AL., 2007), pp. 33–38.

It should be mentioned that among the paratroopers of the Cassinga attack, a number of them are generally tight-lipped about the Cassinga events. Since they are reticent, it is difficult to locate them and listen to their individual stories. Generally, they appear not to entertain the idea of sharing issues of the Cassinga event with people falling outside the former SADF niche. Nonetheless, their dormant position or low public profile pertaining to issuing individual accounts of experiencing the Cassinga massacre, may be deciphered in terms of several other meanings.

In the first place, their silence may be understood as a way of protestation and of distancing the self from the SADF mainstream of the official discourse of the Cassinga massacre. That is, these individuals may be disenchanted with what happened in Cassinga and hence prefer to stay out of the Cassinga public spat. Their silence may indeed suggest compliance with the former SADF enforced restrictions that forbade individual soldiers or any other person from making public statements about personal experiences of violence in the war zones. In fact, Section 118 of the South Africa Defence Act states, among other things:

> No person shall publish in any newspaper, book or pamphlet, or by radio or any other means ... any information relating to the composition, movement or dispositions of the SADF ... or any statement comment or rumour calculated directly to any member of the SADF or any force or any activity of the SADF ... calculated to prejudice or embarrass the government in its foreign relations or to alarm or depress members of the public, except where publications thereof has been authorized by the Minister or under his authority.[49]

However, it appears implausible to link this prevailing silence to former SADF conventional norms of repression against those found guilty of contravening the stringent codes of the Army, such as the unauthorized disclosure of censored and restricted sensitive information about the possibly deplorable things that the SADF carried out in conflict zones. It is difficult to accept that the stringent code of conduct or service in the SADF should have any effect today. However, I would like to think of it, silence, as acting in response to individual moral values, peer influence, negativity about the foregone political and ideological orientations, as well as disappointment and embarrassment with the old order of doing things in the name of apartheid and colonial oppression. My thinking has been influenced by the barricades and challenges, outlined below, I encountered in trying to find and interview a number of the Cassinga paratroopers. It would have been important to sit down with the ex-paratroopers and listen to their individual stories of the Cassinga experience. It is possi-

---

49 Tony Weaver, "The war in Namibia: social consequences." In Gerhard Totermeyer, Vezera Kandetu and Wolfgang Werner (eds.), *Namibia in Perspective* (Windhoek: Council of Churches in Namibia, 1987), p. 239.

ble that what is written and spoken through the media or other medium of communication about them, as a collective, could break up into dissimilarities when narrated by the participants themselves as individuals.

The number one challenge in trying to find those who appear to choose to remain silent has been where to locate the former Cassinga paratroopers more generally. The second issue has been how to establish a line of communication, or how to introduce myself to them in such a way that they would welcome and trust me as someone they can openly talk to about their divergent experiences and interpretations of the Cassinga event. The third, and most difficult, challenge has been how to introduce my background, possibly unacceptable to many of them: namely telling them that I grew up in the SWAPO camps and I am a former PLAN combatant, perhaps a "terrorist' still to them. At the time of completing the research for this book, I have succeeded in reaching out to a few of the former Cassinga paratroopers through intermediaries. As might have been noticed earlier, the reception from those few who responded through emails was individually commendable but generally embarrassing and discouraging. I felt rejected by the apprehension and, occasionally, unfriendly responses I received. This emerges in the email correspondences I exchanged with some of the paratroopers involved in the Cassinga massacre.

One of such paratroopers, for example, notified me that he would accept the interview on the condition that I meet certain requirements as elaborated in the following excerpt:

> I take note of your request in a positive light. Can you please, however, give me more details about yourself, e.g. ID no: R.S.A.; Namibian or Angolan; Date of birth; Domicile; Religion; Academic and Military background etcetera, as well as your planned meeting place with me ... I could agree to be interviewed on the condition that no questions are asked about how many people I killed at Kassinga.[50]

Many readers would like to know "how many people" this paratrooper killed in Cassinga. However, it appears that, among other issues, the uneasiness about openly disclosing how many people he killed in Cassinga carries the aura of disgrace embedded in the gruesomeness of the violence. As it emerged from my correspondence with individual paratroopers, as well as by reaching out to a few of their immediate family members, the Cassinga massacre left many paratroopers riddled with psychological problems. This trouble is evident in some of the responses I received from individual paratroopers, harbouring strong or inflammatory language. In one of such email correspondences, the correspondent promised menacingly to "fuck [me] up before he speaks to (me)"[51] or accept an interview. In the logic of things however, this individual's verbalized anger does not intend doing to me what it

---

[50] Email exchange with anonymous Cassinga paratrooper, February, 2010.
[51] Email exchange with anonymous Cassinga paratrooper, February, 2010

exclaims it will do or intends doing. Instead, this genre of verbal assault can be ascribed to the fact that following the fall of apartheid, ex-service men were abandoned, many of them suffering from emotional and psychological trauma.[52] There had never been "formalized counselling" or support for the soldiers who returned from the war zones. Many of them returned perturbed by the senseless violence they committed or carried out. The SADF did nothing to stop the onset of Post Traumatic Stress Disorder (PTSD),[53] especially in considering the soldiers who were returning from places where extreme violence was unleashed, such as in the case of the Cassinga massacre.

It is important to note that the SADF was a ruthless entity even to its own employees and their families. This relates to the fact that the public and indeed many families remain (even to this day) in the dark[54] about what their family members experienced or went through at the fronts. Consider the following statement:

> My wife did not understand the context or the logical sequence. She knew I had been in the war, but knew I didn't speak about it. By writing it (post-war), it's given both of us a better understanding.[55]

Since nobody was expected to say anything about the madness of the border war, it was impossible for friends and families, including spouses, to suspect that returning soldiers were suffering from difficult memories that required individual families' understanding and finding ways to help and assist the victims. Instead, many families, it appears, interpreted that their family members were proud and happy when they returned from the front. Consider the following naive interpretation by one of the spouses upon her husband's return from the Cassinga massacre:

> Eventually, my husband came home ... he was wounded (on) his wrist ... The paratroopers talked often about that day and their experiences and I did not always take in what they said. But, I knew that this was a day in their lives they would never forget but somehow I thought it was just another episode in their military lives. Something they were proud of because they are not only soldiers of the best quality but paratroopers prepared to go and do their duty and lose lives for the sake of others.[56]

---

52 A statement by Cliff Holt, in "Soldiers relive apartheid war in surge of writing: post traumatic stress prevented many from talking about it till now," *Weekend Argus*, 14 October 2006, p. 15.

53 A statement by Cliff Holt, "Soldiers relive apartheid war in surge of writing: post traumatic stress prevented many from talking about it till now," *Weekend Argus*, 14 October 2006, p. 15; Karen Batley (ed.),*A secret burden: memories of the border war by South African soldiers who fought in it* (Johannesburg: Jonathan Ball Publishers, 2007).

54 Jan Breytenbach, *Eagle strike*, pp. 384–387.

55 A statement by Cliff Holt, "Soldiers relive apartheid war in surge of writing: post traumatic stress prevented many from talking about it till now." In the *Weekend Argus*, 14 October 2006, p. 15.

56 Statement by Jan Breytenbach's wife. In Jan Breytenbach, *Eagle Strike*, pp. 384–387.

One assumes that many other families and women married to soldiers in the service of the SADF shared perceptions and experiences such as that of Mrs. Breytenbach. Ironically, soldiers returning from the war front or episodes like Cassinga were not "proud of their duty" as their families perceived them to be. Crucially important, however, is noting that the predominant presence of psychological problems, presumably among many ex-SADF members, is not only confined to the suffering of individuals alone. Such individual problems discharge far-reaching negative effects within the radius of family circles, workplace and other interactions in the public space, such as in the response I got from Dolf that he would "fuck" me up before he accepts that I interview him.

An anonymous daughter (name withheld) of a former Cassinga paratrooper disclosed in email correspondence through an intermediary, that her father is "very angry with the SADF ... (he was) heavy handed ... and exceptionally strict on (us) when (we) were growing up."[57] Nevertheless, this lady does not understand or know the things that made her father particularly angry with the SADF or why he had been harsh with his children. An anonymous former SADF conscript suspects that the absence of the "peace of mind" of this former paratrooper means that this individual probably "carries a burden of having killed excessively for many years. If he can speak up, he would find some peace of mind."[58] It is, however, important to note that the former SADF paratroopers' anger and discontent with the SADF reflects the fact that there has been no acknowledgment for what they (ex-SADF members) did in service, and no mourning for their losses. As things turned around at the end of the conflict, it became apparent that the SADF did not only lose the war but also fought "an unpopular war - one that was not politically correct."[59]

Another category of the Cassinga paratroopers consists mainly of individuals whom Mike McWilliams rightly describes as "emotional about the facts being published [by senior officers] because (such facts) do not match"[60] individual paratroopers' experiences of witnessing Cassinga as it took place. This category aspires to narrate and present testimonies of the previously untold individual stories of paratroopers' experiences of the unfolding of the Cassinga attack on the ground.[61] However, they risk victimization and ostracization by the deniers of the Cassinga massacre for disclosing in public events that the SADF wants to keep concealed. The deniers accuse those who disclose the "truth" about the Cassinga attack

---

[57] Email exchange with anonymous daughter of a former Cassinga paratrooper, February 2010.
[58] Interview with an anonymous former SADF military conscript, 2010.
[59] In the *Weekend Argus*, "Soldiers relive apartheid war in surge of writing," 14 October 2006, p. 15.
[60] http://www.sainfantry.co.za/e107_plugins/forum/forum_viewtopic.php?166
[61] See anonymous soldier statement. In *The Star*, 8 May 1993. footnote

of being disloyal, disrespectful of the army and their former commanders, and ridicule them as "junior officers (who) suffer from delusions of adequacy."[62]

In recent times, there have been explosive exchanges of conflicting accounts of the Cassinga experience among the Cassinga paratroopers themselves. This tension is recognizably between the extreme paratroopers, deniers, who deny the massacre (and require individual paratroopers to keep the secrets), and the moderate paratroopers who feel that they "have spent a long time digesting" their bitter experiences of the Cassinga attack. The moderates are unhappy with what they call the "astounding accounts" of Cassinga by senior officers. These debates unfold in newspaper articles, journals, books, and the SADF veteran websites such as the South African Infantry Association website.[63] In one of these, Reconnaissance Commando Lt HP (Pierre) Hough (retired) rebuked the absence of the "many defining moments" in the paratroopers' published accounts and writings of the Cassinga massacre. Hough argues that:

> Cassinga Day is overshadowed by its tragic results: many innocent women and children or non-combatants died! ... Unfortunately, it is surprising that the paratroopers' published materials on Cassinga ... all missed ... first-hand evidence ... on the defining moments at Cassinga.[64]

The central argument in this book regarding the impossibility of any text to elicit tangible evidence of brutal violence, is in fact one of Hough's major concerns. He is possibly dismayed and astonished by the fact that the unapologetic paratroopers' articles and memoirs omit practical realities that took place at Cassinga. For example, he is specifically concerned with Breytenbach's book, the *Eagle Strike,* which he describes as not an "honest reporting"[65] of what actually unfolded during the Cassinga attack.

On the contrary, the paratroopers who disagree with the version that Cassinga was a civilian camp want the public to believe that no paratrooper disagrees with the SADF official (which this book finds incorrect) version of the Cassinga massacre. This is the context of the following statement:

> Except for one senior paratrooper, a Brigadier General [Edward George McGill Alexander] and so-called 'Master jumper' ... not a single paratrooper from among the 367 who took part in the Cassinga "massacre" had stepped forward to confess that his conscience had finally forced him to spill the beans.[66]

---

62 http://www.sainfantry.co.za/e107_plugins/forum/forum_viewtopic.php?166
63 http://www.sainfantry.co.za/e107_plugins/forum/forum_viewtopic.php?166
64 http://www.sainfantry.co.za/e107_plugins/forum/forum_viewtopic.php?166
65 *Ibid.*
66 Jan Breytenbach, *Eagle Strike,* p.xv.

Breytenbach and others are stuck in the argument that the deniers' version of the Cassinga event is the "fundamental truth ... unvarnished by the wishful and supine thinking of some contemporary ex-soldiers and politicians."[67] Interestingly, proponents of the Cassinga massacre argue that any narration of the Cassinga event that falls outside, or is critical of the SADF official version, is untrue and misleading. For example, when Mike McWilliams learned about Hough's intentions to write his own account of what he experienced in Cassinga, he argued that Hough would never articulate or divulge any tangible truth through descriptive writing of the Cassinga experience. Why? Because, "words ...cannot ... tell it."[68]

Similarly, in a case involving Brigadier General McGill Alexander's MA thesis, "The Cassinga Raid," Jan Breytenbach was "perturbed" when the author (a former paratrooper) raised issues of the paratroopers' ruthless killing of women and children in Cassinga. Breytenbach argues that Alexander:

> Failed to research this aspect (Cassinga) usefully and critically as any researcher should have done. Instead, he ignored what I and my paratroopers had to say about the matter by lending his ears out to hysterical accusations from the opposition, including the new SANDF in which he had served while preparing his thesis. Irremediable damage had already been done to the good name of the paratroopers and the Air Force of the old SADF and Alexander (formerly a respected paratrooper) blatantly reinforced the damaging perception that we acted like a bunch of bloodthirsty murderers and rapists. How do we rectify it? I doubt if we can ever put the record straight.[69]

Breytenbach continued with the following lines:

> In my mind he (Alexander) has no loyalty [for breaking the silence] to his former paratrooper comrades in arms. As a paratrooper myself, I therefore, no longer wish to be associated with Brigadier General McGill Alexander because of a Masters Cum Laude degree he had acquired at the expense of the good name of the paratroopers of which he too was once a commander.[70]

The trouble here involves one central issue. Why anoint it as the "fundamental truth" when Cassinga is constructed as part of a military infrastructure, but ridicule it as "false" when other paratroopers express concern that the SADF official version is "overshadowed" by not conceding the spilled blood of "many innocent women and children"? These attacks illustrate the bitter relationship between those who deny the SADF killing of civilians and those who disagree with it, within the SADF circle. These are some of the complicated issues that this chapter has attempted to explore and thereby challenge the reader to pursue to the

---

[67] Mike McWilliams, *foreword* to Jan Breytenbach's book, *The Eagle Strike*.
[68] http://www.sainfantry.co.za/e107_plugins/forum/forum_viewtopic.php?166
[69] Jan Breytenbach, *The Eagle Strike,* p. 544.
[70] *Ibid.*, p. 561.

next level. In addition, it should be borne in mind that the higher the rank or commanding role that one played in making Cassinga a success for the SADF and apartheid regime, the greater the degree of negativity towards acknowledging that Cassinga planned to massacre innocent civilians.

Lastly, it should be noted that the systematic mass killings of civilians in Cassinga did not only result in the victims' never-ending emotional suffering, individual paratroopers left Cassinga with painful and disquieting memories about the inhumane and unacceptable violence which they unleashed on defenceless civilians in Cassinga. The following statement by one of the paratroopers may illuminate this scenario:

> There were just too many wounded .... Some conscious, some were not. We found this woman clutching her screaming baby ... (with) terrible wounds inflicted by an Air Force bomb. There was no hope for her. I had to shoot her ... I don't know how many people I shot that day. ... I can never describe what it did to me. It was too much. I later broke down.[71]

So, if the Cassinga attack has left the perpetrators emotionally wounded, as suggested in the statements of the anonymous paratrooper above, how much damage and suffering did it cause to the victims of the Cassinga massacre? The following chapter might help answer this question.

---

[71] Anonymous soldier, *The Star*, 8 May 1993.

6 The Aftermath of Violence, Framed Reconciliation, and Injustice

It has become a tradition for modern nations, societies and states, emerging from violent conflicts to implement reconciliatory projects. These are intended to reconcile former adversaries, propel peace and forgiveness. However, such practices do not always work in favour of victims of violence. In Namibia, amnesty is applied as a substitute for reconciliation. This is, however, the opposite of reconciliation, which in a literal sense should treat both perpetrators and victims as equals. In this light, it is evident that the type of reconciliation that the SWAPO government declared at independence glossed over restorative justice and the dignity for the victims of the war for Namibian independence. Amnesty, when it is not preceded by justice, degrades forgiveness and perpetuates the victims' suffering. As Gerhard Totemeyer rightly put it, true reconciliation should be a process that involves "the admission of guilt, repentance and forgiveness and the application of restitution and reparation.[1]

Namibia has unfortunately sidestepped all the requirements underlined above. In fact, in postcolonial Namibia, power means everything. The former SADF echelons remain politically and economically powerful. This elite class has the power to say whatever they want to say and get away with it. There is no accountability for the violence committed against innocent civilians during the Namibian war for independence. The victims experience endless suffering and anger as the agency, state, that transformed power from colonialists and oppressors has become an agent that shields from prosecution those who have been accused of gross human violations of civilians during the war.

As discussed in the earlier chapters, the most disturbing scenario underlines the fact that many of the perpetrators of violence are not apologetic for any crimes they committed against Namibians. As such, they continue to deny the killings and maiming of many innocent Namibians. This chapter is therefore concerned with the problematic relationship between reconciliation and amnesty following the end of the war for Namibia liberation in 1990. In particular, it attempts to explore a number of political issues that compelled post-colonial Namibia to ruin the victims' justice in return for unconditional amnesty for the perpetrators of violence. It should be understood that, while the focus of this book is on the victims of the Cassinga massacre, it does not lose sight of the victims of colonialism and apartheid in Namibia in general.

---

[1] Gerhard Totemeyer, *Obstacles to reconciliation and stability in the Namibian state and society*, Namibia Institute for Democracy, 2013, p. 7.

As I elaborate on later, the Namibian state is the benefactor of amnesty, the unconditional pardon granted to perpetrators of violence when the country went to war for independence. The state stance on amnesty, which undermines a harmonious relationship between reconciliation and victims of violence, is fully supported by its beneficiaries who are the former perpetrators of violence against colonial subjects. This support appears unwavering despite numerous reports and claims of unacceptable violence that apartheid South Africa committed against innocent civilians during the war for Namibia's independence. For example, the TRC reported that the Cassinga massacre amounted to "a breach of humanitarian law."[2] In a literal sense, this violation of humanitarian law includes other acts of violence against Namibian civilians during the war. Thus, following the collapse and fragmentation of colonial rule in Namibia, which arguably signaled the imminent fall of apartheid in South Africa, the victims of war and other forms of colonial violence hoped that independent Namibia would initiate criminal proceedings against those who perpetrated violence and brutalized the Namibian people in many ways.

Therefore, in examining the Cassinga massacre, I have argued that the victims' unending suffering and anger are not only a testament to, and a belated or extended traumatic experience of, the Cassinga event alone. Their ongoing suffering is linked to other traumatic experiences across the landscape of violence in Namibia and in the neighbouring countries where many Namibians sought refuge. For example, many of the Namibians who returned from exile had the misfortune to find their families killed and their homesteads destroyed.[3] Civilians, particularly in the operational areas, the former war zones in northern Namibia, Owamboland,[4] were frequently and deliberately killed, harassed, intimidated, beaten and their homesteads and property destroyed by the South African security forces. This was especially true of the Koevoet,[5] a counter-insurgency unit, based on the Rhodesian Selous

2   *Truth and Reconciliation Commission of South Africa Report*, "The state outside South Africa between 1960 and 1990," Vol. 2, Ch. 2 (1998), Cape Town, pp. 50–58.

3   John Liebenberg & Patricia Hayes, *Bush of ghosts*, pp. 180 & 259.

4   Owamboland is located in the north central part of Namibia (along the border with southern Angola). It was the major combat zone between the South African troops and SWAPO fighters. For details about some accounts of colonial violence in northern Namibia read: Ellen Namhila, *Kaxumba KaNdola: man and myth. The biography of a barefoot soldier* (Basel: Basel Africa Bibliography, 2005); Ellen Namhila, *Tears of courage: five mothers, five stories, one victory* (Windhoek: Archives of Anti-Colonial Resistance and the Liberation Struggle Project, 2009); Ellen Namhila, *The price for freedom* (Windhoek: New Namibia Books, 1997).

5   In addition to the Koevoet (a special police counter-insurgency unit), there was also the South West Africa Territorial Force (SWATF), formed at the beginning of the 1980s. It conscripted Namibians into the force with intent to Namibianize the military conflict. Boys as young as 14 years old were targeted for recruitment to fight against SWAPO combatants – their own brothers – who had taken up arms to liberate the country. Visits by the SA security forces to schools (sometimes interrogating and beating up teachers and students) prompted many students to stay away from

Scouts model.[6] Established by Brigadier Hans Dreyer of the South African Police's Security Branch in June 1979, Koevoet was widely perceived as being more brutal than the SADF "because of its bounty or cash for corpses policy."[7]. Its top echelons comprised of the battle - hardened veterans of the Rhodesian war - among them Colonel Eugene de Cock and Eric Winter, Captain Sakkie van Zyl and Beachball Vorster, Lieutenant Frans Conradie and Warrant officer Snakes Greyling. The Koevoet unit was arguably responsible for numerous human rights abuses, before Namibian independence, and operated with impunity.[8]

Unacceptable stories are told about how the Koevoet and other South African Security Forces[9] stopped at nothing to force information out of people. They raped women, razed homes, abducted people from their homes, tortured and shot civilians at will, and killed domestic animals deliberately. Especially when the Security Forces discovered the tracks of SWAPO guerrillas, the local people were intimidated and tortured to disclose the whereabouts of the "SWAPO terrorists." Captured SWAPO fighters who refused to cooperate with the security forces were tortured badly, often unnecessarily shot dead,[10] or ended up in notorious places such as the Oniimwandi detention camp east of Oshakati. The former Oniimwandi military and detention camp is where, according to oral sources, many victims who were suspected of rendering assistance to SWAPO fighters as well as captured SWAPO soldiers were harshly interrogated, severely tortured and where many of them disappeared.

---

schools. In particular, it was mainly male students who stopped going to schools as rumours were spread that they would be recruited into the enemy forces. This resulted in many of us (both boys and girls) seeking ways to flee Namibia and join SWAPO in exile, as a way of avoiding forced recruitment into the South African security forces and to seek opportunities to complete our studies. This political harassment, the fear of being forced to join the SWATF or SWAPOL (the South West African Police Force) explains why the beginning of the 1980s experienced the largest exodus of children and youths, most of them leaving their parents behind for exile. See Peter Stiff, *The Covert War: Koevoet operations, Namibia 1979–1989* (Johannesburg: Galago Publishers, 2004).

6   Peter Stiff and Ron Reid. *Selous Scouts-Top Secret War as told to Peter Stiff* (Alberton: Galago Publishers, 1982).

7   *Truth and Reconciliation Commission of South Africa Report*, "The state outside South Africa between 1960 and 1990," Vol. 2, Ch. 2 (Cape Town: 1998), pp. 50–58.

8   *Truth and Reconciliation Commission of South Africa Report*, "The State outside South Africa between 1960 and 1990," Vol. 2 / Ch. 2 (1998).

9   Locally, the security forces were called *omakakunya*, which means merciless and brutal forces. It is a local slang originating from the earlier period of the South African rule of Namibia when the government institutionalized chiefs or headmen in place of customary kings among different ethnic communities of northern Namibia. The chiefs were protected by local Tribesmen, Home Guards, vested with the ruthless power to strip people naked for buttocks flogging. *Epokolo*, the thorny rib of the palm tree was the commonest tool of enforcing punishment by flogging. Such floggings were, by and large, politically motivated and men were primarily subjected to such public humiliations.

10 See the *Truth and Reconciliation Commission of South Africa Report*, "The State outside South Africa between 1960 and 1990," Vol. 2, Ch. 2 (1998), Cape Town, p. 75.

Each Koevoet involved in the killings received a monetary reward between R 1000 and R 2000 kopgeld[11] which means "cash for corpses." According to the TRC:

> At the height of the war, in the early to mid-1980s, Koevoet alone claimed a kill rate of around 300 to 500 people a year, for which its members were paid a bounty per corpse ... Koevoet ... kept no proper or official records of the identities, numbers or whereabouts of people it killed ... These practices were confirmed by journalists who were allowed to travel with security force units ... As the war progressed, South African security forces, especially Koevoet, resorted increasingly to summary executions of captured combatants. The payment of bounty served as an incentive for the extra-judicial murder of captives. The representative of the International Committee of the Red Cross in South West Africa said in 1981 that 'it simply does not happen in any conflict or battle that you have a clash with 200 people and forty-five killed and no prisoners or wounded are taken.'[12]

The mutilated dead bodies were displayed publicly as a psychological weapon to intimidate local populations from supporting SWAPO. In his amnesty application in December 1996, Lance Corporal Sean Callaghan described his experiences of serving with the Koevoet in the operational areas in northern Namibia as follows:

> I can remember loading bodies onto and off casspirs (armed military vehicles). After a contact, we tied bodies onto spare tyres,[13] bumpers, mudguard, and left there until we got back to the base camp, until they could be unloaded. This could be (after) days of driving through thick bush, and the skin could be worn right off the bodies.[14]

When I carried out interviews about the secret war graves in northern Namibia between 2000 and 2005,[15] interviewees who witnessed the exhibition of mutilated and spoiled bodies in northern Namibia by the security forces showed me different places where unknown people had been buried in these secret graves, many of them in unmarked shallow mass or single graves. In most cases, according to oral accounts, when the SADF dumped spoiled bodies of alleged SWAPO fighters near Cuca shops or school grounds, security forces forced

---

[11] *Ibid.*, 264 & 268.

[12] *Ibid.*, pp. 68–70.

[13] John Liebenberg & Patricia Hayes, *Bush of ghosts*, pp. 47, 97& 247.

[14] *Truth and Reconciliation Commission of South Africa Report*, "The State outside South Africa between 1960 and 1990," Vol. 2, ch. 2 (Cape Town, 1998). Also see a report by Christof Maletsky, "Koevoet killed for hell of it: teams kept scoreboards of death." Online at http://www.bnvillage.co.uk/black-roots-village/81294-koevoet-killed-hell.html. See Appendix K for Callaghan's testimony to the TRC.

[15] The history research project was funded by the Ford Foundation to collect and document material culture and oral history in the former Owamboland. It conducted interviews with local people about local cultures in north central Namibia and the impact of war violence on individual lives. The project also hosted a weekly radio program, published booklets and organized exhibitions.

the public to view them and sometimes instructions were given for the corpses not to receive burials.[16]

A number of international organizations confirmed such horrific reports. For example, in 1981, a delegation from the British Council visited Namibia and "conducted extensive interviews with church and community representatives. They reported that torture and intimidation were widespread. Their documentation of more than twenty individual cases included incidents where corpses of alleged guerrillas were dragged through villages behind military vehicles."[17]

As civilians feared for their lives, many abandoned their homes and communities and fled or attempted to flee the violence to neighbouring countries, such as independent Angola. The SADF pursued them with massive force to capture or eliminate them. In either case, civilians had always been, by and large, the victims. The SADF carried out regular air raids of the settlements where displaced Namibians established themselves into organized communities of exiled civilian populations. Such communities in refugee camps, particularly in Angola and Zambia,[18] received logistical support from the international community, including the significant role played by UNICEF and the UNHCR, who sponsored many Namibian refugee children to complete their studies in foreign countries.

In attempting to contextualize some of the issues raised above, I argue that the aftermath of the post- Cassinga massacre lies not so much in the victims' remembering of the traumatic past. The recurring intrusion of survivors' distressing moments is connected to postcolonial Namibia's own mistakes of dealing with the past justly and fairly. This state of affairs causes the burden of rumination, which refers to survivors' regular reflections on the difficult and unwanted traumatic experiences or moments of the Cassinga massacre and its aftermath. In this context, rumination relates predominantly to the survivors' disappointments about their unfulfilled expectations. Such emotional pain about the victims' disrupted expectations activate and bring about memories of traumatic experiences. The derailing of the victims' expectations, therefore, has negative implications for the survivors' aspirations to come to terms with the Cassinga killings and perpetuates human suffering. This disruption creates the bond between traumatic violence and the evolving emotional anger. For example, the failure of the state to demand from the perpetrators an official ac-

---

16 Interviews with Festus Kaapanda KaNangolo, David Iilende, Shivute Sebulon, Selma Nangolo, Julia Nuulimba and many others.

17 *Truth and Reconciliation Commission of South Africa Report,* "The State outside South Africa between 1960 and 1990," Vol. 2, ch. 2 (1998), Cape Town, pp. 47, 97 and 247.

18 The following were some of the Namibian refugee settlements outside its border: Cassinga, Kwanza Sul, Sumbe, Ndalatando, Kabuta, Namibia Health and Education Centre near Lubango (Angola); Nyango, Kitwe (Zambia); Loudima in Congo (Brazzaville).

knowledgment and apology for the massacre unravels, time and again, the "traumatic knot," thereby creating an enabling space for the survivors' endless suffering.

Literally, without political will on their side, the victims find themselves pushed into formidable and precarious situations. Their individual tenacities and ability to engage in "active coping" with traumatic stress succumbs to the prolonged existence of emotional and physical suffering in isolation. This is contrary to the victims' aspirations to free their lives from the burden of traumatic memories and emotional distress, which gives rise to rumination, arising in response to the blocking of valued goals. To put it differently, traumatic emotions arise "when schemas are disrupted." In this case it is the broken "schemas" of unfulfilled victims' values and expectations following the end of violence. Hence, when post-violence conditions are in conflict with established expectations of the victims, an emotional impulse is generated. In this way, traumatic experiences are reconnected, reactivated and stay active as long as the machinery that evoked the human suffering is let loose or not held accountable.

It is important to recognize that, although the tension created and sustained by the victims' disrupted expectations are emotionally traumatic, such situations serve as a useful "impetus in seeking solutions" to unresolved traumatic experiences. In other words, tensions emanating from disrupted expectations can draw the victims closer to each other and encourage them to collectively respond to issues of collective suffering and seek common ways of dealing with the sources of the recurring emotional traumas.

7 The Abandoned Cassinga Mass Graves and Breytenbach's Visit

As presented in the previous chapter, Namibia as a national state has closed its eyes to a number of war memories and historic sites that the formerly oppressed population groups consider important to ignore. One key sensitive issue pertains to the dividing wall between the Cassinga mass graves, family members and Namibians in general. When the process of repatriating 41 000 Namibian exiles[1] began in June 1989 under the auspices of the United Nations Transition Assistance Group (UNTAG), SWAPO and the international bodies involved in this exercise appeared not to have outlined measures regarding the preservation and protection of the graves of Namibians who died in exile from war and natural causes, especially in the refugee camps of Angola and Zambia. Perhaps the issue of dealing with the welfare of the war graves and human remains in exile awaited the attention of the government of an independent Namibia. Sadly, after over twenty years into independence the human remains of those Namibians killed in the course of the liberation struggle, particularly with regard to the Cassinga mass graves, have not yet received the recognition and treatment they deserve. This state of affairs negates the United Nations General Assembly Resolution that calls for every nation emerging from violence to abide by the protocol of accounting for the graves of missing persons after hostilities end and thereafter protecting them.[2]

The question of the human remains of the Cassinga victims is one of the emotional issues that survivors and affected families want resolved. During the Cassinga commemorations held at UN Plaza, Katutura, in Windhoek on May 2006, Agnes Kafula, a survivor of the Cassinga massacre, asked the "government to consider allowing survivors to visit the mass grave(s) of those who died"[3] at Cassinga. During the 2007 Cassinga commemorations in Windhoek, she (Agnes) again, speaking on behalf of other survivors, "urged the government to take the initiative to bring back the remains of those comrades who perished in the liberation struggle so that they [can] get a proper burial."[4]

---

[1] William Claiborne, "Namibian exiles begin to return home," *The Washington Post* (June 13, 1989).
[2] "Article 34 of the Geneva Convention of 12 August 1949. It must be noted however that local residents at Cassinga have tended the graves. Both mass graves have the inscription "Massacre at Cassinga 4 May 1978. We Will Always Remember Them." See Jo Ractliffe, *As Terras do Fim do Mundo* (Cape Town: Michael Stevenson, 2010), pp. 27 and 115.
[3] See Appendix L: "Cassinga events need to be documented."
[4] See, Appendix M: "Don't scrap Cassinga Day."

Fig. 9: A photographic scene of one of the Cassinga mass graves. This photograph was taken in 2009.
It suggests that the Cassinga mass graves are in a poor and abandoned condition.

The Cassinga mass graves are not only in very poor condition,[5] they are also abandoned and disconnected from the living world related to them. The families, relatives and comrades of those thought to have died in Cassinga and buried in the mass graves have not visited them since their burial there. The survivors urge that the government should coordinate things in ways that "allow survivors" and families "to visit the mass grave(s)." This request is entrenched in the prevailing disturbing disconnectedness between the dead and their loved ones, as well as a reference to the victims' improper and dishonourable burial in the mass graves. Generally, survivors and many families whose loved ones disappeared during the war and who suspect that the Cassinga human remains could be those of their missing relatives and friends feel they have the obligation to visit the dead and connect with them physically and spiritually.

In fact, it is wrong to perceive the identities of the Cassinga human remains as belonging to unknown Namibians. Although the victims buried in the Cassinga mass graves are generally unknown to many Namibians, the fact remains that every person killed in Cassinga was

---

5   Jo Ractliffe photographs of the Cassinga mass graves, online at http://www.artnet.com/magazin-eus/reviews/pollack/jo-ractliffe-at-the-walther-collection-4-15-11_detail.asp?picnum=4

known to individual survivors. It is valid to point out that the violent manner in which the killings took place damaged survivors' knowledge of their comrades killed in the massacre and the ways they could ascertain their burial in the mass graves. Nonetheless, the mental picture or "mental snapshots" of friends and comrades' names and faces remain. It is this preservation of the survivors' mental pictures, reflective of the individual identities and names of the comrades, that survivors want to retain in reclaiming the presence of the dead. One way of doing this would be erecting a monument at the site of the massacre bearing the names of the dead. Another way would be to build a museum at the site, to tell stories and exhibit images about the event, in memory of the victims of the Cassinga massacre.

While the Namibian government is yet to pronounce its commitment, long overdue, for those who feel bereaved and unconsoled, it is the survivors generally who initiate the process of preserving the Cassinga historic site. They initiate breaking the silence and ano-nymity surrounding the myth of the nameless people who disappeared as a result of the Cassinga massacre, and who did not return home when the violence ended. As the agency entrusted with different obligations by the dead in different individual capacities, survivors are enthusiastic about listing the names and ages of their comrades who were missing following the massacre. It is the preference of most survivors that the retrievable names and photographs, as traces of the missing physical identities of the dead, should be inscribed at the site of the mass graves. In this way, the Cassinga historic site could possibly rise above the existing silences and disconnectedness from the living world into a rich and fathom-less exploration ground of the missing people, their identities and their untold traumatic experiences.

It is important to emphasize that the search, albeit in vain, for those people, mainly children, whose fate remains unaccounted for ever since the end of the conflict that divided and displaced families particularly in northern Namibia, is a way of attempting to find a remedy for the injuries that are still open. Further, the initiative to turn the Cassinga mass graves into a quest for a ground or space consecrated to the missing peoples' identities and untold narratives of their terminal injuries and painful deaths is reflective of the SWAPO declaration in the immediate aftermath of the Cassinga massacre. On 1 June 1978, Sam Nuuyoma, the founding president of SWAPO and first President of Namibia stated the following:

> The names of hundreds of Namibian men, women and children who were murdered in cold blood by the fascist troops of racist South Africa at Kassinga ... will forever re-main imprinted in the pages of Namibia's history as heroes and martyrs of freedom and human dignity.[6]

---

[6] Sam Nuuyoma's Foreword. In the "Massacre at Cassinga: climax of Pretoria's all out campaign against the Namibian resistance," Special bulletin of the South West Africa People's Organization

Literally, there is a remarkable degree of softness or flatness in the way the Namibian ruling party, SWAPO, appears to have compromised the liberation struggle ideals concerning the preservation of the Cassinga historic site. Thus, while SWAPO as a liberation movement promised "social justice" for the victims of colonial violence when Namibia is independent, it is unfortunate that postcolonial Namibia has not fulfilled these promises. The issue is not that the suffering and traumatic memories of Namibians affected by the massacre have dissipated, rather that the two periods, the liberation struggle and postcolonial Namibia, appear to be remarkably characterized by a set of dissimilar values and meanings attached to those who sacrificed their precious lives for a free Namibia. This reality is applicable also to the values of SWAPO as a liberation movement and as a political party.

When this situation is assessed culturally, as well as biologically, it is difficult for the bereaved families to find closure and serenity in the presence of the frontiers of division between the world of the dead and of the living. Furthermore, it is believed that the bodies of the dead cannot "rest in peace"[7] until they connect with and feel the recognition and warmth of the living world. By contrast, the Namibian national government naively perceives the issue of the Cassinga human remains, iipongo, as not being a priority of the state:

> In respect of the heroes and heroines who died at Cassinga, [the] government has already done its part in collecting the soil from the mass graves in southern Angola and placing it at [the] Heroes Acre in the capital.[8]

Generally speaking, the majority of those affected by the Cassinga massacre do not agree with the government's stance regarding the issue of the Cassinga human remains. In particular, the metaphor of the "soil," a symbolic gesture, as a substitute for the dead as the state appears to argue, undermines the spiritual and physical connections between the living and the dead. In the context of Namibia, such a practice is unethical: it does not conform to any of the Namibian local cultural practices and it is therefore unrecognizable and cannot help comfort individual families still adversely affected by the Cassinga massacre. The point of concern is that survivors and affected families were not consulted. The government acted without any consultation about how best Namibia could pay tribute to the human remains of the liberation struggle. Consultation with the general public and the affected families and communities should not have been overlooked, since the loss of human lives affects

---

SWAPO, 1978.

[7] Thomas M. Hawley used the concept of "rest in peace" in reference to the body remains of the unknown American soldiers of the Vietnam war: Thomas M. Hawley, *The remains of war: bodies, politics, and the search for American soldiers unaccounted for in Southeast Asia* (Durham & London: Duke University Press, 2005), p. 4.

[8] See, "Don't scrap Cassinga Day," in Appendix M of this book.

individuals, families and clans (some with unique norms of burying and paying tribute to members of their clans) more than it affects the nation as a collective entity.

Nonetheless, the appropriate ways that should be followed in honouring the dead at Cassinga received varied proposals from survivors and relatives of the missing victims with whom I have raised this issue. There are those who feel that the proper way of paying tribute to the Cassinga victims is by exhuming the human remains, identify the bones, repatriate them to Namibia for a proper burial in the home soil closer to their families and communities. However, others contest initiatives to dig up the mass graves, exhume and repatriate the human remains back home. They are of the opinion that if a monument were to be erected at the site of the violence and in the neighbourhood of where the victims have been buried, visitors would feel more connected to the actual suffering and experience of the dead. However, they expressed concern that as the Cassinga human remains are across the border of another sovereign state, the Namibian government may experience some challenging bilateral issues and limitations in developing this historical site the in way it would like, and at its own pace.

While it proved extremely difficult for the comrades and affected families to visit the Cassinga mass graves during the Angolan civil war that lasted until 2002, this is no longer the case. However, any project aimed at developing and preserving the Cassinga heritage site depends on the support and willingness of the Angolan government to allow Namibians uninterrupted access to utilize and develop Cassinga into a place of documenting and preserving the history of that historic site. In this context, I personally feel that Cassinga should be recognized as an international shared space where people of different nationalities lost their lives and loved ones. Not only Namibians died during the Cassinga attack, some Angolan civilians living in the area of Cassinga also died during the massacre. Equally so, the Cuban international forces lost many soldiers who tried to come to the rescue of Namibians.[9] South Africans, according to their own sources, reported their own human losses in Cassinga. Therefore, not only Namibians lost their loved ones there; Cassinga is coupled with shared transnational traumatic memories. The importance of Cassinga to other countries and individuals who were involved in the war for Namibia's independence and the Angolan civil war can be elucidated by Jan Breytenbach's recent visit to Cassinga as represented below:

It was in May 2009 when Breytenbach, the commander of the Cassinga massacre, and seventeen others, according to an anonymous source who was in the group, visited the

---

[9]   Reportedly "around 150 Cuban soldiers were killed." This number accounted for the Cubans single biggest casualty rate during its military involvement in Angola. See, Edward George McGill Alexander, "The Cassinga raid;" Jan Breytenbach, *Eagle strike,* pp. 321–359.

Cassinga mass graves in the Huila Province, Angola. According to a reliable source for this information, the group that visited Cassinga said prayers at the graveside and Breytenbach was observed weeping as he stood in front of one of the Cassinga mass graves. Very interestingly, Breytenbach's visit to Cassinga followed the launch of his publication, *The Eagle Strike* in 2008, in which he blatantly denied the Cassinga massacre, attacked critics of the Cassinga massacre such as Edward McGill Alexander, himself a former SADF paratrooper, and audaciously and unapologetically defended his role as the ground commander of "Operation Reindeer." When examined closely, Breytenbach's publications, including his several articles about the Cassinga attack,[10] and his visit to Cassinga may posit interesting but conflicting meanings. His written accounts of the Cassinga attack, on the one hand, refute that there was ever a massacre of civilians at Cassinga. This is whilst his visit to Cassinga can be translated as a therapeutic search for the ongoing suffering caused by the immense bloodshed and loss of lives of hundreds of innocent civilians. Indeed, as the ground commander of the Cassinga massacre, the unacceptable violence against civilians would have certainly affected him. Whatever the case, it is without a shred of doubt that he considers himself individually implicated in the killings of so many innocent Namibians. In a literal sense, the initiatives to kill or not to kill when confronted with the practicality of noncombatants in the camp rested squarely on him.

Seeing Breytenbach through different spectacles and performances, such as a self-constructed visitor to the mass graves of the people killed under his orders, is testimony to the "embattled self." Put differently, these different pictures situate Breytenbach in the complex and parallel positionalities of victim, perpetrator and witness. Whilst the different pictures of the perpetrator and witness mirror Breytenbach's role of executing and experiencing the horrible massacre, at the same time, it is the simultaneous position of the "victim" that is most interesting here.

The concept of the perpetrator as a victim of the violence that he orchestrated is important to explore. Why did Breytenbach make such a surprise visit to the mass graves at Cassinga? Fundamentally, Breytenbach's return to Cassinga appears embedded, as said earlier, in an individual hunt for closure. The visit could also be interpreted as making a strong public statement about the unsettled issues of the Cassinga massacre, which the perpetrators are circumventing and dodging. In examining testimonies of the French soldiers of the Great War, Leonard Smith suggests the following: "the experience of violence [that] ... Cendrars

---

10 Such as the "Cassinga battle account reveals biased claptrap"; "Airborne assault on Cassinga base, 4 May 1978;" "Bullets do not lie, but it appears people do;" "Foreword" to Graham Gillmore's book, *Pathfinder Company: 44 Parachute Brigade 'The Philistines,'* 2010.

... lived was never 'overcome,' in the sense of being comfortably resolved."[11] In this context therefore, Breytenbach's return to Cassinga thirty-one years after the killings, appears to reveal something of his struggle with the burden of the never-overcome emotional distress and the urge to find "closure" for his role in the Namibian armed conflict since 1966.[12]

This interpretation implies that, since traumatic events are unbearable in their horror and intensity, the perpetrators' long-term suffering and personal struggle with traumatic memories of the crimes they committed compel them to consider taking a new path, perhaps towards accepting their wrongs in subtle ways. The visit to Cassinga by a group of former SADF members heralds the former soldiers' attempts to understand violence beyond the political frontiers that manipulated and compelled them to repress and digest painful violent experiences.

It is important to see this visit in the context of the fact that the SADF has abandoned its soldiers[13] when the conflict ended on a fragmented chapter of apartheid rule in South Africa and colonialism in Namibia. As such, individual soldiers are left alone to seek individual ways of dealing with their postwar predicaments. This might explain why many former SADF soldiers are frustrated and angry with the way the SADF told them lies during the war about the 'enemy' they were fighting.

In an interview with the *Cape Times* Newspaper, some former SADF soldiers said they were brainwashed by the apartheid rulers to believe that SWAPO, like the then-banned African National Congress, posed a terrorist threat to Namibia and South Africa. Now that the two movements are ruling in Namibia and South Africa respectively, former soldiers have come to realize that they were fighting for nothing:

> We were fighting the swart gevaar (black danger) and communism. But now SWAPO and the ANC have the most democratic constitutions in the world, a former Koevoet member, Herman Grobler, said ... And the people we were fighting against weren't communists. They were ordinary people ... It was our war we forced on them ... The memories of the past and the public condemnation have taken their toll [on the ex-SADF members] ... some have had nervous breakdowns, and many have committed suicide ... They felt that they had no purpose in life ... Nobody thinks you have any right to exist. It is the Vietnam syndrome. You are not being acknowledged for who you are - that you fought as a soldier for your country.[14]

---

[11] Leonard V. Smith, *The embattled self,* p. 12.
[12] See Appendix J of this book: Breytenbach's role in the Namibian armed conflict and other places.
[13] This is in spite of the fact that the majority of the former soldiers required counselling and other assistance to help them deal with individual suffering and traumatic experiences arising from the problematic things they did in the war zones.
[14] Emsie Ferreira, "Koevoet: it was a luvverly war," *Cape Times*, Thursday, September 28, 2000; Also, see the Republic of Namibia, *The constitution* (Windhoek: Government Printers, 1989).

In the context above, former SADF soldiers, at least those with resources, are searching for ways of dealing and coming to terms with the nightmares of the war that betrayed their cause. Nevertheless, the act of the perpetrators visiting Cassinga challenges, ridicules and reminds Namibians of their long-overdue obligation to visit, which has not been publicly done since the Cassinga massacre, and pay tribute to their own people. It is also a rebuke to the poor state of the mass graves. In view of this embarrassing state, Brigadier-General Dick Lord interviewed in 2009 on SABC radio about their trip to Cassinga in Angola, indicated that some of the former Cassinga paratroopers have begun initiatives to raise money to erect a memorial at Cassinga to honour the dead. Not underestimating the complexities and contestations that may arise from different quarters of the public with regard to the perpetrators' initiatives to erect a monument at Cassinga, such an idea is good as it challenges the way Namibia, and specifically the Namibian government has, for very long, neglected and abandoned the Cassinga historic site.

It is important to reiterate, as I approach the end of this chapter, that the former South African soldiers' experience of the "border war" and their realization of coming to terms with emotional traumas by opening up to the public have given birth to several websites. This is in fact important for Namibia, with its rich, but largely untold, traumatic stories of colonial violence. One example of such sites is the 61 Mechanised Infantry Battalion Group Veterans Association, which I noted in the preceding chapters.[15]

Such sites, which are dedicated to the collection of the ex-soldiers' stories of the border war experiences, vindicate individual soldiers' attempts to deconstruct and disconnect their personal experiences from political realities. Crucially important is noting that such stories, regardless of their position or inclination, stir up new opportunities that can accommodate different dimensions and realities about contested events[16] such as Cassinga, in a way that inspires critical public dialogue. For example, reading various accounts of war experiences by former SADF soldiers inspires further interrogation into why, for instance, certain individual paratroopers continue to deny the violence while others disclose emotionally about the unpleasantness of the border war experiences. The dissemination of such accounts invites different responses from the other side, in such a way that both sides can open up to each other, place the past and the present in the face of each other, engaging each other in debates, encouraging more public openness and finding a common ground for the understanding and acceptance of each other beyond the political divide.

Another obvious element emanating from the public dissemination of the ex-servicemen's heralding of the war experiences is that it allows individual efforts to find solace in

---

[15]   Visit: *http:www.61mech.org.za*
[16]   Willem Steenkamp. *South Africa's border war 1966–1989* (Gilbraltar: Ashanti Pub., 1989).

each other's shared experiences of the violence. As individuals, abandoned and forgotten by apartheid, they aspire to make their individual traumas less burdensome by drawing strength from others' similar experiences and ways of coping with individual traumas of the apartheid war and violence. As human beings, we can generate strength and courage in confronting our challenges in life when we, for example, learn and become aware that others do experience similar challenges in life.

This brings me to another salient point, as this chapter ends. That is, the dissemination of the war stories is not only a way of helping each other, as ex-soldiers, to manage the traumatic memories of the war, it means that some of these ex-soldiers feel that sharing their stories, testimonies of the war and violence with the wider public could be a way of acknowledging one's mistakes and of seeking public dialogue for acceptance and forgiveness.

8 Conclusion

This book has grappled with a number of complicated and challenging issues arising from the ongoing pain of the victims of the Cassinga massacre. It has been argued that the Cassinga massacre represents the darkest chapter in the history of the Namibian liberation struggle. In particular, survivors of the Cassinga killings continue to bear the brunt of that deplorable moment. Yet, the perpetrators walk freely. Sadly, those I term deniers of the Cassinga massacre, in particular some of the paratroopers who were personally involved in the killing of innocent civilians, continue to enjoy the gruesome moment of their killing-spree. For the survivors of the Cassinga massacre and affected families, the ongoing war rhetoric is another form of violence. The denial of the Cassinga massacre inflames the victims' anger and bitterness, and makes it difficult for these people to accept the national policy of reconciliation as genuinely fair. Ironically, the political stability that Namibia experienced since independence is attributed to the so-called working policy of national reconciliation. On the contrary, the reality of the Namibian policy of reconciliation is perceived by many Namibians as entrenched in the erroneous "power of enforcement."[1] The victims of colonialism and apartheid brutality insist that the policy of reconciliation without litigation is brutally violent: one which compels the wounded body and memory to become a mere political tool; one which is shrouded in political hypocrisy, as it does not recognize the dignity of the victims but obliges them to dance to the tune of the perpetrators of colonial violence. In this context, many perceive the Namibian national policy of reconciliation as a façade, one that is politically correct but which, in reality, is patronizing and hurtful to many people, repressing the victims' voices so they do not raise issues of social justice. The victims raise genuine concerns, yet their issues and protestations are largely individual and circumvented by being confined to private spaces. Clearly therefore, there is a "collusion" between reconciliation and the injustice of the supreme laws of the land. This is especially so when reconciliation deprives the victims of their rights to appeal to, and even sue, perpetrators of violence against innocent civilians for the untold damage to human beings and property.[2]

---

[1]   Elaine Scarry, *The body in pain*, p. 120.
[2]   Related to these resentments is the issue of the Kenyans who are on the verge of suing the UK government for the alleged torture by British colonial authorities during the Mau Mau struggle for the independence of Kenya from the British rule about 50 years ago. See for example, "Mau Mau Kenyans allowed to sue UK government." Visit: http://www.bbc.co.uk/news/uk-14232049.

It is worth reiterating that, although the victims are conscious of the fact that reconciliation is biased against their sufferings, they are entangled in the chains of "passive victimhood." In the first place, the state of passive victimhood means that the victims emerged from the Cassinga violence too debilitated, till now, to resist the post-Cassinga pathos and the enduring suffering which causes more prolonged pain than the actual massacre that was short-lived. Secondly, the notion of suffering in silence is inherent in the culture of enduring pain quietly during decades of colonial violence. Brutal violence unleashed by the SADF against the local population of civilians, particularly in the former war zones, was an everyday experience.[3] Nevertheless, the perpetrators were untouchable. They were beyond questioning, let alone being prosecuted.

The fact that apartheid and colonialism had for decades suppressed the victims so that they endured their suffering in silence appears to have a strong influence on the victims today. That culture is arguably central to the interrogation and understanding of the prevailing passive victimhood of the formerly colonised. This is notwithstanding the fact that the victims freely raise their suffering in one-to-one conversations, such as when I approached them to tell me their stories. When speaking to those willing to listen, survivors aspire to reach a wider audience, in particular the government. One of the things that trouble survivors and which they want communicated to the government is their great unhappiness about the sweeping amnesty extended to the perpetrators of the Cassinga massacre. Consider the following:

> These people have permanently damaged our lives beyond repair. We did not do them any wrongs ... they must apologize for what they did to the innocent people ... Why don't they bring them here [in Namibia]? They [the perpetrators] owe us so much, we have so many unsettled issues with them ... we want to communicate with them, to remind them of the merciless and racial killings of the unprotected civilians and the maiming of so many of us... we want to remind them that we did not provoke them in any way, but they were brutally violent and indiscriminately killed defenseless people including babies and pregnant women ... should they have done that to fellow whites? Most of the victims were women and children and the enemy knew that plain fact ... they have damaged so many lives. Justice must prevail if we are to forgive them.[4]

---

[3] "Before we are all wiped out," *Dateline: Namibia*, Issue No. 3 (New York: New York Times Company, 1982). Interviewed about his visit to Namibia and South Africa, Carl Mau, the General Secretary of the Lutheran World Federation stated that "the South African government and its forces in Namibia are committed to eradication and not giving up – with very little conscience anymore ... They are now determined to go forward and care very little anymore about who gets hurt in the process ...The present administrator general ... has very little sensitivity anymore to the massive human suffering going on in the territory for which he bears responsibility." In *Dateline: Namibia*, Issue No. 3 (New York: New York Times Company, 1982).

[4] Author's interview with Lazarus Namutenya Cornelius, Etunda, February 2008.

It is particularly painful for the victims that the perpetrators are given political pardon without acknowledging and apologizing for the untold crimes[5] they committed against innocent Namibians. In spite of the deplorable issues that the victims of the Cassinga massacre raise, things are not co-ordinated beyond the confines of the individual. There is no open platform, such as an organized body for the victims of the Cassinga massacre, where the victims can coherently and collectively express their disappointments and difficulties.

Nonetheless, the deeper meaning as to why postcolonial-apartheid laws, in both Namibia and South Africa, are lenient towards the perpetrators of apartheid violence must be explained by the uncompromising ties or relationship between politics, law and economy. The 19th Century French philosopher and politician, Pierre-Joseph Proudhon, characterized laws as follows:

> We know what they [laws] are, and what they are worth! They are spider webs for the rich and mighty, steel chains for the poor and weak, fishing nets in the hands of the government.[6]

For many victims of the Cassinga massacre, these words resonate. In democratic Namibia, it is virtually the elite who exercise influence on the laws and politics of the country. Hence, in the case of Namibia and South Africa, those with financial and economic power, mostly the formerly ruling minority whites and their external allies, as well as the emerging or already well established black elites and politicians, have the power to influence and navigate the laws and the political landscape of the state in ways that suit the welfare of the minority - the rich and powerful. Nevertheless, the question whether social justice (for example, if the perpetrators were to be prosecuted, pay reparations for the damage incurred) can bring about recovery and reduce the recurrences of traumatic memories is a topic for a different research undertaking.

On memory and testimony, my focus has been specifically limited to the application and understanding of the two concepts in relation to the interviews conducted with survivors of the Cassinga massacre. I have struggled to draw the distinction between the two concepts in accordance with the challenges and insurmountable difficulties which survivors experienced as they tried to come to terms with the violence through different ways of narration. The process of interviewing survivors presented me with the discovery of considerable differences or distinctive separations between testimony and memory. This dichotomy became evident when the interviewees' attempts to elicit violence through testimony proved contra-

---

[5]   The crimes that the SADF committed in Namibia against civilians such as in the case of the Cassinga massacre and many other atrocities not highlighted in this study are commonplace among many communities in Namibia and widely reported in the press.

[6]   Visit: http://thinkexist.com/quotes/pierre-joseph_proudhon/

dictory and unworkable. Thus, while memory stands for the tangible picture of the violence which continues to hurt the victims, causing repeated injuries and perforating old wounds, testimony, on the other hand, belongs to the range of unsuccessful techniques such as narration or storytelling which survivors used in attempts to elicit the actual world of endless injury and pain. Testimony is unacceptably "annoying," according to survivors, it frustrates them deeply because it is in conflict with what they want the world to see and understand.

Survivors describe testimony as considerably shallow, immaterial and inauthentic. It is trivial, tacit and conceals many practical things which survivors observed directly and aspire to show the inexperienced world. Testimony reaches the intended audience unsubstantiated by the violence that survivors bemoan and want the world to experience and understand. In the same vein, survivors' endless nightmares and traumatic flashbacks of the Cassinga killings become slippery when survivors attempt to show these pictures to those of us who might be sceptical of these everyday experiences since the Cassinga massacre. In view of the inconsistency between testimony and memory or the organic picture of the Cassinga massacre and the excruciating aftermath, the public should not embrace testimony (spoken, written, visual, etc.) as communicating the entirety of the horrific experience of the Cassinga massacre and the terribly unresolved long traumatic aftermath.

On photographs, the central argument has been that visual images obscure many secrets. Photographs, be it those taken by the SADF or by SWAPO allies during, or in the immediate aftermath of the Cassinga massacre, can eclipse and hide more than what they disclose to the viewer. Since the available photographs of the Cassinga massacre obscure the untold experiences and memories of the dead, they produce shadows of darkness rather than disclosing the memories and narratives of the particular scenes of violence they claim to represent. In this context, I have argued that to photograph violence as in the case of the Cassinga open mass grave is not to capture the reality of the actual mass graves. Instead, to photograph is to frame, and to frame is to taint and obscure the face of the natural violence.

The tainted images that photographs of the Cassinga massacre promulgate evaporate evidence and nourish inconclusive dialogues between different witnesses, writers and commentators of the Cassinga event. Therefore, in working against the eclipsing of the untold violence that the photographs of the Cassinga massacre entails, the viewer should become aware that the actual experience of the Cassinga massacre was more diverse and complex than the marginal realities which photographs show. Instead of embracing photographs as authentic representations of the situation or states of world they appear to designate, photographs should be instead examined as standing in front of the material world they intend to designate. Nonetheless, this is not to say that photographs from Cassinga are generally "stilted or unconvincing. However composed and staged, they bear witness to real events."[7] They are in some sense testimonies to the actual SADF heinous violence against civilians, even when these images fail to reveal the totality of that event.

It has been argued in this book that Namibian democracy has closed its eyes to a number of issues that the formerly oppressed population groups consider problematic to ignore. One key sensitive issue pertains to the dividing wall between the Cassinga mass graves, family members and Namibia in general. The mass graves are monumental sites in the history of the Namibian liberation struggle. For many Namibians, generally, it is inconceivable that the mass graves remain inaccessible since Namibia became politically independent. Surprisingly, this happens as Namibia marks every anniversary of the Cassinga massacre as a national mourning day. Perhaps this suggests that the recitation of the Cassinga stories is more significant than the tragedy and victimization of the dead in the apparently forgotten Cassinga mass graves.

To draw a more general picture, Namibia's approach to the remains of the war for Namibia's liberation is shockingly disappointing, if not shameful. I am saying this in response to many troubling questions at the back of my mind. For example, is there a marked grave(s) for the hundreds of people (both civilians and SWAPO military cadres such as Wilbard "Nakada" Tashiya and others) killed during the raid of the Vietnam camp on 4 May 1978? What about the remains of the Oshatotwa attacks in Zambia on 11 November 1976? Equally so, what is the state of the graves of thousands of Namibians who died of natural and other causes in camps such as Cassinga, Kwanza-Sul, Ndalatando and at different other places (mainly in Angola and Zambia) where Namibians settled in exile? Graves of several SWAPO cadres are identifiable in Angola and Zambia,[8] but if Namibia cannot follow South Africa's route of repatriating all cadres home, something else should be done to give such Namibians proper burials even when they have to remain buried in foreign lands.

The historic burial sites in exile are not the only important sites which postcolonial Namibia is idly watching fall apart and disintegrate. At home, sites of traumatic memories of the liberation struggle collapse and disappear, while Namibia shamefully watches the disintegration of these historic sites. Some of these sites include the unmarked graves of PLAN combatants who died fighting inside the country and were secretly buried by local

---

[7]   Alan Trachtenberg, *Reading American photographs*, p. 73.
[8]   These include, to list very few of them, Putuse Meekulu Apollus, Lineekela Hailundu Kalenga, Peter Eneas Nanyemba, Greenwell Matongo, Kapuka Nauyala, David Kamwi, Jason "Wanehepo" Hamutenya Ndadi, Augustus "McNamara" Nghaamwa, Isack "Pondo" Ndeshitiwa Shikongo, Natalia Ndahambelela Mavulu, Nabot Helao Nafidi, Homateni Kalweenya and many other. Some names of the people who died under the SWAPO care, their causes and places of death (in some cases) are listed in the SWAPO Party publication: *Their blood waters our freedom: glory to the heroes and heroines of the Namibian liberation struggle* (Windhoek: Namib Graphics, 1996).

communities in the areas where they operated. There is a concern that when initiatives were taken to mark some of the war graves in the former war zone, this was done without proper consultation with the people involved in the burials of the PLAN combatants. As a result, in many ways the plinths marking the grave sites are misleading as they simply read, "a Namibian hero is resting here" when, in many cases, more than one person is buried at the site.[9]

This book has argued that the ongoing suffering, unhappiness and despair of the victims of apartheid's brutal violence in Namibia should not be simply understood as belated relics of the dark moments or trying times when apartheid unleashed violence on civilians to prevent black rule and the independence of Namibia. Such pathos should be read as firmly anchored in the painful memories of postcolonial Namibia's failure to deal with the aftermath of colonial violence in an unbiased and fair manner. In particular, there is a need to deal accordingly with the obstinate and arrogant perpetrators who for no justifiable reason continue to disseminate the denial of the Cassinga massacre in different public avenues. So, as the spectres of apartheid's brutal violence threaten to cast a pall into the future, it is important to attempt to get to the bottom of some of these difficult issues and conditions. It is necessary to interrogate the situations and mechanisms which reinvigorate the ongoing suffering of survivors and affected families of the missing. In view of some of the survivors' registered worries and demands there is, among them, an urge for Namibia to revisit things, to juxtapose the past and present to make them interrogate each other and do things based on reason and frankness. This does not only call for a collective and united voice of the victims. Above all, political will and commitment is pertinent. Nonetheless, it is critical that the victims are consulted and regarded as experts in matters concerning their damaged lives.

It is crucial that the victims' ongoing suffering and trauma, especially in the case of survivors of the Cassinga massacre, should rise above the concept of a "shared heroic sacrifice." This understanding is political and therefore problematic: the notion of the "heroic sacrifice" suggests closing the chapter of the unresolved issues of the violence. This is because the embedded political association or marriage between the shared violence and political heroism constitute an urge to discourage survivors and affected families from pursuing justice for the violated rights of the victims. This is one reason why so many years of prolonged silence have elapsed as survivors embrace "passive victimhood" due to political manipulation. This perilous situation overlooks the fact that when traumatic memories experience

---

9   Vilho Shigwedha, "turning in their graves."In *The Namibian Weekender,* 24 August, 2001; Vilho Shigwedha, "Commemorating the Combatants," online at http://www.namibweb.com/commemorate.htm; Vilho Shigwedha, "Ondeshifiilwa." Online at: http://www.namibweb.com/ondes.htm

repression for a protracted period of time, the burden of memory becomes heavier for the victims to manage. And, with time, these ticking bombs will definitely explode, become contagious and affect future generations. The Herero and Nama issue with the Germans regarding the 1904 - 1908 genocide which is now simmering between these two communities and the German government is an important lesson to learn.[10] Most importantly, every individual victim of colonial and apartheid violence has every right to rise above the lines of political subordination, exploitation and abuse of the victims' inalienable human rights. They have all the right to demand that the South African government acknowledges and takes responsibility for the "collateral damage" permanently inflicted on the lives of innocent people. Otherwise, legal channels to sue the government of the Republic of South Africa for the severity of the unacceptable acts of violence to civilians and their property should be explored and debated.

---

[10] Jeremy Sarkin. *Colonial Genocide and reparations claims in the 21st century: the socio-legal context of claims under international law by the Herero against German for Genocide in Namibia, 1904–1908* (Westport: Praeger Publishers, 2009).

Appendix A

Statement by the Administrator-General for SWA, Judge MT Steyn

Through consideration of all possible factors and the requests of various politicians in this area I have consulted with the South African government and with their permission have asked the army to launch a limited operation in South Angola to destroy certain terrorist bases. The pressure exerted from the northern leaders like Pastor Njoba and Mr. Alphens Majevero have in recent times increased after members of their tribes came under terrorists attack by members of SWAPO. I have repeatedly invited SWAPO on numerous occasions – and I am still doing it – to participate peacefully in the political process of this country, but such a process can't take place if headmen are kidnapped, women are assaulted, scholars kidnapped and members murdered by people that come across the border. I would not be able to do my duty if I did not give adherence to law and order in this country. I trust that the world will realize that we can resolve the problems in this area democratically and around a confederation table that will be mutually beneficial to all the inhabitants as well as to ensure prolonged stability. The security forces that are represented here will at all times adhere to law and order and will not tolerate any intimidation or any other form of terrorism. In this case there were no measures taken against SWAPO, but against those elements in SWAPO that were revolutionary in controlling this country through violence and who hold no respect for country borders. I trust that everyone who considers the welfare of the inhabitants of Southwest Africa/Namibia to be of importance will support me in the decision I am forced to take. My thanks, and thanks to the peaceful people and to each member of the army that fights in our interest against the forces of anarchy and the revolution.

Source: Chief of the SADF (Top Secret); PSYAC planning directive No. 3/78, Appendix B to PSYAC No. 3 / 78, SANDF Archive, Pretoria.

Appendix B

Statement by the Commander General, Commander Southwest Africa, General Major JJ Geldenhuys, S.M.

On request of the Administrator-General ... Southwest African troops (sic) and troops of the SA Army initiated a limited operation several hours in Southern Angola with the instruction to destroy bases occupied by terrorists. The troops (including parachute troops) received instructions not to act under any circumstances against members of the local population or against any of their property. It was also relayed to our troops to avoid any confrontation with the Angolan government forces. Notwithstanding the reasons given by the Administrator general for this drastic action, the patience of the security forces have been tested in recent times to the utmost extremes by a large number of illegal border crossings and acts against our patrol guards and temporary bases near the border. Terrorists have initially avoided contact with the security forces and were determined on intimidating and damaging business of the local population, but in recent times they have acted in larger patrols against smaller SA patrols – to ensure safe passage over the border. ... We trust that in a couple of hours that everything will be finished and that the Angolan troops will abstain from becoming involved in this ... internal case. Gradually as the operation is progressing news will be available on a regular basis to the press.

Source: Chief of the SADF (Top Secret); PSYAC planning directive No. 3/78, Appendix B to PSYAC No. 3 / 78, SANDF Archive, Pretoria.

Appendix C

Suggested approach for statement by Minister of Defence & The Guidelines for statement by GOC SWA

TOP SECRET

SUGGESTED APPROACH FOR STATEMENT BY MINISTER OF DEFENCE

1. <u>General</u>. It is suggested that the first announcement of
the operation comes from SWA because:

    a.   It indicates that the decision is primarily
        an SWA matter.

    b.   It places the matter in a low profile regional
        perspective.

    c.   It allows the RSA government room for manoeuvre
        in that the outside world must first <u>react</u>, be=
        fore the RSA government states its attitude.

    d.   It could suit our ends should Angola/SWAPO decide
        to play down the effect of the operation and their
        reaction to it. This is unlikely to happen if the
        operation is initially announced by the Minister.

2. <u>Approach</u>. Should the Minister decide to make a statement,
it is suggested that the following broad approach be followed:

    a.   Confirm that the RSA government had been consulted
        and requested to support the operation.

    b.   That the Angolan government was aware that its terri=
        tory was being used as a base for aggression against
        the peoples of SWA but, notwithstanding protest, had
        failed to stop such internationally unlawful activity.

    c.   That SWAPO had been dealt a heavy blow in the inter=
        ests of SWA democratic progress.

    d.   Latest operational details.

    e.   That the RSA, in the future as in the past, will
        always give serious consideration to any request
        for support in maintaining law and order in SWA
        and promoting democratic progress to independence
        in SWA.

DEFENCE INTELLIGENCE
DECLASSIFIED

2 2 JAN 2007

J.A.L. STEINMANN
72563596PE WO1

TOP SECRET

GUIDELINES FOR STATEMENT BY GOC SWA

1.   General. This statement may be made in conjunction with
or separately from a statement by the AG, SWA. It should be
issued as soon as success has been confirmed and withdrawal has
commenced. The following general guidelines apply.

2.   Profile. The operation must be presented as having been
a self defence operation. It is the latest of a series of hot
pursuit operations.

3.   Justification. The operation is motivated by:

     a.   The increasing intensity of border violations
          culminating in the serious incident of D minus 1.

     b.   The history of SWAPO intimidation of the Owambo
          people and the murder of elected political figures.

     c.   SWAPO statements and evidence of a pending SWAPO
          offensive to forestall democratic elections in the
          territory. The role of Cassinga in the SWAPO in=
          frastructure.

     d.   The above called for preventative self-defence
          operations to protect Namibian lives and property
          from SWAPO.

4.   Consultation. The operation was preceded by consultation
with the relevant bodies in SWA/Owambo.

5.   Results. An indication of the results of the operation and
he nature of own casualties.

TOP SECRET

Source: Chief of the SADF (Top Secret); PSYAC planning directive No. 3/78, Appendix B to PSYAC
No. 3 / 78, SANDF Archive, Pretoria.

Appendix D

Some photographs taken by the SADF during the Cassinga attack.

Source: SANDF Archive, Pretoria.

Appendix E

Extract from the transcription of the author's interview with Rev. Samwel Mateus Shiininge about his experience of the 'Vietnam' attack.

In the interview, Rev. Samwel Mateus Shiininge told me that he was born on September 10, 1923 at Onakayale in Ombalantu, northern Namibia. At the time of the 'Vietnam' attack, he was the head of the Evangelical Lutheran Owambokavango Church (ELOC) – now known as the Evangelical Lutheran Church in Namibia (ELCIN) – mission at Oshikango sha Popawa. This place is located about 25km from the Angolan southwestern border with Namibia. Rev. Shiininge was sent there in 1974 to, according to the interview, "plant the seeds of Christianity" among communities in southern Angola.[1]

Oshikango sha Popapwa, also called Osheetekela is the same place where SWAPO established the 'Vietnam' military camp. The area was suitable for the SWAPO combatants in considering its proximity to a perennial water point, etale, and a dense forest called omufitu gwa Sheetekela or the jungles of Sheetekela. SWAPO military camp at that place was strategically located as it was closer to the Namibian border. For that reason, it provided a reception to many civilians (before they were transported to Cassinga) who were escaping from Namibia by the northwestern route entering into Angola.

The Lutheran Mission home and the church were located a stone's throw from the SWAPO base at Vietnam. Rev. Shiininge recounted his experience of the SADF attack of the SWAPO camp at Vietnam as provided by the following excerpt:

> The attack took place on the Ascension Sunday, May 4, 1978. I had just returned home from the church that afternoon. And, as I was lying down, for a siesta, on a mat or oshiinda, under a pawpaw tree shade I was awoken by a thundering noise. I got up quickly ... bombs were exploding all over the place and dust was oozing everywhere. The attack was unexpected. The SWAPO soldiers were loosely in and outside the camp. Some of them were at the kitchen when the attack happened as it was lunchtime ... The bombers retreated towards the northeastern direction of the

---

[1] "The Evangelical Lutheran mission work began in southern Angola led by the Rhenish missionary A. Wulfhorst from 1891 to 1915. Due to political circumstances, the Lutheran Christians left Angola in 1915 for northern Namibia, thinking that they belonged to the same ethnic group as the people located south of the Namibia border. In 1933, Angolan Lutherans returned to Angola and were served under the administration of the Evangelical Lutheran Church in Namibia (ELCIN). In 1954 Simon Ndatipo became the first ELCIN pastor to work in Angola permanently, and in 1962, Rev. Noa Ndeutapo of ELCIN replaced Rev. Ndatipo. The Evangelical Lutheran Church of Angola erected its first church building at Shangalala in 1965. It became a member of the Lutheran World Federation in 1997 and today has 29,000 members." Visit: http://www.elca.org/Who-We-Are/Our-Three-Expressions/Churchwide-Organization/Global-Mission/Where-We-Work/Africa/Angola/Mission-History.aspx

camp and never returned ... as soon as the bombing planes left, a reconnaissance plane moved in and began circling the camp continuously. At the same time, the ground forces moved in with armed vehicles. A heavy fight erupted between the Boers and the SWAPO soldiers. Some of my family members and I escaped from the mission home ... we went to hide in the middle of the omahangu field. It was a good harvesting season and the tall and thick omahangu stalks provided good cover for us but not protection.

While hiding in the omahangu field, the fight intensified and we felt very much unsecured ... A group of young girls also joined us. The crowd was getting bigger ... we feared that the enemy might find us there, but it was also unsafe to move away ... When the fight subsided ... we decided to vacate that position. I suggested that the best place to find protection was to run inside the thick forest that surrounded the camp ... but my wife, meme Hilya Martin [late], warned against possible dangers inside the jungles. That idea was revoked ... alternatively, we decided to take the direction where we could find Angolan homesteads ... We came to the homestead of Nghidulika Komukwiyu, but no one was in the house ... People fled for fear of their lives ... We came to the second homestead, which belonged to Paulus and still we found no people in the house. Late in the afternoon, we found a man, his name was Ndongili. He was riding a horse ... I did not remember to take my shirt and shoes when I fled from the house and as it was getting cold ... Ndongili gave me a shirt and left us there ...

From there, we went to the homestead of Sarafi yaNangombe. He accommodated us for weeks. He also gave me shoes and clothes to wear... The big trouble was my mother-in-law, Ruth Shooya [late] who was not with us. We left her inside the missionary home when we escaped. She was very old and we could not take her with us ... Two days later, my conscience compelled me to go back to the camp to try and find her. I was escorted by two villagers, members of my parish ... I also wanted to assess possible damage to the church and to the mission home ... we found the church and the homestead completely destroyed ... some people went inside the church for protection, thinking that the attackers would not tamper with and cause harm to the church building. They were mistaken as the church and the mission house were all bulldozed and razed to the ground by the casspirs and other armed vehicles.

My mother-in-law was nowhere to be located ... We searched all over the camp expecting to find her body ... we later learnt that the Boers, attackers, found her in the homestead. They accused her of being a SWAPO's medicine woman – a witch or *omulodhi*. She was an elderly woman, but they tortured her so badly and took her back to Namibia. We stayed in the dark about her whereabouts for months... we presumed that she was killed in the attack. Months later, I got a clue, through our mission station at Oshaangalala, that she was alive but kept in prison in Namibia ... she did not receive proper medical treatment for her injuries while in prison. As a result, her health deteriorated while incarcerated ... the church intervened and she was released after spending about a year in detention ...

After her release, she lived with Simon Ndatipo in Ombalantu, but her health deteriorated further. In 1980 I sent for her to come and stay with us at Osheetekela. But her health did not get any better. She died in 1982 and we buried her there in Angola (Vietnam) ... Anyway, I should tell you that what I saw in the camp when I went back to the mission church and house is very difficult to describe ... people's bodies were scattered everywhere in the camp ... What exactly happened to their bodies and whether the bodies of prominent commanders whom I knew like Nakada (Wilbard "Nakada" Tashiya), Mbango and others were ever recovered for burial I do not know, as I did not go back there until things settled ...

Source: Rev. Samwel Mateus Shiininge's interview with the author, Etunda, 2007.

Appendix F

UNICEF report on Namibian refugees at Cassinga before the attack.

In mid-April 1978 – just three weeks prior to the South African attack – a delegation from the United Nations Children's Fund (UNICEF) visited Kassinga. They observed a flood of refugees coming directly from Namibia under pressure and repression from the South African army, which is currently attempting to establish a no-man's-land on the Angolan-Namibian frontier. The delegation estimated the number of Namibians between 11, 000 and 12, 000. With regard to the composition of the refugee population, the mission found that the young population, that is to say, adolescents, children and infants constitutes the majority. The percentage of women also seems to be considerable. Thus, the mission concluded, the vulnerable groups apparently represent approximately 70 per cent of the total population [...]. The remainder [...] is composed of adults, with very few elderly persons. The school going population was estimated close to 2, 500. As would be expected in any rapidly growing refugee settlement, the UNICEF mission identified a number of problem areas, however, it was positively impressed by SWAPO's organization and administration, as well as by the determination shown by the refugees: one is struck by the organization of their health services, their education and sanitation ... [programmes]. Therefore, in the rational essence of the actuality of Cassinga, it is evident that it was indeed a Namibian refugee centre, administered by SWAPO with the assistance of the United Nations and protected by a small SWAPO military force, which included a senior SWAPO commander. Representatives of the United Nations High Commission for Refugees and the World Health Organization who visited Cassinga three weeks after the raid ... verified on the ground ... the extreme savagery, the attempted annihilation, and the systematic destruction wrought upon a group of refugees under the protection of the High Commission for Refugees. ... That these people were civilians is attested to by all the evidence that this UN mission has been able to gather ... All the facts (on the ground) that this UN delegation have been able to verify reveal that what happened in Cassinga must be described as criminal in legal terms and savage in moral terms. It reminds us of the darkest moments of modern history.

Source: Tor Sellström, *Sweden and national liberation in Southern Africa: solidarity and assistance 1970–1994, volume 11: solidarity and assistance 1970–1994* (Nordiska Afrikainstitutet, 2002), pp. 352–363.

Appendix G

"Cassinga battle account reveals biased claptrap: a former SADF Colonel who led forces in controversial battle speaks out"

I have followed the Sunday Independent letters between Mike McWilliams and Randolph Vigne of Cape Town concerning the Battle of Cassinga. I am totally in agreement with Mike McWilliams since I too was there – in fact, as Mike's commander on that fateful day.

Concerning Annemarie Heywood's accusation in her The Cassinga Event: An Investigation of the Records, it can be stated categorically that the battlefield was carefully prepared by South West Africa People's Organisation (Swapo) and People's Armed Forces for the Liberation of Angola (FAPLA) troops before the international press arrived. Thus, there was no reliable evidence to be obtained from a subsequent photograph of a so-called "mass grave" to show the bodies of "the great majority of women and children" slaughtered by the paratroopers or the Air Force.

Nor could there be because there never was such a grave to photograph. There was and still is, however, one photograph – and one only, of a so-called mass grave, which shows a great majority of men, all them combatants, with only three women barely recognizable among the lot and, significantly, without any evidence whatsoever, of dead or mutilated children.

This is the photograph that is used by Heywood, Vigne and others to accuse my paratroopers of butchering women and children indiscriminately, pregnant women having their stomachs ripped open by bayonets, after they had been raped, of course, to get at the unborn as well.

If there had been a photograph sent into the world showing a huge heap of women and children massacred by the "Boers," John Vorster's government would have become history overnight and the concerned five western nations would have given up the whole attempt to come to a peaceful solution for the South West Africa Namibia problem.

They and others would have instituted a water-tight sanctions plan, perhaps even a blockade of the South African and South West African coastlines, even used military force to kick the South African Defence Force (SADF) out of South West Africa Namibia. And even the Security Council would have been driven to accept Swapo as the only legitimate government of SWA / Namibia.

But there was no such photograph of hundreds of massacred innocents, if not the thousands, because the rumoured mass grave had, unfortunately, already been covered up before the first camera arrived on the scene

It would, of course, have been sacrilege to reopen the grave of such a tragic event just for the sake of photographic evidence. So they had to make do with what they had and rely on Goebbels-type hype and propaganda to sway the ignorant masses and their "not-so-ignorant" leaders by embroidering the alleged atrocities committed by barbaric, crazed paratroopers.

The only photograph they could produce had to serve, but no matter. An energetic propaganda offence would change the shortcomings of this photo, as pointed out above, into an instrument of almost gospel truth.

For Vigne's information, my paratroopers did not carry bayonets or any other sharp instruments with which to slaughter women and children, a fact he could have verified with General Constand Viljoen himself, since he had taken the infantry's bayonets away some years before Cassinga.

Incidentally, Viljoen also arrived on the scene of battle, unexpectedly, and the least Vigne could have done was to confirm his perceived details with the general who started it all, a man who was pronounced by Nelson Mandela himself as one of a very few totally honourable and honest men he has ever dealt with during his remarkable life.

I nevertheless refer Vigne, again, to the extremely prejudiced Cassinga Event, authored by Heywood, which he unequivocally favours, and specifically to the photograph I have mentioned, which is the only one ever used to accuse us of a genocidal massacre.

Then there is, of course, also the Truth and Reconciliation Commission report Vigne can go and dig up. He will discover that even the biased truth commission found that there was no substantial evidence, in spite of Heywood's accusations, that we, the paratroopers, had wiped out a refugee camp while pretending to attack a Swapo base.

If that is not enough information for him, I, as honourary colonel of the Legion of Associated Airborne, Republic of South Africa, invite him to a night out with paratrooper veterans in Benoni, or here in Sedgefield, to have a snort or two and to discuss his reservations with men who were there. I can assure him that the men are always on their best behaviour so that he [sic] need not fear being given a torrid time.

A less dodgy approach would have been to buy an older colleague, namely Willem Steenkamp, a malt whiskey and to tap his brains on many aspects of the border war.

Vigne is perhaps ignoring the fact that Steenkamp was a brilliant war correspondent for the Cape Times and that he wrote a book called Border Strike which covers, among others, the Reindeer and the Cassinga battles extensively.

This is by far a much more reliable and balanced account from the pen of a cool and calm reporter with impeccable integrity – compared with the prejudiced horror story told by a biased, almost hysterical Heywood.

So Vigne's excuse that only Heywood's less-than-salubrious effort should be considered is, to tell the truth, dishonest and holds no water at all with me.

Vigne knows about Steenkamp, where he comes from and where he can be found. What is more, Steenkamp is a Capetonian and thus easily accessible to a fellow Capetonian like Vigne.

On the other hand, Vigne can wait for my own telling of the Cassinga event to see the light of day in the near future. In this book, which he will have to buy (no freebies from me), I have gone out of my way to expose the manufactured evidence Heywood had used to project a deliberately skewed account into the world with the specific objective to discredit the whole SADF as baby killers and thus to cover up the vitally important fact that Swapo had badly lost the most strategic battle, ever, up to that point, in the history of the border war.

Unfortunately, the author of the masters thesis referred to by Vigne also relied, to some extent, on Swapo and Heywood claptrap, especially in some critical areas, to substantiate a somewhat watered down "accidental" killing scenario of civilians – the so-called "collateral damage" profile the Americans are so fond of using when justifying especially bombing raids, while discussing events during the Vietnam and Iraq wars.

My book has been written specifically to contradict the "baby killer" tag and a host of other serious accusations made by the author of the masters thesis and, by extension, by Heywood et al. – thus also by people like Vigne who make ill-considered statements without proper research and cross-checking.

I have meticulously researched my book over a much wider spectrum than any previous pontificators on the Cassinga battle with the almost inevitable result that none of us really come out of the Cassinga battle smelling of roses. Nevertheless, we emerge with our humanistic reputations and our pride, as paratroopers and air men, still very much intact.

Lots went wrong on that day, up to a point when imminent disaster became almost a certainty, but the fighting spirit of all my paratroopers and some very brave pilots and aircrews pulled us through, so that we could go home more or less intact to claim a most remarkable victory.

Colonel Jan Breytenbach was first commander of 44 Parachute Brigade and commander of the paratroopers during the Cassinga battle.

Article authored by Colonel Jan Breytenbach. Source: *Sunday Independent* 3 February 2008.

Appendix H

Ellen Namhila's response to Jan Breytenbach's article

"I was at Cassinga and it was not a military base"

I refer to the correspondence in your columns re: Cassinga.

I am a Namibian survivor of Cassinga, which was a Swapo refugee camp attacked and bombed by the South African Defence Force's (SADF's) air force and paratroopers on May 4 1978.

I was there when it was bombed and I, and many of my friends whom I lost in the bombing were not military people. We did not study military matters and did not have guns to fight anyone. I can state categorically that Cassinga was not a military base.

We had run away from Namibia because of apartheid repression. Swapo established a refugee camp for us at Cassinga. It was a camp for children and youths like myself, and there were elderly people who were responsible for cooking our meals and doing the administrative work of the camp, such as nurses, gardeners and teachers. Our teachers did not carry guns.

The SADF is fully responsible for its own casualties, which might have been due to their own miscalculations. We the residents of Cassinga did not have guns to kill anyone. The air force dropped bombs all over the place and put the life of their own personnel in danger.

Why didn't they attack Swapo military camps? What did we do to them to be bombarded like that?

It is strange that in today's world we still have people who are trying to earn their glory out of merciless killings of innocent lives and that newspapers such as yours should give space for a disgraceful regime to claim the glory over those of us who are still recovering from the trauma of the Cassinga massacre.

Ellen Namhila, Namibia

Source: *Sunday Independent*, 9 March 2008, p. 6.

Appendix I

"Bullets do not lie," Jan Breytenbach's response to Ellen Namhila's letter.

Bullets don't lie, but it appears people do

I have read with amused astonishment Ellen Namhila's description of the attack by South African paratroopers on Cassinga on May 4 1978 ("I was at Cassinga and it was not a military base", *The Sunday Independent*, March 9).

What really tickles me is her interpretation that we South Africans had been shooting ourselves during the ensuing "massacre", which obviously accounted for our own casualties.

There were no weapons anywhere to be found in the Cassinga "refugee camp", according to Namhila.

I will only discuss this aspect as the rest has been covered a number of times by both the former paratroopers and, of course, the helpless "refugees" that survived this "atrocious" slaughter by the bloodthirsty Boers.

I was, according to Namhila, shot through the wrist by one of my own men. It could only have been with an AK-47, which the paratrooper who did the dirty deed had to have smuggled in since his service rifle, a good old 7.62 R1 rifle would have taken my whole hand away.

Similarly, Backhouse, who was badly wounded, having his aorta severed, obviously by an AK, SKS or more likely a PPSH, would have had his whole heart system and most of his chest cavity shot away if it had been one of his own mates who had done him in with an R1.

Norman Reeves had an incoming bullet stopped by a pencil flare projector in his top pocket.

If it was a R1 rifle (Nato 7.62 bullet) it would have carried this pencil flare deep into his chest cavity which would have meant the end of Norman Reeves.

Likewise, Dries Marais, our intrepid Buccaneer pilot who had come to our rescue, collected a number of anti-aircraft holes in his plane, two shots through his two Rolls Royce Spey engines, but nevertheless kept flying because of the ruggedness of the plane.

If it had been one of our 20 mills he would, however, not have made it.

Thus, the three of my men killed, the one MIA believed killed and the dozen or so wounded were done in by paratroopers behaving like a bunch of cowboys during a drunken brawl.

Perhaps I had the very substantial numbers of AK-47s, PPSHs, SKSs and other weaponry parachuted in to create the impression, through pictures taken at the time, that Cassinga was a South West Africa People's Organisation military base and not a refugee camp as claimed.

Jan Breytenbach
George

Source: *The Sunday Independent*, 16 March 2008.

Appendix J

Jan Breytenbach's role in regional and other conflicts

Jan Breytenbach was the SADF number one [paratrooper], experienced, of proven ability and deserved all respects of the SADF. According to Edward George Alexander, the Chief of the South African Army, General Constand Viljoen tasked Jan Breytenbach "to plan the 'assault' on Cassinga and to train the troops for it. ... There was no one else (in the SADF) with the proven combat leadership of Jan Breytenbach. ... In 1966 he (Breytenbach) commanded the paratrooper contingent that participated in the first action of the war in Namibia when a helicopter assault was carried out on the SWAPO base at Ongulumbashe .... In 1969, he and three other hand-picked paratroopers who were under his command, were sent on a top-secret mission, masquerading as mercenaries, to assist the Biafrans in the Nigerian civil war. For his part in (Biafra) War Breytenbach was decorated by the President of Gabon. This adventure led directly to the founding of South Africa's first special force units, 1 Reconnaissance Commando ('The Recces') with Jan Breytenbach as its commander. In this role he led clandestine operations into Zambia, Tanzania (raiding Dar-es-Salem harbour from a submarine), Angola and Mozambique ... On 22 January 1974, Breytenbach and five of his Recces parachuted into Mozambique with 35 Rhodesian SA paratroopers in an operation against ZANLA (Zimbabwe African National Liberation Army) guerrillas only weeks before the coup in Portugal. ... When South Africa became involved in the Angolan civil war in 1975, Breytenbach was the first training team commander sent to assist the FNLA (Frente Nacional de Libertação de Angola – National Front for the Liberation of Angola). He formed the battalion of FNLA forces known as 'Bravo Group' and led them as part of Task Force Zulu, participating in phenomenal advance across southern Angola to the coast, then up towards Luanda, fighting one battle after another, first against the MPLA and then against the Cubans. ... When the South Africans withdrew from Angola, Breytenbach brought Bravo Group with him and eventually engineered their absorption into the SADF as the notorious 32 Battalion. He commanded them ... conducting ... counter guerrilla operations into Angola ... At the time of ... Cassinga ... Colonel Jan Breytenbach was probably the most experienced combat commander in the SADF. Certainly he was the most highly decorated soldier in the SA Army and one of the very few to have first hand experience of parachute operations. He had an intimate knowledge of the fighting capabilities of SWAPO, the MPLA (and) the Cubans."

Source: Edward Alexander, "The Cassinga Raid," pp. 96–102.

Appendix K

The SADF torture and deliberate killing of the suspected SWAPO fighters as told by Lance Corporal Sean Callaghan & Warrant Officer John Deegan, former SADF soldiers:

"The third specific incident that I remember is chasing a SWAPO unit commander or political commissar. We picked up his spoor and chased him for two days ... this was typical of the style of contacts that I was involved in. Five Casspirs, fifty men chasing one or two people running on foot. We finally did catch him, hiding in a kraal. The unit commander ... lined up a bunch of Koevoet people next to the hut he was in and drove over the hut with the Casspir. Everyone then fired into the rubble ... The SWAPO commissar was pulled out of the rubble and given to me to keep alive. He had been shot in the arm and the leg and had been driven over ... because he was a commissar, he would have been carrying a handgun. John [Deegan, acting unit commander] started to interrogate him while I was putting up a drip. The purpose of this interrogation was to find the handgun ... We never found the handgun because John shot him in the head out of frustration while I was still attending to him. The incident and the face of this SWAPO commissar haunted me in dreams for years." [Statement by Lance Corporal Sean Callaghan, amnesty application, December 1996].

"[The SWAPO commissar] was a veteran ... he would have been an excellent source of information but he was so fucked ... each team had an army medic and Sean started patching up this guy while I was busy interrogating him ... and he was just going 'kandi shishi' (I don't know anything), even at this stage he was denying everything ... and I just started going into this uncontrollable fucking rage and he started going floppy and I remember thinking 'how dare you, I'm talking to you, how dare you ignore me ... why don't you answer me' and then this is what I was told afterwards. I had my 9 mm in my hand and I was just pushing my way through the team ... and apparently what happened was I started ripping ... Sean had put a drip into the guy's arm and started plugging the bullet hole to get him together ... he would have pulled through ... I ripped all the bandages, the drip off the guy, pulled out my 9 mm, put the barrel between his eyes and fucking boom I executed him ... and they told me afterwards I was just screaming, I was raging ... " (Statement by Warrant Officer John Deegan).

Source: Lance Corporal Sean Callaghan & Warrant Officer John Deegan – accounts of an incident to the Truth and Reconciliation Commission's conscript hearing, Cape Town, June 1997. In the "Truth and Reconciliation Commission of South Africa Report: Volume Two, Chapter Two, The State outside South Africa between 1960 and 1990."

Appendix L

"Cassinga events need to be documented"

It wasn't the first time the story had been told, but judging from the age of many in attendance and the silence during its telling, one could have believed that it was.

"We heard a strange sound coming from the south-eastern side of the camp," Cassinga massacre survivor Agnes Kafula started, recounting the events of 28 years ago, which left hundreds of Namibians dead. Kafula was speaking at the annual commemoration of Cassinga Day in Windhoek yesterday, which was held at the UN Plaza in Katutura. She recalled how they quickly learned that the sound came from South African Defence Force (SADF) aircraft which proceeded to drop bombs onto the southern Angolan town, and send in forces.

"Many were shot at close range. Small kids thrown against trees and big stones," she said, losing her voice at times. "Our wounds have healed," she finally said after narrating how she, along with other survivors, some of whom stood behind her holding candles, managed to escape the onslaught. "But our scars remain. May their souls rest in peace." Kafula asked the government to ensure that the history of Cassinga was documented "in the form of a booklet" to ensure that what happened does not become lost to future generations. She also asked Government to consider allowing survivors to visit the mass grave of those who died, while asking that those who were instrumental in saving the lives of survivors be recognised as national heroes and heroines.

Former Prime Minister Hage Geingob also stressed the need for this part of Namibia's history to be documented, regardless of how painful it might be. "Many want us to forget what we went through. They want us to believe that Namibia started on March 21 1990. But history is about everything, the good and the bad," Geingob said. "We must be careful in this country not to play down certain events. We must not take our reconciliation for granted." In conclusion, Geingob cautioned Government to become more proactive in addressing issues of land and economic empowerment, in order to avoid possibly dangerous consequences. "There are many Namibians who are angry. Angry also with their leaders who say let's forgive and forget. Let's address the land issue, the economic issue, before it's too late," he said. The plaza was filled with Namibians young and old, who sang songs of remembrance between the speeches.

Source: *The Namibian*, 5 May 2006.

Appendix M

"Don't Scrap Cassinga Day."

Windhoek – Deputy Prime Minister Dr. Libertina Amathila outrightly dismissed some public sentiments that Namibian holidays, including Cassinga Day, should be scrapped because there are too many holidays, arguing that the country's independence came at a very high price.

Addressing hundreds of Namibians at the UN Plaza in Katutura on Cassinga Day on Friday, Amathila stressed that each citizen must never forget that the independence that they have enjoyed for the past 17 years was won the hard way by those who died in the war of liberation. "We will not allow their sacrifices to be forgotten or be reduced to insignificancy and we will not reduce holidays. We value our freedom and we value the contribution made by our fallen heroes and heroines," said Amathila.

The latest sentiment by the Deputy Premier, who was addressing the crowd on behalf of President Hifikepunye Pohamba, comes in light of some suggestions from various quarters in the country that there are too many holidays. It is being suggested that these holidays be scrapped, including Cassinga Day. However, Amathila was quick to dismiss these suggestions. "I wish to use this opportunity to dispel those suggestions with the contempt they deserve and I want to remind those persons making these suggestions that the blood of the victims of Cassinga as well as other victims of the liberation war, waters our freedom!"

The significance of Cassinga Day dates back to 29 years ago, on May 4, 1978, when thousands of innocent Namibian civilians were brutally attacked and hundreds killed by the South African apartheid military forces at Cassinga, a Swapo refugee camp in southern Angola. The commemoration on Friday was graced by the presence of the Founding Father of the Nation Dr Sam Nujoma. Amathila noted that the hard-won independence and sacrifices made should not be taken for granted, but rather respected through hard work. "As people, we must always be mindful that the virtues of peace, tranquility and political and social stability are building foundations for a prosperous and strong nation. We must never take these virtues for granted," said Amathila. Cassinga Day should be seen as a day of reflection on the country's historical journey to freedom and for looking at the way ahead in addressing the daunting challenges of poverty, unemployment and social disparities. "It is about reminding ourselves, individually and collectively, about the challenges we still need to address and to re-awaken our sense of national consciousness and dignity," she said. In respect of the heroes and heroines who died at Cassinga, government has already done its part in collecting the soil from the mass graves in southern Angola and placing it at Heroes

Acre in the capital. Steps are also under way to construct a monument at the mass gravesite at Cassinga, in memory of those who died for the liberation of the country.

Earlier that day, Amathila laid a wreath in honour of the Cassinga heroes and heroines at Heroes Acre. Speaking on behalf of the group of close to 20 Cassinga survivors present at the commemoration, Councillor Agnes Kafula said the 4th of May was a very sad day in the history of the country. "This was a barbaric act of cowardice by the South African apartheid regime. Although our wounds are healed, the scars remain and the pain and anguish that we have gone through 29 years ago is still fresh in our minds," said Kafula. She added that as Cassinga survivors, the spirit of those who sacrificed their lives in the liberation struggle such as at Cassinga would not rest until their remains are brought back home. "Therefore, we urge our government to take the initiative to bring back the remains of those comrades who perished in the liberation struggle so that they get a proper burial," said Kafula, adding that plans are under way to set up a Cassinga Trust.

Source: *New Era*, 7 May 2007

Abbreviations

ANC	African National Congress (of South Africa)
FAPLA	Forças Armadas Popular da Libertação de Angola (People's Armed Forces for the Liberation of Angola)
MPLA	Movimento Popular da Libertação de Angola (People's Movement for the Liberation of Angola)
NAPLA	Namibian People's Liberation Army
PLAN	People's Liberation Army of Namibia
SADF	South African Defence Force
SWALA	South West Africa Liberation Army
SWAPO	South West Africa People's Organisation
SWAPOL	South West African Police
SWATF	South West Africa Territorial Force
TRC	Truth and Reconciliation Commission of South Africa
UNITA	União Nacional para a Indepêndencia Total de Angola (National Union for the Total Independence of Angola)

List of Figures

Bibliography

1. List of interviewees

Amakali, Shimwandi (Cassinga survivor). Interview with the author, Oshakati, 29 December 2007.

Amukoto, Michael (Cassinga survivor). Interview with the author, Onaniki,2 May 2002.

Anonymous, daughter of a former Cassinga paratrooper. Interviewed by email (through intermediary), 6 February 2010.

Anonymous, former Cassinga paratrooper. Interviewed by email (through intermediary), 28 March 2010.

Anonymous, former SADF conscript. Email interviews with the author, 6 February 2010; 10 February 2010; 28 March 2010 and 30 March 2010.

Ashuunda, Nashima Paulus (Cassinga survivor). Interview with the author, Oshinyadhila, 11 January 2008.

Festus "Kaapanda kaNangolo"(Ongulumbashe battle veteran). Interview with the author, Omukondo Noshilulu, 20 August 2002.

Kathingo, Gideon Paulus (Vietnam survivor). Interview with the author, Uukwamatsi, 12 January 2008.

Hamaambo, Ottilie (Cassinga survivor and wife of the late Dimo Hamaambo). Interview with the author, Uuvudhiya, 5 December 2007.

Haulyondjamba, Elise (former SWAPO combatant). Interview with the author, Oshakati, 20 August 2003.

Helmut, Paulus "Uncle Paul" (retired politician). Interview with the author, Windhoek, 5 November 2007.

Homateni, Lotto (Ongulumbashe battle veteran). Interview with the author, Oshakati, 22 August 2002.

Iilende, David (retired teacher). Interview with the author, Oluteyi, 22 April 2002.

Iiyambo, Kaarina (Vietnam survivor). Interview with the author, Uukwamatsi, 12 May 2008.

Kaapanda, Junias Vaino "Kaunda kaZambia" (retired pastor and community activist). Interview with the author, Uukwanampembe, 12 March 2001.

Kamati, Lena (Cassinga survivor). Interview with the author, Oshakati, 29 December 2007.

Kapolo, Tjapaka Mathew (pastor and community activist). Interview with the author, Oshakati, 22 May 2001.

Kiiyala, Hendrina (Cassinga survivor). Interview with the author, Oshikuku, 21 December 2007 & at Oshiku sha Shipya, 11 June 2009.

Lazarus, Cornelius Namutenya (Cassinga survivor). Interview with the author, Etunda, 5 February 2008.

Martin, Magdaleen (GwaMartin)-Kapolo (wife of Adam Kapolo who disappeared on Robben Island). Interview with the author, Elondo, 9 September 2005.

Aune Kapolo. Interview with the author, Elondo, 9 September 2005.

Max, Nangulohi Selma (Paavo Max's wife). Personal communication with the author, Efindi Lyomulunga / Efidi, 2008, 2009, 2010 and 2011.

Max, Paavo (Cassinga survivor). Interview with the author, Efindi Lyomulunga / Efindi, 2007, 2008, 2009, 2010 and 2011.

Mbango, Simeon (Cassinga survivor). Interview with the author, Onandjokwe and Oshakati, 2 May 2004.

Mwanyekange, Vahongaifa Ignatius (Cassinga survivor).Interview with the author (including follow-up email interviews with the author) 21 September 2008; 27 February 2009 and 27 March 2009.

Mwatilifange, Ndamona Martha (Cassinga survivor).Interview with the author, Oshakati, 19 December 2007.

Nakambwela, Hilka (Cassinga survivor). Interview with the author, Okadhila, 29 December 2007.

Namhila, Ndeshi Ellen (Cassinga survivor).Interview with the author, Windhoek, 26 January 2007.

Nangolo, Selma (victim of the SADF violence inside Namibia). Interview with the author, Okapuku, September 2003.

Ngula, Titus "Kasindani" (retired pastor and community activist). Interview with the author, Oshitayi, 29 April 2004.

Per Sanden (archivist, photographer). Interview with the author, Windhoek, 23 November 2007 (including follow up email interviews).

Prinsloo, Gerald W. (archivist, SANDF archive, Pretoria). Interview with the author, 30 September 2009 (including follow-up email interviews).

Sebulon, Shivute (community member). Interview with the author, Ondongwadhiya, August, 2002.

Sellstrom, Tor (visited Cassinga with the UN observer team following the attack). Email interviews with the author, 26 and 27 February 2009.

Shaghala, Josaphat (Bishop of the Evangelical Lutheran Church in Namibia, Western Diocese). Interview with the author, Okahao, 2004.

Shiininge, Samwel Mateus (retired pastor and Vietnam survivor). Interview with the author, Etunda, 5 February 2008.

Shikongo, Darius "Mbolondondo" (Cassinga survivor). Interview with the author, Ondangwa, 23 December 2007.

Shimbindja, Pius (Cassinga survivor). Interview with the author, Oshakati, 21 December 2007.

Shitangi, Ndatila Rauha (Cassinga survivor). Interview with the author, Okadhila, 29 December 2007.

Shixuadu, Helena Iipinge (Cassinga survivor). Interview with the author, Oshakati, 1 December 2007 & on 7 January 2009.

Shomagwe, Pinhas Andreas (pastor-captured by the SADF near Vietnam while trying to escape from Namibia to join SWAPO in Angola. This happened on the date of the Cassinga attack, 4 May 1978). Interview with the author, Okahao, 14 January 2008.

Tshoome, Ashighono Ishaka (Ongulumbashe battle veteran). Interview with the author, Okuwale, 2007; 2008; 2009; 2010; 2011.

Uupindi, Sabina (Cassinga survivor). Interview with the author, Ombafi, 29 December 2007.

Vatileni, Lonia "Ndjeimo" (Cassinga survivor). Interview with the author, Ongwediva, 22 December 2007.

Nandenga, "Kommanda Zulu" (ex-PLAN combatant and former regional commander of SWAPO). Interview with the author, Oshakati, 20 August 2003.

2. Published books and chapters in books

Armstrong, Sue. *In search of Freedom: the Andreas Shipanga story as told to Sue Armstrong* (Gibraltar: Ashanti Publishing, 1989).

Asmal, Kader (et al.). *Reconciliation through truth: a reckoning of apartheid's criminal governance* (Cape Town and Johannesburg: David Phillip and Mayibuye Books, 1997).

Baines, Gary & Peter Vale (eds.). *Beyond the border war: new perspectives on southern Africa's late-cold war conflicts* (Pretoria: University of South Africa printers, 2008).

Batley, Karen (ed.). *A secret burden: memories of the border war by South African soldiers who fought in it* (Johannesburg: Jonathan Ball Publishers, 2007).

Blonsky, Marshall (ed.). *On signs* (Baltimore: Johns Hopkins University Press, 1985).

Breytenbach, Jan. *Buffalo soldiers: the story of South Africa's 32 Battalion 1975–1993*, (Johannesburg: Galago Books, 2004).

Breytenbach, Jan. *Eagle Strike: the story of the controversial airborne assault on Cassinga* (Sandton: Manie Grove Publishing, 2008).

Brothers, Caroline. *War and photography: a cultural history* (London and New York: Routledge, 1997).

Caruth, Cathy. *Unclaimed experience: trauma, narrative and history* (Baltimore: Johns Hopkins University Press, 1996).

Clausewitz, Carl von. *On war.* Edited / translated by Michael Howard and Peter Paret. (Princeton: Prinston University Press, 1976).

Cliffe, Lionel (et al.). *The transition to independence in Namibia* (Boulder and London: Lynne Rienner, 1994).

De Gruchy, John. *Reconciliation-restoring justice* (London: SCM Press, 2002).

Delbo, Charlotte. *Days and memory.* Translated and with a preface by Rosette Lamont (Evanston: Marlboro Press-Northwestern, 2001).

Department of Information and Publicity (SWAPO of Namibia).*To be born a nation* (Luanda and London: Zed Press, 1981).

Dinur, Benzion. "The displacement of testimony." In James Young, *Writing and rewriting the holocaust: narrative and the consequences of interpretation* (Bloomington and Indianapolis: Indiana University Press, 1988), p. 31.

Dobell, Lauren. "SWAPO in office." In Colin Leys and John Saul (eds.). *Namibia's Liberation Struggle: The two-edged sword.* (London: James Currey, 1995), pp. 171–195.

Dobell, Lauren. *SWAPO's struggle for Namibia, 1960– 1991: war by other means* (Basel: P. Schlettwein Publishing, 2000).

Du Pisani, Andre. "Liberation and tolerance." In Henning Melber (ed.). *Re-examining liberation in Namibia political culture since independence* (Uppsala: Nordiska Afrikainstitutet 2003), pp. 129–136.

Du Pisani, Andre; Reinhart Koessler; William Lindeke A. (eds.). *The long aftermath of war-reconciliation and transition in Namibia* (Freiburg: Arnold Bergstraesser Institut, 2010).

Els, Paul. *Ongulumbashe: where the bush war began* (Wandsbeck: Reach Publishers, 2007).

Fanon, Franz. "Concerning violence." In *Wretched of the earth.* Translated by Constance Farrington (Harmondsworth: Peguin, 1990), pp. 35–59.

Feitlowitz, Marguerite. *A lexicon of terror: Argentina and the legacies of torture* (New York and Oxford: Oxford University Press, 1998).

Felman, Shoshana & Laub Dori. *Testimony: crises of witnessing in literature, psychoanalysis, and history* (New York and London: Routledge, 1992).

Geldenhuys, Jannie. *A general's story: from an era of war and peace* (Johannesburg: Jonathan Ball, 1995).

Geldenhuys, Jannie. *At the Front: a general's account of South Africa's border war* (Johannesburg: Jonathan Ball Publishers, 2009).

Gewald, Jan-Bart. *Herero Heroes: a socio-political history of the Herero of Namibia 1890–1923* (Oxford: James Currey Ltd., 1999).

Gillmore, Graham. *Pathfinder Company: 44 Parachute brigade 'the Philistines'* (Johannesburg: 30 Degrees South Publishers, 2010).

Gleijeses, Piero. *Conflicting missions: Havana, Washington* (Pretoria: Galago Publishers, 2003).

Gorggin, Peter N. & Maureen Daly Gorggin. "Presence in absence: discourses and teaching (in, on, about) trauma." In Shane Borrowman (ed.). *Trauma and the teaching of writing* (Albany: State University of New York, 2005), pp. 29– 51.

Groth, Siegfried. *Breaking the wall of silence* (Wuppertal: Peter Hammer, 1996).

Groth, Siegfried. *Namibia – the wall of silence: the dark days of the liberation struggle* (Cape Town: David Philip, 1995).

Gutman, Roy; Rieff, David; Dworkin, Anthony (eds.). *Crimes of war: what the public should know* (New York: W.W. Norton & Company Inc., 2007).

Halbwachs, Maurice. *Memory and history.* Translated by Francis J. Ditter, Jr. and Vida Yazdi Ditter (New York: Harper and Row, 1980).

Hamilton, Carolyn (et al.). *Refiguring the archive* (Cape Town: David Philip Publishers, an imprint of New Africa Books, 2002).

Hangula, Lazarus. *The international boundary of Namibia* (Windhoek: Gamsberg Macmillan Publishers Limited, 1993).

Hawley, Thomas M. *The remains of war: bodies, politics, and the search for American soldiers unaccounted for in Southeast Asia* (Durham & London: Duke University Press, 2005).

Heywood, Annemarie. *The Cassinga event* (Windhoek: National Archives of Namibia, 1996).

Hodges, Andrew. *Into the deep – the hidden confession of Natalee's Killer* (Birmingham: Village House Publishers, 2007).

Hoffer, Pamela M. *Reflets reciproques: a prismatic reading of Stephane Mallarne and Helene Cixous* (New York: Peter Lang Publishing, 2006).

Holt, Clive. *At thy call we did not falter: a frontline account of the 1988 Angolan war, as seen through the eyes of a conscripted soldier* (Cape Town: Zebra Press, 2005).

Jabri, Vivienne. *Mediating conflict: decision-making and western intervention in Namibia* (Manchester: Manchester University Press, 1990).

Jaster, Robert S. *South Africa in Namibia: the Botha strategy* (Lanham, New York and London: University Press Oof America, 1985).

Johnson, Allen. *The historian and historical evidence* (New York: Charles Scribner's sons, 1926).

Kaela, Laurent. *The question of Namibia* (London: Macmillan Press Ltd., 1996).

Kameeta, Zephania. Cited by Gerhard Totemeyer, "the Role of the church in Namibia: fostering a discourse on reconciliation." In Du Pisani, A. R. Kössler & W. A. Lindeke (eds.). *The long aftermath of war-reconciliation and transition in Namibia* (Freiburg: Arnold Bergstraesser Institut, 2010), p. 131.

Katjavivi, Peter (et. al). *Church and liberation in Namibia* (London: Pluto Press, 1989).

Katjavivi, Peter H. *A history of resistance in Namibia* (London and Paris: James Currey, 1988).

Kimberly, A. Nance. *Can literature promote justice? Trauma narratives and social action in Latin America testimonio* (Nashville: Vanderbilt University Press, 2006).

Koessler, Reinhart. "Public Memory, Reconciliation and the Aftermath of War: a Preliminary Framework with Special Reference to Namibia." In Henning Melber (ed.). *Re-examining liberation in Namibia political culture since independence* (Uppsala: Nordiska Afrikainstitutet, 2003), pp. 99–112.

Kracauer, Siegfried. "Photography." In *The mass ornament: Weimar essays.* Edited and translated by Thomas Y. Levin (Cambridge: Havard University Press, 1995), pp. 47–64.

Kratz, Corinne A. *The ones that are wanted: communication and the politics of representation in a photographic exhibition* (California: University of California Press, 2002).

LaCapra, Dominick. *Writing history, writing trauma* (Baltimore: The John Hopkins University Press, 2001).

Lalu, Premesh. *The deaths of Hintsa: postapartheid South Africa and the shape of recurring pasts* (Cape Town: Human Sciences Research Council, 2009).

Langer, Lawrence L. *Holocaust testimonies: the ruins of memory* (New Haven and London: Yale University Press, 1991).

Leys, Colin and John Saul (eds.). *Namibia's liberation struggle: the two-edged sword* (London: James Currey, 1995).

Leys, Colin and Mahmood Mamdani. *Crisis and reconstruction – African perspectives: two lectures* (Uppsala: Nordiska Africainstitutet, 1997).

Liebenberg, John & Patricia Hayes. *Bush of ghosts: life and war in Namibia 1986–1990* (Cape Town: Umuzi, 2010).

Lister, Martin and Liz Wells." Seeing beyond belief: cultural studies as an approach to analysing the visual." In Theo Van Leeuwen and Carey Jewitt (eds.), *The handbook of visual analysis* (London: Sage, 2001), pp. 61 - 91.

Malan, Magnus. *My life with the SA defence force* (Pretoria: Protea Books House, 2006).

Malkki, Liisa H. "Speechless emissaries: refugees humanitarianism, and dehistoricization." In Alexander LabanHinton (ed.), *Genocide: an anthropological reader* (Malden: Blackwell Publishers, 2002), pp. 344 - 367.

Mamdani, Mahmood. "The truth according to the TRC." In Ifi Amadiume and An Na'im Abdullahi (eds.). *The politics of memory: truth, healing and social justice* (London: Zed Books, 2000), pp. 176– 183.

Mamdani, Mahmood. *Saviours and survivors: Darfur, politics, and the war on terror* (Cape Town: Human Sciences research Council Press, 2009).

Mamdani, Mahmood. *When does reconciliation turn into denial of justice?* (Cape Town, Human sciences research council Press, 1998).

Mburumba, Kerina. *Namibia: the making of a nation* (New York: Focus Books, 1981).

McQuire, Scott. *Visions of modernity: representation, memory, time and space in the age of the camera* (London: Sage, 1998).

Melber, Henning (ed.). *Transition in Namibia: which changes for whom?* (Uppsala: nordiska Afrikainstitutet, 2007).

Mendez, Juan E. "Latin America experience of accountability." In Ifi Amadiume and An Na'im Abdullahi (eds.). *The politics of memory: truth, healing and social justice* (London: Zed Books, 2000), pp. 127–141.

Merewether, Charles (ed.). *The archive* (London: Whitechapel Ventures Limited, 2006).

Miescher, Giorgio (et al.). *Posters in action: visuality in the making of an African nation* (Basel and Windhoek: Basler Afrika Bibliographien & National Archives Namibia), 2009.

Morris, Rosalind C. *Photographies east: the camera and its histories in east and southeast Asia* (Durham and London: Duke University Press, 2009).

Namakalu, Oswin O. *Armedliberation struggle: some accounts of PLAN's combat operations* (Windhoek: GamsbergMacMillanPublishers (Pty) Ltd., 2004).

Namhila, Ellen N. Kaxumba KaNdola: *man and myth. The biography of a barefoot soldier* (Basel: Basel Africa Bibliography, 2005).

Namhila, Ellen N. *Tears of courage: five mothers, five stories, one victory* (Windhoek: Archives of Anti-Colonial Resistance and the Liberation Struggle Project, 2009).

Namhila, Ellen N. *The price for freedom* (Windhoek: New Namibia Books, 1997).

Nuuyoma, Sam S. *Where others wavered: the autobiography of Sam Nuuyoma: my life in SWAPO and my participation in the liberation struggle of Namibia* (London: Panaf Books, 2001).

O' Brien, Tim. "How to tell a true war story." In *The things they carried* (New York: Broadway Books, 1990), pp. 82.

Pink, Sarah. *Doing ethnography: images, media and representation in research* (London: Sage, 2001).

Pinney, Christopher. *Camera Indica: The social life of Indian photographs* (London: Reaktion books, 1997).

Ractliffe, Jo. *As Terras do Fim do Mundo* (Cape Town: Michael Stevenson, 2010).

Republic of Namibia, *The constitution* (Windhoek: Government Printers, 1989).

Sarkin, Jeremy. *Colonial Genocide and reparations claims in the 21st century: the socio-legal context of claims under international law by the Herero against German for Genocide in Namibia, 1904–1908* (Westport: Praeger Publishers, 2009).

Scarry, Elaine. *The body in pain: the making and unmaking of the world* (New York: Oxford University Press, 1985).

Sellström, Tor. *Sweden and national liberation in Southern Africa: solidarity and assistance 1970– 1994, volume 11: solidarity and assistance 1970–1994* (Nordiska Afrikainstitutet, 2002), pp. 350– 352.

Shane, Borrowman (ed.). *Trauma and the teaching of writing* (Albany: State University of New York, 2006).

Silvester, Jeremy and Jan-Bart Gewald. *Words cannot be found: German colonial rule in Namibia, an annotated reprint of the 1918 blue book* (Leiden: Brill, 2003).

Silvester, Jeremy (et al.). *The colonizing camera: photographs in the making of Namibia history* (Cape Town: University of Cape Town press, 1998).

Smith, Leonard V. *The embattled self: French soldiers' testimony of the Great War* (Ithaca and London: Cornell University Press, 2007).

Sontag, Susan. *Regarding the pain of others* (New York and London: Penguin Books Limited, 2003).

Soyinka, Wole. *The burden of memory, the muse of forgiveness* (New York and Oxford,: Oxford University Press, 1999).

Soyinka, Wole. "Memory, truth and healing." In Ifi Amadiume and An Na'im Abdullahi (eds.). *The politics of memory: truth, healing and social justice* (London: Zed Books, 2000).

Steenkamp, Willem. *Borderstrike: South Africa into Angola 1975– 1980* (Durban: Just done Productions Pub., 2006).

Steenkamp, Willem. *South Africa's border war 1966–1989* (Gilbraltar: Ashanti Pub., 1989).

Stiff, Peter. The Covert War: *Koevoet operations, Namibia 1979–1989* (Johannesburg: Galago Publishers, 2004).

SWAPO Party. *Their blood waters our freedom: glory to the heroes and heroines of the Namibian liberation struggle* (Windhoek: Namib Graphics, 1996).

Tagg, John. *The burden of representation: essays on photographies and histories* (London: Macmillan, 1988).

Tal, Kali. *The world of hurt: reading the literature of trauma* (Cambridge, University Press, 1996).

Thompson, J. H. *An unpopular war, from afkak to bosbefok: voices of South African national servicemen* (Cape Town: Zebra Press, 2006).

Trachtenberg, Alan. *Reading American photographs: images as history Mathew Brady to Walker Evans* (New York: Hill & Wang, 2001).

Tutu, Desmond. *No future without forgiveness* (New York: Doubleday, 1999).

Vigne, Randolph. "The moveable frontier: the Namibia–Angola boundary demarcation." In Patricia Hayes, et al. (eds.). *Namibia under South African Rule: mobility & containment 1915-1946* (Oxford: James Currey, 1998), 289–304.

Von Clausewitz, Carl (ed.). *On war.Translated by Michael Howard and Peter Paret.Commentary by Bernard Brodie* (Princeton: Prinston University Press, 1976).

Walter, Benjamin. "The Author as Producer." Reprinted in Victor Burgin (ed.), *Thinking photography* (London: Macmillan, 1987).

Weaver, Tony. "The war in Namibia: social consequences." In Gerhard Totermeyer, Vezera Kandetu and Wolfgang Werner (eds.). *Namibia in Perspective* (Windhoek: Council of Churches in Namibia, 1987).

Winter, Jay. *Sites of memory, sites of mourning: the Great War in European cultural history 1990* (Cambridge: Cambridge University Press, 1996).

Ya Nangolo, Mvula & Sellstrom Tor. *Kassinga a story untold* (Windhoek: Namibia Book Development Council, 1995).

Yerushalmi, Yosef Hayim. *Zakhor: Jewish history and Jewish memory* (Seattle and London: University of Washington Press, 1982).

Young, James E. *Writing and rewriting the Holocaust: narrative and the consequences of interpretation* (Indiana University Press, 1988).

3. Journal Articles

Barnard, Leo. "The Battle of Cassinga, 4 May 1978: a historical reassessment Part 1: the course of the battle and ensuing controversy." *Journal for contemporary history*, Vol. 31/ 3 (December 2006), pp. 131–146.

Barnard, Leo. "The Battle of Cassinga, 4 May 1978: a historical reassessment Part 2: Interviews with two SADF soldiers," *Journal for contemporary history*, Vol. 31/ 3 (December 2006), pp. 147–160.

Conway, Paul. "Truth and reconciliation: the road not taken in Namibia." *Online Journal of peace and conflict resolution*, Vol. 5/ 1 (Summer 2003), pp. 66–76.

Dobell, Lauren. "Silence in context: truth and/or reconciliation in Namibia." *Journal of Southern African studies*, Vol. 23/ 2 (June 1997), pp. 371–382.

Dzinesa, Gwinyayi A. "Postconflict disarmament, demobilization and reintegration of former combatants in Southern Africa." *International studies perspectives*, Vol. 8/ 1 (2007), pp. 73–89.

Edwards, Elizabeth. "Photographs and the sound of history." *Visual anthropology review*, Vol. 21/ 1 and 2 (Spring 2005), pp. 27–46.

Erichsen, Casper. "Shoot to kill: photographic images in the Namibian liberation struggle / bush war." *Kronos: Journal of Cape history*, Vol. 27 (November 2001), pp. 158–182.

Gleijeses, Piero. "Moscow's proxy? Cuba and Africa 1975–1988." *Journal of cold war studies*, Vol. 8/ 2 (Spring 2006), pp. 3–51.

Grunebaum, Heidi - Ralph. "Re-replacing pasts, forgetting presents: narrative, place, and memory in the time of the truth and reconciliation commission." *Research in African literatures*, Vol. 32/ 3 (Autumn, 2001), pp. 198–212.

Hallet, Robin. "The CIA in Angola." *African affairs*, Vol. 78 (1979), pp. 559–562.

Hallett, Robin. "The South African intervention in Angola 1975–76." *African affairs*, Vol. 77 (July 1978), pp. 347–368.

Hayes, Grahame. "We suffer our memories: thinking about the past, healing and reconciliation." *American Imago*, Vol. 55/ 1 (1998), pp. 29–50.

Hayes, Patricia. "A review article."Kronos, special issue: Visual history, *Journal of Cape history*, No. 27 (November 2001), pp. 27–243.

Howe, James. "Argument is argument: an essay on conceptual metaphor and verbal dispute." *Metaphor and symbol*, Vol. 23/ 1 (2007), pp. 1–23.

Lalu, Premesh. "The grammar of domination and the subjection of agency: colonial texts and modes of evidence." *History and Theory*, Vol. 39/ 4 (December, 2000), pp. 45–68.

Malkki, Liisa H. "Speechless emissaries: refugees humanitarianism, and dehistoricization." *Cultural anthropology*, Vol. 11/ 3 (1996), pp. 377–404.

Pohlandt-McCormick, Helena. „I Saw a Nightmare...": Violence and the Construction of Memory (Soweto, June 16, 1976). *History and Theory*, Vol. 39/ 4 (December 2000), pp. 23–44.

Saunders, Christopher. "The transition in Namibia 1989–90 and the South African Case," *Transformation*, Vol. 17 (1992), pp. 8–18.

Tapscott, Chris. "National reconciliation, social equity and class formation in independent Namibia." *Journal of Southern African Studies*, Vol. 19/ 1 (March 1993), pp. 29–39.

Williams, Christian A. "National history in Southern Africa: reflections on the 'remember Cassinga?' exhibition." *Kronos: Southern African histories*, Vol. 36 (November 2010), pp. 207–250.

4. Archival documents

SADF Chief of Staff Operations. "Operation Reindeer" (Top Secret).Ref. No.H Reer / 309/1 DD MRT 78 by HS OPS/ 301/ 2. Source: SANDF Archive, Pretoria.

Chief of the South African Defence Force. "SWAPO ontplooiing in suid-Angola ten noorde van Owambo" (Top Secret). Ref. No. AANH A by H / LeeR/ OPS/ 301/2 DD, February 1978. Source: SANDF Archive, Pretoria.

Chief of the South African Defence Force. "Military Politieke Situasie in Suidwes-Afrika" (Top Secret).Ref. No. HS OPS/301/2, February 1978. Source: SANDF Archive, Pretoria.

"Memorandum from Chief of the South African Army to the Chief of the SADF" (Top Secret).Ref. No. H Leer/309/1, 8 March 1978. Source: SANDF Archive, Pretoria.

"Vernietiging van SWAPO basisse" (Top Secret). Ref. No. HS OPS/310/4/KOSTUUM. Source: SANDF Archive, Pretoria.

Chief of the SADF. "Guidelines for statement by GOC SWA: Appendix A& B to PSYAC planning directive No. 3 / 78: suggested approach for statement by the Minister of Defence" (Top Secret). Source: SANDF archives, Pretoria.

"Memorandum from Chief of Staff Operations to the Chief of the SADF" (Top Secret).Ref. No. HS OPS/310/4/ Reindeer, 21 April 1978. Source: SANDF Archive, Pretoria.

"Media Analysis." Appendix B to HS OPS 310 / 4 / Reindeer," 8 August 1978 (Top Secret). Ref. No. CSI'S Media Analysis document MI / 205/13/1/1. Source: SANDF Archive, Pretoria.

Chief of the SADF. PSYAC Planning Directive No. 3 / 78. Operation Reindeer, Phase Three
– Media coverage (Top Secret). Source: SANDF Archive, Pretoria.

The SADF Chief of Staff Operation. "Militer Politieke Situasie in Suidwes Afrika (Uiters
Geheim).Ref. No. HS OPS/ 301/ 2. Source: SANDF Archive, Pretoria.

Chief of the SA Defence Force. "Press release by the Commander General, Cmdmt SWA
General Major J. J Geldenhuys." Ref. No. H3 0PS/328/3/3/1/2/1. Source: SANDF archive,
Pretoria.

Chief of SADF."PSYAC Planning Directive No. 2 \ 1978. Operation Bruilof, Phase Two" (Top
secret). Source: SANDF Archive, Pretoria.

Chief of the SADF. PSYAC Planning Directive No. 3 \ 78. "Operation Reindeer, Phase Three
– 25 April 1978" (Top Secret). Source: The SANDF Archive, Pretoria.

Chief of the South African Defence Force. "DG OPS/ 159/ April 78" (Top Secret).Ref. No. HS
OPS\310\4\Reindeer.

Chief of SADF. "PSYAC Planning Directive No. 2 \ 1978, Operation Bruilof: Phase Four"
(Top Secret). Source: SANDF Archive, Pretoria.

"General Reports of the Cassinga Camp Committee," June 1976. Source: BAB SWAPO Archives, Basel, Switzerland.

5. Newspapers

"Concentrate on the issues." *The Namibian*, 5 November 1999, p. 5.

"Don't force our hand: Govt." *The Namibian*, 12 September 2007.

"National reconciliation – lip service or reality?"*New Era*, 15 August 2008.

"The strike into Angola." *The Natal Witness*, 9 May 1978, p. 8.

"Cassinga remembered." *The Namibian*, 5 May 2009.

"Who Killed Clemens Kapuuo?" *The Namibian Weekender*, 20 July 2001.

"460 in mass grave at scene of Angolan raid." *The Cape Times*, 10 May 1978, p. 1.

"Desolation reigns as SWAPO buries dead." *Daily Dispatch*, 10 May 1978, p. 1.

"A timely and necessary blow." *Financial Gazette*, 10 May 1978, p. 6.

"SA bombs still lie unexploded in SWAPO camp." *The Star*, 10 May 1978, p. 19.

"SWAPO defies the West." *Eastern Province Gerald*, 10 May 1978, p. 12.

"Did SA have to play soldier?" *The Star*, 11 May 1978, p. 10.

"The propaganda war." *Daily Dispatch*, 10 May 1978, p. 6.

"SWAPO veg voort in SWA." *Die Volksblad*, 10 May 1978, p. 3.

"Minister to get wider control of land on borders." *The Argus*, 2 March 1978, p. 1.

"Strike to the West's advantage?" *To the point,* 12 May 1978, p. 36.

"Despite Raid Pretoria wants Western support." *To the Point*, 12 May 1978, p. 36.

"I was at Cassinga and it was not a military base." *Sunday Independent*, 9 March 2008, p. 6.

"Partial Sources colour the Cassinga story." *Sunday Independent*, 17 February 2008, p. 8.

"Cassinga criminals should be brought to justice."*Informante*. Thursday, 30 April, 2009, p. 17.

"Cassinga battle account reveals biased claptrap." *Sunday Independent*, 3 February 2008, edition 1, p. 6.

"Bullets don't lie, but it appears people do." *Sunday Independent*, 17 February 2008.

Sunday Independent, 17 February 2008.

"Soldiers relive apartheid war in surge of writing: post traumatic stress prevented many from talking about it till now." *Weekend Argus*, 14 October 2006. p. 15

The Star, 4 June 1996.

Sapa, 3 June 1996.

The Star, 8 May 1993.

"Koevoet: it was a luvverly war." Cape Times, 30 September 2000.

"Battle of Cassinga still rages on," *The Star*, 19 May 2007, p. 11.

"Namibian exiles begin to return home,"*The Washington Post*, 13 June 1989.

New Era, 25 August, 2010.

"Don't scrap Cassinga day," *New Era,* 7 May 2007.

Cape Times, Thursday, 28 September 2000.

New Era, Thursday 30 April 2009.

"Cassinga events need to be documented," *The Namibian*, 5 May 2006.

"Koevoet: it was a luvverly war," *Cape Times*, Thursday, 30 September 2000.

6. Theses, Papers, Brochures and Reports

Addison, G. N. "Censorship of the press in South Africa during the Angolan war: a case study of news manipulation and suppression," Rhodes University, 1980.

Akawa, Martha. "The sexual politics of the Namibian liberation struggle" (University of Basel: Doctoral Thesis in history, 2010).

Alexander, Edward. "The Cassinga raid" (UNISA: MA Thesis in history, 2003).

Baines, Gary. "The battle of Cassinga: Conflicting narratives and contested meanings." Working Paper, presented at the Basler Afrika Bibliographien 11 December, 2007.

Dateline: Namibia, Issue No. 3 "Before we are all wiped out." (New York Times Company, 1982).

Grunebaum, Heidi Peta. "Spectres of the untold: Memory and history in South Africa after the Truth and Reconciliation Commision" (University of the Western Cape: Doctoral Thesis in history, 2006).

International Defence & Aid Fund for southern Africa (IDAF). "Namibia the facts" (IDAF publications Ltd., 1989).

International Defence & Aid Fund. "Apartheid's army in Namibia: South Africa's illegal military occupation." *Fact Papers on Southern Africa, No. 10* (London: Canon Collins House, 1982).

International Defence & Aid Fund. "Remember Kassinga and other papers on political prisoners and detainees in Namibia." *Fact papers on Southern Africa, No. 9* (London: Canon Collins House, 1982).

International Defence & Aid Fund for Southern Africa (IDAF). "This is Namibia: a pictorial introduction (London, 1984).

Moosage, Riedwaan. "The impasse of violence: writing necklacing into a history of liberation struggle in South Africa" (University of the Western Cape: MA Thesis in history, 2010).

Oloko, Joe-Onyango. "The Status of human rights in sub-Saharan Africa, Namibia," Human rights library, University of Minnesota.

Saunders, Christopher (ed.). "Documenting liberation struggles in southern Africa: selected papers from the Nordic Africa documentation project workshop, 26–27 November 2009," Pretoria, South Africa.

Special bulletin of the South West Africa People's Organization SWAPO, "Massacre at Cassinga: Climax of Pretoria's all-out campaign against the Namibian resistance." 1978.

Truth and Reconciliation Commission of South Africa Report (1998)."The state outside South Africa between 1960 and 1990," Vol. 2/ Ch. 2.

Truth and Reconciliation Commission of South Africa Report presented to President Nelson Mandela on 29 October 1998. "Institutional hearing, the Faith Community," Vol. 4 / Ch. 3.

Truth and Reconciliation Commission of South Africa. "Political party submissions, transcript of the National Party, party political recall in Cape Town, 14 May 1997."

Vester, Frederich J. "Ex-SADF Special forces officer's testimony to the commission, 4 July 1997." In "the Truth and Reconciliation Commission of South Africa report: The State outside South Africa between 1960 and 1990," Vol. 2 / Ch. 2.

Williams, Christian. "Exile History: An ethnography of the SWAPO camps and the Namibian nation" (University of Michigan: Doctoral Thesis in anthropology and history, 2009).

7. Websites

Andén-Papadopoulos, K. "The Abu Ghraib torture photographs: news frames, visual culture, and the power of images" (University of Stockholm: Sage, 2008). Online at http://jou.sagepub.com/content/9/1/5.

Andén-Papadopoulos, K. "The Abu Ghraib torture photographs: news frames, visual culture and the power of images." In P. Lashmar (ed.), *Journalism: Cutting edge commentaries on the critical issues facing journalism at the practical, theoretical and media industry level* (London: The Marketing & Management Collection, Henry Stewart Talks Ltd., 2010). Online at http://hstalks.com/go.

"1988 Oshakati bomb blast." Online at http://www.spiritus-temporis.com/1988-oshakati-bomb-blast/.

"ANC Daily News Briefing." Online at http://www.e-tools.co.za/newsbrief/1996/news0606

"Cassingastring/facebook.' Online at http://et-ee.facebook.com/topic.php?uid=40615219623&topic=15512

"Castro in Africa: Cuba's Operation Carlotta." Online at http://www.thepanamanews.com/pn/v_14/issue_03/travel_03, accessed on 19 September 2010.

"Coming to terms with the border war in post-apartheid South Africa." Online at http://moo.sun.ac.za/mailman/listinfo/armytalk/, accessed on 7 June 2009.

"Govt appeals for info on mass graves." Online at http://allafrica.com/stories/20051114140.

"Iraq Body Count." Online at http://www.iraqbodycount.org/databae.

"Koevoet killed for hell of it." Online at http://www.bnvillage.co.uk/black-roots-village/81294-koevoet-killed-hell.html.

"Mau Mau Kenyans allowed to sue UK government." Online at http://www.bbc.co.uk/news/uk-14232049.

"Metaphysical statements." Online at: http://www.thefreedictionary.com/metaphysical

"Namibia struggling with the past." Online at http://www.mopanetree.com/human-rights/473.

"Necklacing" and other acts of violence under apartheid South Africa. Online at http://www.justice.gov.za/trc/hrvtrans/submit/np2.htm.

"State Security policy and proxy wars in African." Online at: http://www.nps.edu/Academics/Centers/CCC/Research-Publications/StrategicInsights/2010/Jul/SI_V9_I1_2010_Craig_3.pdf.

"The battle for Cassinga." Online at http://eprints.ru.ac.za/946/1/baines_Cassinga.pdf

"The the National Archives of South Africa Act No. 43 of 1996." Online at *http://www.national.archives.gov.za/dir_entries_pg3.htm.*

"Transcript of the National Party, party political recall in Cape Town – 14 May 1997. Online at http://www.justice.gov.za/trc/special/party2/np2.htm;

"Lessons of Norway attacks." Online at http://edition.cnn.com/2011/OPINION/07/22/fishman.norway/index.htm

http://www.deseretnews.com/article/252666/De-Klerk-apartheid -apology-was-inadequate-ANC-says.html;

http://www.nelsonmandela.org/omalley/index.php/site/q/03lv02167/04lv02264/05lv02303/06lv02331/07lv02333.htm.

"To bomb and protect." Online at http://english.aljazeera.net/indepth/opinion/2011/03/2011329125911441807.html, accessed on 10 April 2011.

"The Massacre of Cassinga." Online at http://amadlandawonye.wikispaces.com/The+ Massacre+of+Cassinga,+Piero+Gleijeses, accessed on 10 October 2008.

"Apartheid bomber loses court bid." Online at "http://www.dispatch.co.za/article.aspx?id=338529.

Index

A

Aawambo 37, 74
African National Congress (ANC) 31, 62, 83, 88, 93, 116
Afrikaans 16, 88
Aftermath (of Cassinga, violence) 20, 37, 48, 65f., 72, 74, 76, 79, 81, 85, 108, 112, 122, 124
Airborne (assault \ attack \ environment on Cassinga) 92, 95, 115
Akawa, Martha 64
Amputation 66, 68, 71
Amukoto, Gabriel 76
Amukoto, Michael 75f., 78
Amukoto, Nuusiku Lengomwenyo 76
Amukoto, Otto 76
Amwaama, Loide 74
Andén-Papadopoulos, Kari 49
Angola 3 f., 8–16, 31, 37, 39–41, 45, 49f., 75, 80, 82, 86f., 91, 93, 98, 105, 108, 110, 113–117, 123
Anti-Aircraft gun(s) 95
Anti-Apartheid movements 31
Apartheid 3, 15, 17, 43, 46, 51–53, 55, 58, 62f., 71, 73, 80, 82, 84, 87, 90, 93f., 97, 99f., 103–105, 116, 118–121, 124f.

B

Baines, Gary 30f., 35
Barclays Bank 3
Barthes, Roland 23
Basson, Wouter 3
Berlin-Buch 67
Blaauw, Johan 48, 95
Bloemfontein 17, 83, 87
Bloemspruit 12, 18
Boers 5, 7–9, 36, 67, 71, 74f.
Border 4, 11–14, 38f., 55, 57, 60, 75, 80, 82f., 87, 89, 94, 99, 105, 108, 114, 117
Botha, Hannes 47
Botha, Pik R. F 14
Botha, P.W 14, 16f.
Botha, P.W. 14–16, 49
Bothma, Louis 88
Breytenbach, Jan 12, 17, 35, 42, 45, 47, 52f., 55, 57, 59, 61f., 80–83, 88f., 92, 94–96, 99–102, 114–116

C

Callaghan, Sean 107
Canjanla 39
Cape Town 1, 39, 43, 49, 85, 88, 93, 105–108, 110
Casspirs 107

Charter of the United Nations 50
Chetequera 12, 14, 16
Coetzer, Morne 44
Congo (Brazzaville) 108
Conradie, Frans 106
Cuba 4, 8, 10, 17, 37f., 48, 66, 75, 93f., 114
Cubango River 9, 47, 77
Cunene Province 4, 16

D

de Cock, Eugene 106
de Klerk, Frederik Willem 62
Democratic Turnhalle Alliance (DTA) 14
Department of Defence (former SADF) 1, 4f., 8, 10–12, 14–17, 20, 37f., 40, 42–47, 49–53,
     55f., 58, 61f., 80–88, 90–95, 97, 99–102, 104, 106–108, 115–117, 120–123
Dolf (surname unknown) 100
Dreyer, Hans 106
du Plessis, Mike 47f.

E

Eembulu 10
Eenhana 4
Epinga 3
Etunda 13, 55, 58f., 61, 120
Exile 4f., 21, 38–40, 64, 66, 76, 78, 91, 105f., 110, 123

F

Ferreira, Emsie 116
Forças Armadas Populares de Libertação de Angola / People's Armed Forces for the Libera-
     tion of Angola (FAPLA) 11, 37, 39f.
Fougstedt (Sgt. Major) 44

G

Gaetano, Pagano 31
Geldenhuys, Jannie 17, 83, 87
Genocide 32, 61, 125
Gerhardt, Dieter 89
German Democratic Republic (GDR) 31, 66
German Government 61, 125
Gleeson, Ian 47, 87
Gould, Chandre 3
Great Britain 83
Greyling, Snakes 106
Groenewald, Tienie 83

H

I

J

K

L

M

N

O

P

Martha Akawa
The Gender Politics of the Namibian Liberation Struggle

With an introduction by Bience Gawanas

Basel Namibia Studies Series 13
Illustrations, map, index
ISBN 978-3-905758-26-9
eISBN 978-3-905758-50-4
ISSN 2234-9561, eISSN 2297-458X
www.baslerafrika.ch

Women's contributions against apartheid under the auspices of the Namibian liberation movement SWAPO and their personal experiences in exile take center stage in this study. Male and female leadership structures in exile are analysed whilst the sexual politics in the refugee camps and the public imagery of female representation in SWAPO's nationalism receive special attention. The party's public pronouncements of women empowerment and gender equality are compared to the actual implementations of gender politics during and after the liberation struggle.

"It is my contention that unless we rewrite history from a woman's perspective and by ourselves, we will not have a complete recollection of our past and be in a position to negotiate a space on the independence agenda. Martha Akawa has made us aware of this responsibility and asks of us what legacy we as women who fought in the liberation struggles will leave to future generations of women?"
Advocate Bience Gawanas, Windhoek

Printed in the United States
By Bookmasters